Media and Religion

Religion and Society

Edited by
Gustavo Benavides, Frank J. Korom,
Karen Ruffle and Kocku von Stuckrad

Volume 74

Media and Religion

The Global View

Edited by
Stewart M. Hoover and Nabil Echchaibi

DE GRUYTER

ISBN 978-3-11-125469-2
e-ISBN (PDF) 978-3-11-049787-8
e-ISBN (EPUB) 978-3-11-049608-6
ISSN 1437-5370

Library of Congress Control Number: 2021936860

Bibliographic information published by the Deutsche Nationalbibliothek
The Deutsche Nationalbibliothek lists this publication in the Deutsche Nationalbibliografie; detailed bibliographic data are available on the Internet at http://dnb.dnb.de.

© 2023 Walter de Gruyter GmbH, Berlin/Boston
This volume is text- and page-identical with the hardback published in 2021.
Typesetting: Integra Software Services Pvt. Ltd.
Printing and binding: CPI books GmbH, Leck

www.degruyter.com

Acknowledgements

A project such as this has many sources, and many have contributed to this one. We'd first like to thank our scholarly colleagues in the Center for Media, Religion, and Culture. The papers in this volume resulted from one of the Center's conferences, and the depth and significance of that event were due in no small measure to the efforts and reputation of the faculty, graduate fellows, and visiting fellows who continue to make the Center an exceptional place in global discourses on media and religion. The Center also depends on an exceptional staff, including during the course of this project Dona Olivier, Kimberly Donovan, Erin Ashbaugh, Claire Waugh, Valerie Albicker and Helen Gurnee. Finally, and in many ways most importantly, our efforts in research and scholarship would not be possible without the substantial support of the University of Colorado and its new College of Media, Communication, and Information, which came into being while this project was in process. The Dean of the college, Lori Bergen, Associate Dean for research Andrew Calabrese, and Media Studies Department Chair Rick Stevens continue to be important parts of what makes our work possible.

Finally, we want to thank those who contributed directly to this volume. First, the editorial staff at De Gruyter, in particular Alissa Jones Nelson and Sophie Wagenhofer, who have been patiently supportive throughout. We also benefitted from important assistance from Fellows in our center, and want particularly to acknowledge Dr. Ryan Bartlett, who provided invaluable editorial assistance and consultation at key moments in the process.

Stewart M. Hoover
Nabil Echchaibi
Boulder, CO

Contents

Acknowledgements —— V

Stewart M. Hoover and Nabil Echchaibi
Introduction —— 1

Stewart M. Hoover and Nabil Echchaibi
Conjuring the Religious, the Global and the Mediated —— 21

Florence Pasche Guignard
High Tech Mediations, Low Tech Lifestyles: The Paradox of Natural Parenting in the Digital Age —— 41

Deborah Justice
Multi-site Mediated Worship: Why Simulcast Sermons Need Live Local Praise Bands —— 63

Kathleen M. Ryan
Silencing the Tongues of Angels? The Aesthetics of Destruction in Environmental Edens —— 83

Devin Wilson
Anatta in Buddhism and Games: Emptiness and the Magic Circle —— 99

Solmaz Mohammadzadeh Kive
The National Museum and Religious Identity: The "Islamic Period" at Iran's National Museum —— 105

Magali do Nascimento Cunha
Media, Religion, and the Fabric of Culture and Communication in Contemporary Brazil —— 125

Steven Hu
Digitizing Jesus: Expanding Publics and Cultivating Civility with the Jesus Film Smartphone App —— 141

Seung Soo Kim
Digital Media and Imperial Formations: The 2012 Lady Gaga Controversy in South Korea —— 159

Stewart M. Hoover and J. Kwabena Asamoah-Gyadu
Media Curation and Re-emergent Religion in Ghana's Roadside Public Sphere —— 181

Pradip Thomas
Religion, Media and Culture in India: Hindutva and Hinduism —— 205

Contributors —— 219

Index —— 221

Stewart M. Hoover and Nabil Echchaibi
Introduction

Media and Religion: The Global View

The second decade of the 21st Century has become a period of great change across the world. Upheavals in economies and markets, in political sentiments, and in the global flows of populations and peoples have led to upheavals in politics. These have been obvious in, but not limited to, the developed nations of the North Atlantic West. The "Brexit" vote in the United Kingdom, followed by the one-term Trump presidency in the United States, seemed to signal a shift that had already begun earlier in Hungary, Russia, Poland, India, and elsewhere. The rise of so-called "illiberal" and "populist" politics in these settings moved ahead with the election of Jair Bolsonaro in Brazil and the further entrenchment of right-wing movements elsewhere. The twin upheavals of 2020 – the coronavirus pandemic and then the U.S.-generated turmoil over racial injustice that then spread much further – in a sense linked the world in new and unprecedented ways and further roiled these cultural and political developments.

There are interesting parallels among many of these things. One dimension that is present – and increasingly significant – is the role of religion. In many places, religion has taken on a new force and influence, and done so in ways that are also new. It is no longer at the "side." Nor does it remain taken-for-granted or tacit culturally. It has achieved new prominence, and this prominence is a function of another significant dimension: the role and place of media, mediation, media institutions, and media practices in these matters. To a great extent, it is the imagination of religion and its role in broader social imaginaries of meaning and value that is key. The role of social imaginaries in the constitution of power, of meaning, and of the definition of identities and boundaries is of critical importance. And, as should be clear, such imaginaries are deeply inflected with religion, with the memory of religion, with the architecture and the genealogy of religion, and with the historical trajectory of religion. In important ways, the interaction between these various valences of religion and the various valences of media is determinative.

This is the burden of this book. We, and the scholars we present here, are engaged in a deep inquiry into the contemporary constitution of the relations between religion and the media. This is no simple task. All religions have always been mediated in one way or another. All require means by which they are celebrated, shared, recorded, and mystified. Some of these "media" are the traditional ones: song, dance, movement, poetry, painting. But today, we know that many religions are mediated by what we think of as the "modern" media of communication: mechanical, industrial, electronic. These "media" – what we think of as "THE media," are the determinative context of action across social, cultural, and political spaces. The way that these domains today operate within logics of media is a subject of broad public and scholarly comment. There is a great deal said and written about media and politics and about media and economics. There are broad scholarships focused on the role of media in cultural understandings of race, gender, class, and social identities of various kinds.

But, even though it is easy to assume that modern mediation must also impinge on religion, our understandings as scholars and as citizens of how this is the case lag behind these other areas. First, it has been conventional to think of "religion" and "the media" as separate and hermetic spheres of value and action. Second, it has been conventional to think of things primarily in terms of the "effects" of one upon the other. Third, it has been conventional to generalize our understandings of each of these domains based on their functions in what have been thought to be entirely different registers of action. These determinative ideas about religion and media have limited our abilities to fully understand them in a period marked by powerful changes in each.

Change and Evolution

The media have, of course, undergone succeeding periods of restructuring from the time – in the middle of the last century – when the media sphere was marked by a relatively few powerful sources and channels. For much of the world, this was determined by powerful public broadcasting systems of various forms. Elsewhere, such as in the U.S., broadcasting systems were private but were concentrated and in the hands of major industrial corporations. The print media were more widely privatized, but were similarly concentrated in ownership and control. The media, thus constituted and structured, were easy to see and understand as a concentrated center of action, hermetic and self-generating. And media practice further enforced this conception, with a few major voices, such as the BBC and later CNN, coming to dominate and determine the global circulation of news and information.

All of this began to change in the 1970s with the beginnings of a rapid restructuring of the production and distribution of global media. Technological change brought about entirely new sources, contexts, and channels. Satellite transmission opened up opportunities for new systems of distribution both domestically and internationally. The development of small-format video production and the videocassette led to new opportunities for new voices and new networks to form. Driven in part by these trends, new commercial models for media also began to develop, with increasing competition, commercialization, and commodification of media, both news and entertainment. But probably no single factor has influenced the development of global media more than the so-called "digital revolution." Its early impacts were mostly felt in telecommunications, where new distribution means and networks could form, but later, with the development of cellular technology, digitalization led to a wholesale restructuring of systems of production, distribution, and circulation.

These changes in media have led to major changes in the management of media, and in the kinds of material that can be publicly mediated. It is no longer in the hands of a few traditional editorial voices to gatekeep media content. Today, content can emerge from almost anywhere and can be circulated and consumed in a wide array of locations, forms, and contexts. What Henry Jenkins calls "spreadable media" today better defines the media world than older, received notions of media transmission and reception. Digital media can be produced and distributed in traditional ways, of course, and what we now call "legacy" media still exist. But they exist in an increasingly diverse and influential marketplace of many sources and many locations. They also exist in a context of increasing diversity of voices, sources, and practices. The legacy media were not built to account for things such as secondary circulation or "remediation" where consumers of media also become producers at the same time (Bolter and Grusin 2000). They were also not built to account for an emergent array of voices and sources from contexts beyond the global cultural and commercial "centers." What originates and where it originates are today open questions in a way they never before have been. This has led to an entirely new paradigm, that of the "social media," which have taken on an autonomy and form of their own, and have proven themselves to be a voluble context of social action and meaning-making.

These developments are significant to global circulations because the centralized structures of global media typical of mid-century so easily mapped onto globalized structures of political and cultural power. The centralized media were the media of the global centers – and indeed helped to define and instantiate those centers – particularly in the North Atlantic West. American film dominated global film. British and French news dominated global journalism. Systems and structures rooted in colonial legacies of economic and linguistic power were both embodied and reinforced by systems of communication. The technological changes of the latter half of the century began to undo some of those relations, though initially in small ways. For example, India early on pioneered domestic satellite communication. But the real changes have come much more recently as the whole system and structure of communication has taken on more and more of a digital "logic."

It is hard to miss that these changes in the systems and structures of communication have coincided with a radical rethinking of the whole notion of global systems. The spirited debates over the evolution of cultural and economic globalization and the recent renewed interest in articulating rights have revealed systemic and structural evolutions that have come to contest the earlier notions of a unified, totalized global system. They have questioned the whole notion of totalities and generalities in global cultures and economics, suggesting that what were once thought to be general were in fact particular, particular to specific historic relations and locations. The idea that Europe, the center of the world that emerged from the "age of exploration," should in fact be "provincialized" (Chakrabarty 2007) in our thinking, emerged along with vibrant ferment and change in relations of communication and circulation, rooted in the technological changes we've discussed.

The post-modern turn toward particulars has thus found a footing in systems of communicational relations that encourage precisely that sort of thinking. The contestation of received systems of power and authority similarly emerges at a time when the very means by which the globe circulates ideas and symbols is itself moving away from its traditional foundations of authority.

This postmodern turn has been felt in the world of religion as well. This has been obvious in at least two registers of interest to us here. First, religions today seem more diverse and distributed. Even the traditional faiths with their historically-embedded structures of history, memory, structure, and practice are today being riven with "democratic" individualizing impulses which seem to challenge their authority. Religions today can no longer control their own symbols. They can no longer declare a sacred bounded "space" that is uniquely theirs. They can no longer determine the contexts and networks through which their ideas and values are distributed and circulated. Second, scholars who study religion are increasingly seeing these trends in the formal religions and a whole range of other religiously-significant phenomena beside. What could once be conveniently labelled as "informal," "privatized," "implicit," or "quasi-religious" practices are growing in breadth, depth, and reach. Entirely new forms of religion are emerging. This has led to a change in the way religion scholarship is done. Received ideas of "essential" religious forms have given way to studies of practices, materialities, and identities, the locations where religion and spirituality emerge and find their form. This means that the whole definition of religion has changed, away from essentialized categories of belief and behavior to categories of action where religion is being produced and re-produced today. Our task as scholars is to capture and analyze these decentered circulations on a global scale in such a way as to redeem their place and significance in otherwise singular and hierarchical systems of knowledge production.

A Global View

The parallels to the post-modern turn in globalization and in global media are stark and persuasive. At the same time that the global cultures of exchange and value are moving toward emergent particulars, the same markings can be seen in religion. And each, as we would like to argue, is articulated to emergent systems and practices of mediation and communication.

While there are vibrant scholarships in each of these areas: emergent religion, restructuring of media and communication in the digital age, and globalization and post-colonial studies and decolonial theory, none of them have as yet looked at the emerging situation through the lens of their interactions. While there is an emergent field of media and religion studies that focuses on the ways that religions are today mediated, it has looked at the larger, global context only tentatively. As religious studies has thought about issues of modernity and culture, it has not yet looked fully at the contribution of systems of mediation and communication to these realities. Clearly, there is scope for this sort of scholarship and it is long past time when a scholarly focus on media and religion from a global perspective should have been on the table.

There would be a range of implications of such a discourse, over and above what religion scholarship, media scholarship, and post-colonial, de-colonial, and globalization scholarships might learn from each other. A disciplined review of these issues and trends might also help elaborate our understandings of some fundamental issues, such as the question of the nature of contemporary secularization and broader trends in social evolution. Much of what we have described here could look like the progress of secularization in modernity. Theories of secularization have predicted changes in religion that look very much like what we have described in the world of religion. Religious authority is increasingly under pressure, religious participation in the conventional sense continues to decline, particularly in the developed West. Religious discourses have become less and less articulated to the systems of belief of the formal religions. At the same time, though, religion in different forms and in different places seems to be thriving, not least in the emerging global "illiberal" and "populist" political formations. These trends are more obvious as we step back from particular national situations and understand these evolutions on a more global scale.

It should be clear that we do not intend to argue that a global view of media and religion would again reify the received sense that there is a normative category of "the global." Instead, we wish to suggest that no national or regional view is sufficient without some reference to larger systems of mediation and circulation. It simply makes a difference today that any particular or local or national or regional articulation of "the religious" takes place in a context of constant connectedness and possibilities of interaction with larger – even potentially "global" – contexts.

This holds for the articulation of scholarship into these questions. Scholarly conversations about emergent religions and their mediation in various forms have largely been parallel national or regional conversations in and about Europe, North America, Latin America, Africa, the Middle East, or Asia. They have not been as self-consciously articulated to broader contexts. Each has been conscious of the other contexts. But this book asks "what about a global view?" Could there be a fully global view? What would that mean? Must the goal of a discourse that would move toward the global only be about arguing for global universals, new normativities of "the global?" Clearly, such an approach would not have learned much from the postmodern and post-structuralist turns. Instead, we want to suggest that a "global view" can be at the same time more modest than that, and have ambitions beyond.

What we wish to argue and hope that this book will demonstrate, is that a nuanced, historicized, empirical view is called for. It is possible to keep in mind both the contexts where particular meanings are being produced or practices elaborated and broader contexts of meaning and circulation. This view should also be historicist in the sense that it should lodge its understandings in lived histories and in the tracings of those histories across time and location. Practices of religion do not emerge out of nothing and from nowhere. They are each embedded in trajectories of belief, culture, action and context.

It seems obvious that the empirical direction that would most helpfully undergird such a scholarly turn would be one focused on rich, ethnomethodological and historicist case studies. Such cases can and should be seen according to their own trajectories, but also in relation to other trends, causes, and consequences. The situation such scholarships seek to unpack is indeed a complex one, but one that absolutely depends on a view outside their located contexts of action. Such scholarships should also be seen in light of – and add to the critical assessment of – thought about globalization more generally.

As critics such as Said and Chakrabarty have made clear, approaches that particularize phenomena through historicist and culturalist lenses can not only transcend the received framing of a unitary and normative "global," they can also bring into relief critical questions of power. In particular, the legacy of colonialism (and its influence on academic as well as lay thinking) which has been so determinative in our understandings of "the religious" as a category, can be critiqued in entirely new ways.

This Volume

This volume is a contribution to this conversation. It grows out of a conference titled "Media and Religion: The Global view," held at the University of Colorado. The conference brought together seventy scholars from twenty different countries to consider questions of the mediation of religion in the context of global relations of power, culture, and communication. The conference demonstrated the value of empirical and historicist work and led to provocative and productive questions about the nature and epistemology of scholarly consideration of religion and media as they are deployed across a range of contexts. It led to our commissioning of papers that would show the value of focused case studies as contributors to our understanding of these complex trends. We engaged scholars in conversations about these works, and together further developed important ideas and further probed important trends. This volume is the result of those conversations.

These studies range widely in terms of geographic and religious context and indeed in their implicit definitions of both "geography" and "religion." Each seeks to be deeply descriptive, providing valuable insights into its particular materials, but offering perspectives and connections to other cases and other contexts. Like all focused ethnographic cases, they are fascinating for their descriptive detail. At the same time, they point to things outside their own frames of reference and begin to describe a set of themes that can and should guide our thinking moving forward. We intend this volume to demonstrate a "global view" that is epistemically two-dimensional. First, these accounts represent deep and focused studies of their materials in their contexts. They each develop and elaborate understandings of how social, culture, institutional, and technological forces interact in actual settings. They each are also more than mere hermetic cases, isolated and idiosyncratic. But they also afford a second dimension. They give us an opportunity to look back from these settings toward some larger trends and implications. In particular, we point to the way that they collectively help us understand how the contemporary socio-political moment (with which we began) is possible. Much of what appears to be nonsensical or contradictory to our received ways of understanding religion, politics, or media in fact makes more sense when we see things through the lenses of these studies. To take the prominent example with which we began – the way that religion is interpolated into the illiberal "populist" politics of today – these cases help us understand how this has been made possible by conditions and practices in actual locations and through actual social forces.

The volume begins with a critical essay that explores in more detail and depth the emerging theoretical, conceptual, and scholarly issues involved in the overall project here. In it, we locate the project of this volume in a specific context, that of the particularized experience and discourse of North Atlantic imperial and colonial history. While we understand that there is no over-arching context or discourse of history, only a variety of histories, the particular map on which much of what we have known and been told about history results from the North Atlantic trajectory. As Chakrabarty argued, it needs to be particularlized – "provincialized" – to be understood. We want to suggest that, once we have done that – in a sense moving beyond the dead-end that otherwise emerges as we try to look at particular cases and locations on the basis of the received view – then important conceptual and empirical work can proceed.

As the following studies illustrate, and as many of their authors explicitly argue, we need a new understanding of mediation as it occurs in new valences. We are taken, for example, with the formulation Magali Cunha introduces here, based on the work of the influential Latin American theorist Jesus Martin-Barbero (1993; 2012), who argues for a new understanding of media and mediation as "mediatization." This is distinct from other work that uses this same term (primarily in Europe, see for example Couldry and Hepp, 2018; and specifically with reference to religion, Lövheim and Hjarvard, 2019) in that he wishes to suggest that we think about the role of media as transcending most received categories of production, reception, content, etc., and instead understand how media function to integrate and interpolate life, identity, practice and action. For example, the fact of media can itself symbolize things, adding a layer to the meaning processes involved. This complexity is well-illustrated in Cunha's account of the Brazilian religious communication scene, but really in most of the cases we see here. In this approach to media, media are no longer instrumentalized (even in terms of "mediatized" power – a turn that is common in other uses of this term). Instead, we can adopt analytical frames that take them on their own terms and seek to understand how they are both "meaning-making" and "meaning-made." In analyses such as Cunha's we can see the role of media and mediation as complex, layered processes of symbolization and circulation that act in interaction with structure, technology, social meaning and social action to instantiate entirely new forms and valences of "the religious."

In our own essay, we point to the mediatic moment as one that is conditioned, afforded, and coded by media in a socio-cultural regime Echchaibi (2020) has called "hypermediation." Chunha suggests, referencing Douglas Kellner, how hypermediatic religion might look: ". . . it involves and engenders discourses and religious action based on fluidity, immediacy, image privilege, spectacularization of practices, fragmentation, emptying of spontaneity, distancing/virtuality, and an address to audiences." Such a view of religion is indeed revolutionary and paradigm-shifting. The implications for power, both institutional and cultural, are important and far-reaching.

This relationship to power is even more profound when we consider another insight that we can draw from many of the works here: the way that these emergent forms of mediatized (and again, we will use this term in the sense proposed by Martin-Barbero) religion are so tacitly and smoothly interpolated with the larger project of neo-liberal globalization. This is most obvious in the Cuhna, Kim, Justice, and Hoover and Asamoah-Gyadu chapters, centered as they are in contexts where the new media-based Pentecostalism is most obvious. But important strains of this can also be seen in Thomas's chapter, focused on Hindutva and in Hu's study of the global spread of a new mediatized form of Protestant mission. There may be clues here as to the extents and limits of the neo-liberal moment and its embedment in media forms and structures.

Each of the chapters, in its own way, provides evidence of the extent to which such factors as commodification, spectacle, and circulation work in globalized cultural marketplace. We've argued – and Martin-Barbero's paradigm supports – the notion that media forms articulate and enforce certain gestures and practices at the expense of others. We would not argue that these things are necessarily as formal as the "media logics" some theorists identify with contemporary mediatization. Nonetheless, we can see the ways in which the structures and processes of the media have interpolated themselves into processes of knowledge, meaning, and imagination. Ryan's chapter shows how even seemingly archaic or "legacy" forms of mediation (in this case photography) have long insinuated themselves into systems of social meaning and cultural identity. This can be seen in more sophisticated ways in other cases here. Wilson provides a fascinating and subtle reading of how certain media forms can come to privilege certain religious forms and practices. The spectacular expressions of religion in Brazil, the United States, Korea, India, and elsewhere show evidence of this same affordance of "media" and "mediation" for "religion." In the media age, some religions "win" and some "lose" as a result of their interactions with the media environment.

What have been called the "aesthetic formations" (Meyer 2009) or the "affective infrastructures" (Hoover 2019) of media root and instantiate certain kinds of social, cultural, and political formations. This is all very powerful evidence of where we should look to understand the role of religion in the constitution of contemporary "illiberal" or "populist" politics. Many observers have noted how religion's relationship to these movements seems somehow thin or superficial (Marzouki et al. 2016; Norris 2019; Hidalgo 2019). The hypermediatic forms of religion we see here give us insight into how and where these forces are, in fact, substantial.

That we can gain such insights demonstrates the value of the kind of deeply empirical work we present here. Such work is necessary because, in spite of the fact that much of what we see in emerging trends seems so large and spectacular, much of it is also so subtle, nuanced, and layered. This is nowhere more obvious than in Guignard's contribution. In it, she shows how the logics of the hypermediatic age and their implications stretch even into the most intimate realms of daily life. These structured relations of circulation and meaning-making can displace prior sources of normative value – such as the teachings of religion – in favor of modern logics of governmentality even in relation to questions of fertility and women's self-determination. As she shows, this is not a mere matter of media "influence" or manipulation. Instead, it is a particular and located valence of the "mediatization" logics suggested by Martin-Barbero.

There are some consistent learnings from these studies. First, they each demonstrate that there are, while maybe not "media logics" that determine things, the media do seem to "afford" certain kinds of things in certain ways. Aesthetics and aesthetic practices seem to be important and determinative, as Cunha, Thomas, Justice, Ryan, Kim, and Hu show in their respective cases. Second, there is an increasingly prominent role for individual subjectivity and individual practice. Much has been said about the ways that digital and social media have centered the individual and centered at least the claim of autonomy there. But we can see from Thomas's history as well as from Justice's, Ryan's and Hu's work, that this is not a unique providence of digital media. Instead, the whole nature of modern mediation has afforded, for individuals, the right to make their own judgements and form their own religious and quasi-religious gestures, from eco-spiritualities related to photography, to ethno-nationalist identities related to television drama.

Third, a significant implication in each of these studies is in relation to authority, whether historical, institutional, or clerical. They collectively show how contemporary hypermediated systems of meaning-making and circulation which strive toward new imaginaries of practice and belief form cultural or social fields of practice that necessarily displace received power and authority. As we note elsewhere, religions can no longer control their own symbols, boundaries, or discourses. These studies show that the challenges are even more profound than that. Whole geographies of cultural and social practice are becoming reconstituted at their centers by systematic social practices of religiously-significant mediation.

Fourth, this is all happening in relation to the neo-liberal project. Where once there might have been the possibility of a rarefied theological debate about the implications of the commodification of religious (or spiritual) practices and symbols, or of the question of whether religion can remain "authentic" when it is "commodified," those fine distinctions have been swept away by the kinds of developments we see here. Religion as practiced, religious materialities, religious products and services and religious commodities have become naturalized and taken-for-granted. One of the interesting dimensions of this, also obvious in these pages, is that the displacement of religious authority is in fact a case of its relativization in the hypermediated cultural marketplace. This is obvious in the Cunha, Hoover/Asamoah-Gyadu, Thomas, Kim, and Justice chapters, and there are hints of it elsewhere. Religion now finds itself in a neo-liberal marketplace of choice.

As a result, traditional religious institutions and authorities are faced with an existential challenge. Either they fade to the margins or they begin to brand and commodify *themselves*, as Thomas and Cunha show in their respective studies.

These accounts also demonstrate that neo-liberal globalization and the instantiation of digital global cultures have not worked to "flatten" or "homogenize" the world. McLuhan's famous aphorism about the emergent "global village" anticipated such a world, at least to many readings at the time. What we see here instead is the late-modern, contemporary instantiation of the Imperial/colonial project. The world does seem increasingly "flattened" in some ways, and at the same time, from the imperious perspective of Appadurai's (1996) "global ethnoscape" of circulating elites and elite cultures, the world has also become increasingly "secularized."

These chapters demonstrate that such a view is in need of serious nuance and re-thinking. Far from transcending the received social and political structures that have defined what is most often thought of as a progressive view of history, the emerging formations at the intersection of media and religion are deeply embedded in those structures and in that history. The imperial/colonial project defined a unitary vision of global progress and development under a regime deeply rooted in the epistemic turn brought about by the North Atlantic West's "age of exploration." As decoloniality scholars (see Mignolo and Walsh, 2018) have suggested, this history cannot be simply ignored or swept away. It continues to define relations, boundaries, border, identities, and – most importantly – imagination today. Its legacies are in the structures of power and of politics and of economics that continue to structure the world.

While it is beyond the scope of our argument there to explore it in detail, it is important to understand how this history was deeply embedded in, and conditioned by, the twin concerns of this volume: media (or "communication") and religion. It is well known that the imperial/colonial project was in important ways inspired by, conditioned by, afforded by, and imagined by religion. The history is rife with examples of religious imaginaries inscribed in its motivation, in its moral justifications, and in its violence. Further, religious motivations and religious interests have been central forces in its continuing form and shape (Maldonado-Torres 2014). Less reflected on is how communication or media played a role in this history. The very fact of the age was a communicational phenomenon as it was made possible by emergent technologies of communication (the development of maneuverable ships and systems of navigation). What is less thought about is how there was also a political economy of communication production that made the age, and thus the whole colonial project, possible. New cultures of print were emergent at the same time, supported by an early form of the neo-liberal model of cultural markets. These emergent "media" included those with commercial and state-oriented purposes, but – more importantly – they also included cultures and readerships focused on the cultural, moral, and religious dimensions of the project. The religious "other" of the European imagination was a function of these media. Religious forces in the colonial project also were extensively mediated as missional activities focused on literacy, publication, proselytization, and religious advocacy, all of which were increasingly mediated.

So, the religion of the colonial project that structured and continues to structure global "modernities" has always been a mediated religion. And, this mediation has been far more extensive, nuanced, and layered than is implied by the banality that religions "use" media for purposes of faith, ritual, catechesis, and propagation. No, it is more than that and has always been more than that. In fact, a new way of theorizing and understanding the role of media in contemporary religion, politics, and culture (as is called for in a number of places in this volume) is not only relevant to the contemporary situation, it might well be a better way of understanding this deeper history.

A way of looking at the cases in this volume then is to understand them in this larger context. They bear the marks of this history in the interpellation of "the religious" with the "media," the "mediated," the "mediatized" or the "mediatic" (all terms that are proposed in various forms in these pages). This interpellation is, as we have said and these cases show, afforded by the commodities, sensations, spectacles, practices, contexts, networks, and affordances of "the media age." These are large and significant matters and they have large and significant implications if, as we argue, they are part of the cultural architecture that has made the cultural politics of the moment possible. But yet, as with all opportunities to observe and reflect on "media," there is a temptation to be misled that the questions are about smaller things. Two stand out here. First, these studies demonstrate the importance of grasping practices that were once thought of as merely popular, individual, informal, private, ludic, or "implicit" against the presumed "larger" matters of structures, institutions, explicit power, explicit authority, and their aspirations. These studies show that the "smaller" formations have immense significance today. Second, much of the cultural momentum in each of these cases seems to be less about power as formally constituted and more about imagination and "imaginaries" of cultural, moral, and political practice (Alma and Vanheesvijck, 2018). Power is seen in these pages as a consequence of complex relations of materiality, technology, reflexive autonomy, and practice. Ever since Benedict Anderson (2006) pointed it out to us, we've known about the importance of imagination. What we see here are examples of the formation, circulation, and accumulation of imaginative resources in relation to the instruments of modernity most accustomed to imagination: the media. But it is not a simple or banal case of the media affording the triumph of the image. It is instead, as these studies show, a case of systems of mediated generation and circulation often subtly yet deeply conditioning significant (often portentous) cultural formations.

These Contributions

This book is organized so that important themes can emerge – and interact – as the reader proceeds through its chapters. The empirical chapters that follow our stage-setting chapter begin with one that focuses on the role of technology and systems of private regulation and governmentality in the most private of spheres. Personal practices around fertility and parenting have traditionally been affordances of moral cultures, most notably those identified with religion. Florence Guignard writes from and about Francophone Canada, a one-time stronghold of Catholicism. Contemporary individuals and couples there negotiate these important life questions with that in the background, but increasingly search for new modes of practice, such as "natural" parenting. Far from being fully organic, though, the media age affords opportunities to technologize these relations, displacing both the formal voice of the church and other, fully private, options. Here, we can see that practice and imagination articulate with technology to displace or re-articulate sources and values that once were fully the province of formal authority. What emerges is an imaginary rooted in a negotiation between technological, religious, and feminist discourses about the most intimate realms of life.

Deborah Justice's study bridges between the private and the public in relation to youth culture. The importance of music as a medium for identity work among younger age groups is well-known, and she looks at a mediatization of this phenomenon by emergent religious ministries. Music becomes a way of crafting new religious imaginaries that engage a religious demographic that is increasingly unavailable to formal religious bodies. This shares several of the dimensions we've discussed: the turn toward individual autonomy and reflexive action afforded by technology and by aesthetic formations circulating around music. As Justice herself notes, the effect is a de-centering of religious practice away from institutions where the whole sense of membership no longer needs to involve physical attendance. The broader implication that something seemingly ephemeral can in fact have important institutional and structural effects is one that accrues as well across these chapters.

Kathleen Ryan explores the question of the role of sensational forms, aesthetics, visuality, and consumption in her analysis of the role and broader implication of nature photography in constructing senses of moral and social value built around the natural world. It is commonplace (at least in the North Atlantic West) to attribute deeper moral and particularly spiritual value to nature, the environment, and to their visuality. Ryan's work demonstrates how performance of commodification and circulation can form a moral economy of practice that in turn can turn toward the "quasi-religious" contemporary form: "spirituality." This is particularly interesting in light of our earlier point that political economies of media have been embedded in the whole imagination of the Western imperial/colonial project from the beginning. The practices and circulations Ryan describes are thus in a long trajectory that subtly and yet profoundly binds image markets to the broader project of manifest destinies in the U.S. and beyond. The fact that they accumulate an imaginative surplus of moral meaning and moral agency resulting in religious and quasi-religious impulses further supports our accumulating insights here.

Devon Wilson presents evidence from a different religious context entirely. Still focused more on the private sphere of action, he investigates one particular gesture where Buddhism achieves a rather seamless interpolation with digital practice. This has a number of important implications, this time directed back towards what we might begin to understand about how media, in fact, integrate with "traditional" religious practice. His case raises fascinating questions about both which religions might "win" and which might "lose" through their interactions with modern media and processes of mediation. More interestingly and subtly though, his work gestures toward ways that particular practices within religious traditions might also be selected, deselected, formed and/or shaped in and through media affordances. Wilson's chapter also provides us with evidence of how significant careful and focused empirical work can be. Understanding *"Anatta"* and how it might evolve in a digital environment is a small, private, and quiet thing on one level, but profound and predictive on quite another.

A very different way of thinking about the form and context of mediation presents itself in Solmaz Kive's study of Iran's national museum across the period of the country's transition following the 1979 revolution. Thinking of the museum as a medium and curation within that context as a kind of mediation or mediatization, enables us to understand the extent to which the age we live in is one defined by seamless trajectories of mediation, circulation, and meaning-making. Kive presents a particular case of the mediation of religion and religious imaginaries that has deep resonance in our current moment. That is the way that imagination of the nation and identity might be integrated into the structured representations of aesthetics and affect present in the modern museum. She is able to chart this as a process of construction, contestation, and reconstruction, where assumptions about how and under what circumstances certain imaginaries are possible and others are not. As she demonstrates, struggles such as the one she charts have an implication we have seen elsewhere in these pages: that the process of mediating religion in modernity (often with the intention to extend or preserve it) often has the indirect but powerful effect of relativizing and thus diminishing it instead. The struggles over these processes in a (uniquely significant) national museum setting give us important insights into how contemporary cultural and political elites think about the power of aesthetic formations, imagination, and identity.

We've already pointed to Magali Cunha's account of the emergence of mediatized or "mediatic" religion in Brazil. From her descriptions, we can gain some important insights into how mediatization and mediatic formations of sensation and spectacle laid the groundwork for Brazil's entry into the "new politics" of illiberal populism. As in other cases, we can see some outlines of broader implications here. For example, we can see in Brazil how mediatizaton there came to advantage one particular religious form (Protestantism) over others (particularly Catholicism) in part because mediatization allows syncretisms of religious forms that Protestantism has been particularly adept at. More importantly, it is not merely generic Protestantism, but emergent Pentecostalism that has come to the fore. Pentecostalism exhibits a fundamental binding of religion into new forms of circulation, commodification, and markets. We can see here (as we argued above) how it can be thought of as the ideal religious expression of the neoliberal project in that it affords market definitions of value at the same time that it promises salvation that is both material and spiritual. Without belaboring the Brazilian case, we nonetheless see dimensions of this case that are shared by the others. As we see elsewhere, the emergent mediatic religious form also de-institutionalizes, de-territorializes, and de-centers institutions and histories. At the same time, as Cunha argues, it centers the individual (and in an echo of other cases here, it makes traditional religious "participation" less important) as it de-stabilizes or relativizes religious authority and religious institutions. But, this story is not all about disestablishment. These forms of mediatic religion at the same time create religious sensation and celebrity and re-position religion (at least this kind of religion) as part of the public and symbolic repertoire, but in a new register. And this new register makes it uniquely and powerfully accessible to politics, a portent that has been realized in the Bolsonaro era in Brazil (and has powerful echoes in the U.S. context, as well).

Stephen Hu's chapter invites us to think once again about a more private and individual level of action and practice, this time related to the important legacies of global Christian mission work. The role of missions in the project of settler colonialism is widely-known and widely-commented-upon (Cf: Gladwin, 2019). Traditionally, though, these projects have been seen primarily in relation to their institutional roots and provenance, and have been evaluated primarily in those terms. Hu's work focuses on a case of the privatization of these relations by means of a complex mediation. He shows how a decades-old film production (that has achieved a sort of iconic status among Evangelical Christians) can be re-purposed and re-circulated through more modern digital and social-media circulations. As a result, it conditions a certain kind of emergent practice that imagines new subjectivities of both missional "subject" and missional "object." Digital gestures such as those Hu describes share in common with other examples here the capacity to locate this practice in the new context of neo-liberal circulation. As Hu describes it, embedding mission in an "app" affords missional activity both as individual/autonomous and as a set of market relations. At the same time it instantiates very traditional conceptions of the relationship between Christian evangelism and its global objects. The film in question is made into a religious commodity that aspires to global symbolic status so that it can mediate and interpolate this new missional globalism. It claims to flatten relations between the religious "center" and religious "peripheries." Its practitioners can imagine themselves as part of a flattened "networked public" at the same time that power relations between centers and peripheries can remain untouched.

Seung Soo Kim writes about a context where missional Christianity had a profound effect in seeding its largest presence in East Asia. The faith has played a major role politically, socially, and economically throughout Korea's rise to an economic and cultural powerhouse in the region. Its connection with the imperialist project, and later with neo-liberalism, has been largely seamless, until recently. There has perhaps always been an undercurrent of discomfort with Christianity's influence – or so Kim suggests here – a set of relations that have become more and more obvious in recent years. Kim charts a specific incident of media spectacle, a 2012 concert by the global superstar Lady Gaga, as a moment when these relations came into relief in a powerful way. What he describes is a negotiation between global celebrity culture and its presumed gloss of cosmopolitanism, secularism and modernity, and the national instantiation of a movement (Protestantism) that was itself a product of this same global culture, but which now took a position of resistance to what it saw as the moral depravity of Lady Gaga. This ritual of identity, nationalism, and imagined value took place in the media, as Kim observes, but also with the media and by means of the media. This suggests that, in modernity, media affordance is an even more-mixed provenance than has appeared elsewhere in these pages. Curiously, as Kim points out, the resistance against Protestantism that emerged had a seemingly contradictory outcome. The reaction of certain Korean commentators and elites ended up valorizing "an American-style liberal imaginary" which favored a certain "moral economy" that became the standard by which to judge local and national actions and sensibilities. Kim suggests that we might think of these relations as indicating the capacity of mediated discourses and practices to instantiate new emergent imperial formations.

Many of the themes we've discussed so far: the relativization of religious authority and institutions, located identities, commodification, visuality, neo-liberal cultural markets, national and international flows and relations via media, and the capacities of technologies and practices to select certain forms of "the religious" and disadvantage others, come together in a very interesting account presented by Stewart Hoover and Kwabena Asamoah-Gyadu. In it, they detail a unique but broadly provocative example of how modern systems of circulation, commodification, and mediation can interact in new ways and express in new contexts. Their study is focused on Ghana, which is a context of substantive traditional visuality. As they note, the Ghanaian roadside is a context where a nearly-unique form – the realist roadside commercial sign – stands as a unique context for the commodification and circulation of religious and cultural meanings and identities. This context has itself always been commodified as many of these signs were in fact commercial advertisements. But the Ghanaian roadside can now be seen to have always born the markers of mediation and mediatization, interacting with discourses of commercial, social, and religious value, as well as celebrity and spectacle. Hoover and Asamoah-Gyadu further argue that it can now be seen to interact with and be invigorated by emergent global practices of exposure and circulation. They note that this visual and media marketplace – again quite remote technologically from the rarefied atmosphere of sophisticated global "media" – can be seen to represent a political economy of mediation made possible in part by the practices of mediated religion. In Ghana's case, this mediation and mediatization is rooted in the same frame we saw in Brazil – mediatic Pentecostalism. As they note, this movement has had the effect, as in Brazil, of disconnecting religious authority from the center of the public sphere, interposing itself instead. But the focus of their study is a phenomenon which could pose a deep challenge to both these new Pentecostal forces and to the traditional religious authorities of Christianity and Islam. As they note, in recent years the media sphere of the Ghanaian roadside has begun to feature entirely new – and previously suppressed – religious forms: the healers and practitioners of African Traditional Religion. Thus a structure of religious mediation and instantiated public influence has helped to afford the emergence – and banalization – of a formerly-marginalized religious practice and discourse. But, as we've seen in other studies here, in that process that religion (African Traditional Religion) is ironically also changed and re-formulated by its mediatization in the very informal, distributed, location of the Ghanaian roadside.

We return to the larger global themes of emergent religion and emergent illiberal politics in the last study, where Pradip Thomas charts these trends in relation to a specific and particularly significant and portentous context, the rise of Hindu nationalism in Modi's India. In an eerie but distinct parallel to what Cunha has described in relation to Brazil, Thomas is able to show how Hindu nationalism is articulated into media and into mediatic spheres of practice. He presents an historicist analysis of the gradual sedimentation of Hindu-nationalist consciousness in relation to emergent media systems and practices in India across the past several decades. We can see mediatization of the kind we've spoken of here – and which we've attributed to Martin-Barbero – functioning in this case. As Thomas shows, the "media stage" – something to which Hindu consciousness contributed and from which it emerged – has made an entirely new context of activation and activism possible and practical in the era of nationalist *"Hindutva."* The media are the site of imaginaries of nation and of nationalism here, and there have been both explicit and implicit signals of those motifs growing across the past several decades, according to Thomas. In an echo of other studies in this volume, we can also see here signs of the easy accommodation of media systems and structures to this movement and vice versa. As in the West, it might once have been easy to hold the idea that media and religion are somehow incommensurate. In both contexts, that idea seems rather quaint now. Thomas also points to an affordance of media that is particular to the times but can also be said of the Brazilian and U.S. situations: that mediation is an ideal context for "muscular" Hinduism and "muscular" Christianities. But it is more than that, as Thomas suggests, when he looks ahead to the implication of digital cultures in the context he writes about. Like what he saw in reviewing the history of Hindutva and legacy media, he predicts that the emergent virtual sites will become "arenas for the re-invention of tradition . . .." What direction that re-invention takes remains the open question.

Larger Meanings, Larger Projects

These studies reveal a complex, layered, and evolving situation. Contemporary social and political formations present us with deep challenges to interpretation and understanding. It is clear that many of our received ideas are no longer adequate and we search for answers. Among the dimensions that have proven the most provocative at the same time that their importance seems so obvious are the twin concerns of this book and these authors: media and religion. We've argued that new ways of thinking about each are both necessary and helpful for being able to unpack and make sense of the evolving world of the 21st Century. On a very basic level, these conditions have confirmed for us that the received understandings of the world, derived as they are from older, more unitary visions of the progression of history, don't map well onto a situation where things seem to be diversifying under centripetal forces.

But, as we can see here, that is largely the point and the significance of the contemporary situation. What seem so fractured and diverse may well have a logic when we look at them in more detail. As we've suggested, our intellectual myopias about contemporary change in these areas may well be rooted in two things about which we think we've provided insight in these pages. First the impression of complexity and chaos may be a function of the epistemic frames through which we have been conditioned to look at things: the received frames of the intellectual history of the North-Atlantic imperial/colonial project. There are important, even vital, insights there. And, as we've said, we cannot ignore or fully transcend that legacy.

We inhabit that legacy even as we critique it. But, in critiquing it we can gain insights such as those we've begun to develop here. Most importantly that the seeming contradictions and incommensurabilities of things like contemporary politics, make more sense when we look more deeply at actual cases, contexts and histories and do so through located frames of reference.

A second significant condition under which much of the discourse about these things has labored is the condition of hypermediation itself. Our global cultural and social worlds are defined, described, understood, critiqued, and reformed through systems and means of communication that operate today under a regime that can be destabilizing, confusing, and complex and which seemingly accelerates at an ever greater rate. At the same time, humans and human systems continue to find ways to live with it and in it. It is our challenge to not be confused by the ways that what we've come to understand about communication seem to be changing, but instead to look at this as well on its own terms. Careful scholarship is one important way of doing that. We encourage readers to consider the works that follow as examples that kind of work. Scholarship today must be increasingly "public." One important implication of that is that scholarship needs to understand that it does not and cannot operate in a rarefied space of circulation beyond the fray. We are part of the fray and are subject to its conditions and limitations. We must find our voices within it in an increasingly complex world. We want this volume to be an example of that.

Works Cited

Alma, H. and G. Vanheesvijck 2018. *Social Imaginaries in a Globalizing World*. Berlin: deGruyter.
Anderson, B. 2006. Imagined Communities: Reflections on the Origin Spread of Nationalism. London: Verso.
Appadurai, A. 1996. "Disjuncture and difference in the Global Cultural Economy," in *Modernity at Large: Cultural Dimensions of Globalization*. Minneapolis: University of Minnesota Press.
Bolter, J. and Grusin, R. 2000. *Remediation: Understanding New Media*. Cambridge: MIT Press.
Chakrabarty, D. 2007. "The Idea of Provincializing Europe" in D. Chakrabarty, *Provincializing Europe: Post-Colonial Thought and Historical Difference*.
Couldry, N. and Hepp, A. 2016. *The Mediated Construction of Reality*. London: Wiley.
Echchaibi, N. 2020. "What's the Use of Hypermediation?" Working paper, Center for Media, Religion and Culture, University of Colorado, August 1.
Faucault, M. 1984. "What is enlightenment?" in The Foucault Reader, edited by Paul Rabinow. New York: Pantheon Press.

Gladwin, M. 2019. "Mission and Colonialism," in J. Rassmussen, J. Wolfe, and J. Zacchuber, (eds.) *The Oxford Handbook of 19th Century Christian Thought*. Oxford: Oxford University Press.

Hidalgo, O. 2019. "Religious Backgrounds of Illiberal Democracy in Central and Eastern Europe," *Religion and Society in Central and Eastern Europe*, 12(1) May.

Hoover, S. 2019. "Affective Infrastructures," https://hypermediations.net/content/affective-infrastructures (accessed June 9, 2020).

Lövheim, M. and S. Hjarvard 2019. "The Mediatized Conditions of Contemporary Religion: Critical Status and Future Directions," *Journal of Religion, Media, and Digital Culture*, 8(2) September.

Maldonado-Torres, N. 2014. "Race, Religion, and Ethics in the Modern/ Colonial World," *Journal of Religious Ethics*, 42(4) December.

Martín-Barbero, J. 1993. *Communication, Culture and Hegemony: From the Media to Mediations*, London: Sage.

Martín-Barbero, J. 2012. "The Processes: From Nationalisms to Transnationals," in M. Durham and D. Kellner, Media and Cultural Studies Keyworks. London: Blackwell.

Marzouki N., D. McDonnell, and O. Roy 2016. *Saving the People: How Populists Hijack Religion*, Oxford: Oxford University Press.

Norris, P. 2019. *Cultural Backlash: Trump, Brexit, and Authoritarian Populism*, Cambridge: Cambridge University Press.

Meyer, B. 2009. *Aesthetic Formations: Media, Religion, and the Senses*. London: Palgrave.

Mignolo, W. and K. Walsh 2018. *On Decoloniality*. Durham: Duke University Press.

Said, E. 1979. *Orientalism* New York: Vintage.

Stewart M. Hoover and Nabil Echchaibi
Conjuring the Religious, the Global and the Mediated

In 1972, the crew of Apollo 17 took an image that may have forever changed the way we think about the world. Called "the blue marble" or "the earthrise," it iconified human understanding of the planet we inhabit and marked a transformative moment in the history of global consciousness. It was remarkable both for its own aesthetics and for its prefiguring of the role that images and image technologies would come to play in the way we see ourselves and our world. It was also remarkable for what it seemingly unleashed in consciousness and in politics. It has been credited as one of the motivations for Earth Day and the subsequent spread of environmental consciousness. But it also marked a new era in thinking about the world as a whole.

It has become common to use the word "global" to describe a wide range of social and political geographies, a turn that can be traced to a change in consciousness occasioned by "earthrise." The idea of "the global" is of course contested, not because there are not in fact things that transcend region and nation and concern the whole earth, but because the provenance of the received conceptions of "the global" and "globalization" have come under scrutiny. Specifically, we must ask "whose 'globalization' are we talking about?" Much of the rhetoric of globalization is not a property of the whole, but the specific deployment of powerful intellectual, social, and political forces in the developed West. It can be seen as the natural consequence of the long march of North Atlantic social and economic progress. The project of neo-liberal economic globalization has been a central example of this.

However, there are other "globalizations." As Amaryta Sen (2002) has said, what is generally thought of rather unproblematically as a universal and normative "globalization" is in fact a particular construction – a historically situated construction. As he puts it, "In this view, globalization is not only good, it is also a gift from the West to the world . . .." Thus, both its generality and its normativity should be re-considered. In Sen's words:

> From the opposite perspective, Western dominance – sometimes seen as a continuation of Western imperialism . . . has established rules of trade and business relations that do not serve the interests of the poorer people in the world (2002:A2)

To Sen, it is important to understand that there are many "globalizations," or rather that there are many points and locations through history when globally-significant and globe-defining developments emerged in locations outside or alongside the histories of the North Atlantic West. These then spread to the West, and are often not appreciated for their non-Western provenance. Among the examples he points to are paper, the printing press, gunpowder, the crossbow, and of course the world-changing developments in mathematics that had their origins in Asia. There are of course, others. There have been many "globalizations" across history.

The point, of course, is that it is all a question of perspective, of framing, and of who and where there are the capacities to name and to claim properties and processes. Sen, and other critics of the unalloyed and progressive view of Western-managed globalization as universal and normative, want us to think about how such descriptions of the situation emerge, are framed, and are sustained. Italian geographer Franco Farinelli (2014) asks a very simple question in this regard, "Why do we believe blindly in maps?" His answer is that our conception of maps is informed and conditioned by a longstanding cartographic reasoning rooted in a Western and Christian logic that reduces material realities to images of the world, or what the world should be. Maps in this sense deploy a geographical discourse that hides a specific scientific and theological belief system. That is what makes the story of "earthrise" so pertinent. It became a moment when a new consciousness of the unity of the world (and its vulnerability to be sure) emerged as a popular circulation, and its status resulted from a technological mediation – a photographic image made possible by the industrial and military prowess of a Western power – the United States. What is also significant to any consideration of the mediation of consciousness or practice – including the religious – is how in this instance, the provenance of the image and its dominant interpretations made its sources tacit and banal. We simply came to accept the image as a property of a whole – the globe – through which it could look back on itself. This idea of globalism and globalization as unproblematic (while at the same time deeply embedded in certain regimes of cultural, social, and state power) was powerfully persuasive.

As a result we as [newly-constituted] "global citizens" began to think in new ways – and to *want* to think in new ways – about that place shown in the images and increasingly held in the images in our heads. At the same time, these new consciousnesses of something we think of as "the globe" afforded new economic, political, and technological forces that have increasingly taken on this new character of "the global."

It is hard now to remember how revolutionary this was in 1972. Before that time, consciousness of the world outside national borders was defined by categories and terms like "international" or "intergovernmental," or "multilateral." The frame was quite different, and defined by perspectives of specific locations and transactions between them. Even the United Nations – the first truly intentionally "global" body – was defined as a collection of the "nations" that were its members. After 1972, it became possible to think outside these frames, conceiving of perspectives and projects that thought of the world as a whole and something that was larger than the sum of its various parts. At least that was the aspiration. And the idea that there could be an aspiration about these things, that we could aspire to re-think and re-generate our imaginations of national and transnational space, is a unique consciousness typical of modernity. As Giddens suggested, modern social reflexivity puts our subjectivities at the center of collective consciousness and collective imagining. We, as individuals, are centered, and we think of the world as something that is there for us to grasp, to understand, and perhaps to master.

Giddens centered modern means of communication in these relations. Their technologies have made new images and understandings possible and available. Their systems and networks have come to transcend prior frameworks of time and space. Truly international conversations, networks, relationships and publics are possible today, for the first time in history. So, media are implicated in our evolving understandings of the world both because they are part of the fabric and constitution of international relationships and networks, and because they afford new epistemologies, new consciousnesses. They enable and – more importantly – *seek to empower* us to think differently, to position ourselves and our subjectivities and our identities on maps that they seem to make possible and logical and inevitable.

We can think in new ways because the networks of communication in which we are embedded carry with them the implication of perspective and effectivity. We think we know how things work because we've seen behind the scenes through modern mediation. That knowledge is a kind of empowerment. This understanding of communication of course has deep roots in Anglo-American traditions of knowledge and of enlightenment. Knowledge for its own sake is a good thing. And to possess that knowledge is a kind of action – at least to the modern, enlightened mind. And it should be a simple extension of this logic to say that knowledge of the world beyond our own home locations and cultures and nations can necessarily also be mastered. Media – at least information media – seem almost to define liberal enlightenment. And, certain modes of practice seem to be implied. We can look at the world as an extension of our own geographies. We can look at the world comparatively. We can look at it as a set of interacting trajectories of history. We can look at it as a set of exchanges.

It's Complicated

But some things complicate this picture. First, our mediated view of the world is necessarily a *horizontal* one. To think about things only as extensions or comparisons or mixtures of the known implies a homogeneity that is contradicted by real experience. This also blinds us to the role of power in these relations. Second, the same media that give us a superordinate conceptual mastery of what we survey there also increasingly show us that the world is much *less horizontal* and much *more diverse*, and much more multivalent and multifaceted than the easy explanatory frameworks allow. The world, in short, resists our easy practices of definition and mastery. Finally, the media themselves are not so straightforward. In place of a once-dominant media regime defined by established media, channels, and networks we today find ourselves in an era we call "hypermediation" (Echchaibi, 2020). An era marked by an open-ended continuum of technological and social acceleration that is at the heart of an intense process of mediation.

A further complexity is suggested by John Tomlinson in his influential work on globalization. That is that globalization is both a set of concrete social, state, and institutional arrangements, and at the same time a cultural formation.

> the huge transformative processes of our time that globalization describes cannot be properly understood until they are grasped through the conceptual vocabulary of culture; likewise that these transformations change the very fabric of cultural experience and, indeed, affect our sense of what cultural actually is in the modern world. (1991:1)

This means that the complex and layered contribution of media and mediation to "the global" is deeply implicated in its constitution. We would not know about the global in any meaningful sense were it not for the essential integration of media structures and circulations in it. Media are thus multiply articulated into the idea of the global, and always have been. "Earthrise" provides a helpful illustration of this point. It was more than a mere mechanical reproduction. It hailed us into a certain subject position. W.J.T. Mitchell famously asked "what do pictures want?" and earthrise wanted a great deal from us, and opened horizons that were necessary consequences of its appearance at its particular point in history. It lay in a trajectory of development that linked ideas of "the modern" with late-modern versions of American manifest destiny. These were and are all cultural and social formations that are brought into being by this particular media object. To use Tomlinson's formulation, the mechanical, physical object of the earthrise image is made manifest through its cultural articulation.

There are, of course, roiling debates about the projects of globalization and their implications for economy, culture, society, and politics. It is not our intention to wade into those debates in general, but rather in a specific way, and with a specific argument. We want to think about the nature of globalization from the perspective of its mediation through modern networks of communication. We inquire into the ways that mediations both constitute and problematize the easy and taken-for-granted ways that globalization is typically thought about. We do not take on globalization in a normative sense. It is not up to us, or within the purview of our argument to be able to validate it or undermine it in that register. Instead, we want to consider how we must think about "the global" (meaning the translocal, the international, the intercultural, the broad contexts that cross national and cultural boundaries) in ways that can foreground an undervalued set of relations. Those relations are the complex and layered interactions between "the media" and "the religious" in the contemporary cultural moment. As we have noted, our ideas of globalization or of the global do not emerge fully formed from historical roots. They have been *made* through the same set of processes that have produced our ideas of "the West" and of the processes that have constituted the North Atlantic West in its position of global centrality.

There are consequences to these impulses to code "the global" – and religions' relationship to it. As we have said, this has the effect of making a *particular* (the Western narrative of the global) into a *universal* (the conceptual and discursive framing of the contemporary neo-liberal project). Further, it has the effect of mis-directing our collective memory and valuation of a range of contributions that places outside the West have made, which is intellectually both dishonest and lazy. We are poorer for this. Perhaps most important in relation to our developing knowledge and understanding about the contribution of religion, religious discourses, and religious impulses to evolving global cultures comes from Talal Asad (Mahmood, 1996). Asad argues that the received view of the normative global has vilified the local or the desire to preserve local and daily life in such a way that only movement into the future and change are worthy of "making history." This narrow historicity has had a deep impact on how we perceive certain cultures, societies and religions or religious movements.

We wish to argue that media and religion have been deeply interconnected throughout this history, and that this interconnection is both under-understood and at the same time profound. At the same time, we must recognize that many of our received definitions are in fact contingent and partial, rather than substantive and canonical. What has been produced and might be produced in the realm of religion emerges as a production of modernity and late modernity. We will further argue that this places a particular kind of burden on scholarships of religion and of mediated religion that might wish to think of themselves as addressing relations across regional, national, or global contexts. It also points to a set of major framing questions and to theoretical and methodological approaches that seem necessary to understand things today.

Trying Times

In the 21st Century, these shifting relations have taken on new urgency as a set of social, cultural, and political conditions have upended many of the settled understandings of the past. Not least among these are questions of how and where religion will be generated, expressed, and negotiated in an era where it seems to be of increasing profile and importance. For most of the 20th Century, it was a settled matter that a unitary and determinative process of "secularization" was the future of religion (Cf. Inglehart and Welzel, 2003). This was generally thought to mean that the future of religion was in decline. Instead, religion has persisted. But this persistence is a complex matter. In the North Atlantic West generally, traditional religious practice is in decline. At the same time, across a range of contexts, informal religious and quasi-religious practice seems to be on the increase. Outside the Christian North Atlantic West, religious participation remains high, but with a shifting geography of traditional and emerging institutions and movements across the Christian, Muslim, and Hindu worlds. Among these movements, the growing Christian neo-Pentecostal movement is a significant force, as are a variety of movements within both Islam and Hinduism.

But religion persists in another way, one that seems of increasing significance and even portent. It is increasingly not just about traditional doctrines, confessions, and institutions. The North Atlantic West seemingly entered a new era with a series of political developments starting with the 2015 "Brexit" vote in Britain. What has emerged has been a new set of political forces focused on re-imagining Europe and Anglophone North America along more nationalist and national-identity lines. Religion has emerged as a subtle and layered dimension of these developments. This situation is of course much more explicit in the U.S. context, where conservative Christianity has played an increasingly prominent role in national politics for at least the last quarter-century. The so-called "Trump phenomenon" carries within it a significant measure of religion, both in *explicit* and *implicit* forms. The U.S. context can, in fact, provide a broad framework for understanding the place of religion across the larger case of North Atlantic populism and now emergent illiberal populist regimes worldwide, from Brazil to Hungary, to India. In the U.S., both the explicit and implicit registers of religion are obvious, and their relations are intelligible through a historiography of religion in that unique context. It goes without saying that there is more explicit religion present in the U.S., whereas more implicit registers seem more typical in Europe.

In the U.S., religion is explicitly present as a long-term legacy of American colonial and political settlement (Fukuyama, 1995; Lipset, 1996; Morone, 2003; Gorsky, 2017). As noted by observers such as Alexis de Toqueville, the North American colonies were clearly and deeply marked by their religious history, and religious practice was not only commonplace, but articulated into both private and state apparatuses of politics and citizenship (Gorsky, 2017). This characteristic of the U.S. context has persisted, even as formal religious participation has declined. It is still taken-for-granted that religion remains a prominent social marker in U.S. culture, and has always had wide latitude to insert itself in explicit ways in American politics and culture.

In the Trump era, this has been typified by the seeming contradiction of broad conservative religious support for a man whose very persona would seem to contradict some of the most basic and traditional of those values (Weiss, 2018; Posner, 2020). The answer lies in the politics, not so much the religion, of the matter. (If by "religion" we mean traditional doctrine, theology, religious guidance and personal piety). Instead, contemporary conservative Christian politics is about a direct and explicit involvement in movement – and electorate – building around a specific set of values and political goals. American religion – and Protestantism in particular – have always sought to mark the culture in iconic and explicit ways, to the extent that it is thought impossible for someone to seek high office who does not have some level of explicit religious involvement. But in the Trump era, American politics has seemingly moved a step further, to the place where direct and pragmatic (and seemingly morally contradictory) actions seem justified. As one prominent conservative voice put it,

> God must have quite a sense of humor to have brought evangelicals and Donald Trump together. Sometimes the most unlikely people become our staunchest defenders, and he certainly has. Not unlike Ronald Reagan, a divorced former Hollywood actor, who became the champion for evangelicals when our movement first burst upon the national political beaches almost 40 years ago. (Weiss, 2018)

Underneath this pragmatism, however, lies a set of implicit relations that are more directly echoed across the Atlantic. This religious register is pointed to in accounts such as this argument from a proponent of the "Trump turn" in the U.S. Republican Party.

> Republicans have long criticized Democrats for dividing the country into competing grievance groups. Some now realize that the Republican analogue has been to divide the country into radically autonomous individuals based on a cartoonish misreading of libertarianism that replaces the free markets and free minds of Friedrich Hayek with the greed and hubris of Gordon Gekko. But that is changing quickly. There is a renewed emphasis on addressing America and Americans as a community characterized by fraternal bonds and mutual responsibility – what Lincoln called the "mystic chords of memory." (Buskirk, 2018)

These "mystic chords of memory" appeal to a different cultural register than pragmatic questions of politics around specific issues. They bear a resemblance to Raymond Williams's notion of the "structure of feeling," a way of understanding informal, working-class consciousness as something deeply embedded in shared memory, sentiment, and perhaps grievance (Hoover, 2017). In the deeply Christianity-marked contexts of both Europe and North America, religion lurks – again largely implicitly – in these relations. Recent studies show that while explicitly religious belief may not be an important contributor to emerging ideas of the populist right in Europe, implicit religion in relation to national identity, is powerfully present (Pew Research Center, 2018). In both the U.S. and European contexts, conservative and populist movements and interests seem motivated by a desire to have some sort of religious "marking" at the center of culture and politics. This is more obvious in the U.S context, of course (Hoover, 2017). However, it should not be missed in the European context. This is an emergent situation, but can be traced perhaps to such things as the debates over the European constitution in 2004–5, where explicit reference to the Christian roots of the continent were proposed for the document, but ultimately not included, much to the disappointment of forces which have come to more prominence in recent years (The Guardian, 2004).

It should go without saying that these constitutions of religion as an explicit political force (in the U.S. context) and as an implicit one in both the U.S. and Europe, bears a deep debt to the mediation of religion in these contexts. American conservative Protestantism would not exist today as a movement, or in the force it expresses, were it not for its mediations. The American Evangelical movement as a political force owes its existence to its emergence in the 1970s in conjunction with prominent media ministries, including the so called "televangelists" and more conventional religious media figures such as Billy Graham.

Even more interesting and perhaps profound, implicit registers of "the religious" can find their effect today through the functions of "imaginaries" of moral purpose, identity, and community. In fact, it is through media imaginaries that these networks of shared memory and identity can find a kind of perfect expression not possible in the real worlds of social life and politics (Simagine, 2018). These imaginaries, of course, exist, are perfected, and are increasingly circulated through the channels and instruments of media.

We want to argue, then, that any attempt to account for contemporary cultural forms in the North Atlantic West must take account of religion, and of media, and of interactions between religion and media. These relations are layered and complex, and involve both traditional and received categories of analysis but at the same time defy those categories, demanding new analytical framings, new locations of inquiry, and new understandings of theory and method.

Our argument of course can and should be extended beyond the United States or the West more generally. Interrogating these relations and establishing a scholarly platform for their analysis must necessarily look outside those contexts. In the rest of the world, religion and media are involved in the same complex dynamics and patterns of interaction. Of course, there will be differences across national, cultural, and geographic contexts. But the growing similarities of media cultures (under the neo-liberal regime of media globalization) are interrogating societies, individuals, and religious authorities in identical ways.

Shifting Meanings

This argument enters a field where a good deal of discussion and ferment is already the order of the day. Globalization, the notion of the global, the very idea that unitary or total framings of experience are all contested ideas and spaces. Beyond them, of course, is the broader question addressed by Tomlinson. Is globalization or "the global" something that is constituted by economy and markets? There is powerful evidence that it is, and that rather than being historically normative and nominal, is in fact something contingent, resting on the interests of capital and markets. This makes the category of "the global" – even in economic and structural terms – historically contingent and partial. This is part of the reason that the idea has been so open to debate and contestation, particularly since the turn of the Century (for a review of these debates, see Strand, Mueller and McArthur, 2005). Globalization is not a stable concept, but rather a way of articulating a broad range of social and structural trends and – more importantly – a way of encapsulating an emerging range of anxieties about those trends.

The concept of "religion" is also contested turf. As religion scholars know, it is exceedingly hard to define. Common discourse about it (including journalistic accounts) tends to go to essentialized, normative framings. It is about human connection with the divine, for example, or about salvation or the soul, or transcendence. Rudolf Otto and Jonathan Z. Smith have provided normative definitions that have essentialism at their centers. There are also more structural or historical definitions that focus on doctrine, sacred text, clerical authority and hierarchies of power. Each of these approaches has proven inadequate to account for all those things that "bear a family resemblance" to religion today (with a nod to Wittgenstein). Religion – and its binary partner "spirituality" – surfaces in contexts and registers that do not easily fit into these received, essentialized categories. In particular, they do not provide the frameworks or tools to account in meaningful ways with religions' articulations into contexts of (what we once facily called) "secular" power, politics, discourse, and contestation. These approaches – and their cousin, deeply "psychologistic" approaches to religion that attempt to locate it entirely within the human brain or human psyche – don't help us very much to understand things like the evolving location of religion in the neo-liberal project or in North Atlantic Populism. The category of "civil religion," which encompasses politics, ritual, secular space, and religious symbolic and ritual practice is yet another layer of complexity challenging our received ways of seeing things (Cf. Gorsky, 2017). Add to this other layers of complexity about normative definitions of religion, who gets to define religion, and whose religious imaginary prevails, creating a hierarchical index of what is considered 'proper religion' and what is relegated to the realm of the cult. Modern conceptions of religion are vastly informed by a distinct Western experience, debates, and power struggles that are not translatable across religious cultures and practices elsewhere.

"Communication" as a category or concept is also shifting in the new century. The complexity of analyzing it is based in a characteristic identified by media theorist Roger Silverstone (1994) as communication's "double articulation" into other social contexts and processes. By this he meant that processes of communication (most notably, those of *mediation*) are at one and the same time an object for us – we can see and experience communication or mediation – and the means by which we make sense of our worlds in specific and in general situations and contexts. This makes the analytical challenge a profound one. Beyond this characteristic, communication and mediation are increasingly complex and ambiguous in that the means and contexts of communication have so radically shifted in the past century. In the late 19th Century, communication was much more a feature of interpersonal and group contexts. More modern and "mass" means of communication were emerging (in mass production of print materials and the development of film and radio) but they had yet to move from the peripheries of most peoples' everyday experience to the center.

Across the 20th century, this changed dramatically. Early in the period, there was a gradual acceleration of both the proliferation of channels of communication (from print, to visual, to new networks and platforms and means of signal delivery) and their ubiquity. By the 1970s, across the developed West, radio was near full saturation in the audience marketplace, with television close behind. In the latter third of the century, new means of distribution meant that audiences had more and more communicational materials available to them no longer being subject to distribution markets such as film exhibition and terrestrial broadcasting. And then came the digital revolution in communication, which further accelerated these other two dimensions and added a new one: speed. "Modern" communication had always offered increased speed in transmission, but the digital revolution introduced exponential acceleration both in transmission and in a new factor – interactivity.

Part of the problem is that – even in banal and received registers – radically different things can be meant and implied by the idea of "the global." Marshall McLuhan (1964:6) is credited with the neologism that articulated the vision later represented by "earthrise:" that of the "Global Village." At the time of his writing, the earth was seemingly coming together, due largely to advances in communication. But, at the same time that people began to know more and more – and in more intimate ways – about "others" out there, difference also became important. So, was the globe something that was unified, or was it a collection of quite different peoples, locations, and geographies? The legacies of the so-called "Age of Exploration" and of colonialism did stress difference and hierarchy and it was those categories and definitions that were elided by the communication revolutions of the mid-20th Century. The ambiguous and often contradictory relations between these two ways of thinking of the globe are at the root of what remains an unstable and contested idea. And, it is increasingly important to ask the question, "who is asking?" or "in whose view?" when we move toward normative definitions. Whose Globality are we talking about?

This challenge has been recognized by voices such as Gayatri Spivak (2003) who proposes to replace "the globe" with "the planet." Her aim is to expand our vision of the world away from a 'one-world' mindset. We are first planetary beings and planetarism, she argues, refers to "an undivided 'natural' space rather than a differentiated political space" divided by lines and characterized by a uniform system of exchange. While globalization segregates and isolates, planerarity can potentially liberate us from identity politics and polarizing logics. More radically – to Spivak – planetarity marks an end to the logic of geography.

The whole project of establishing a normative or consensual view is itself a product of the structures of hierarchy and power through which the elites of the globe some to account for it. Those with the power to make the definitions, to draw the maps, and to engage in the rarified atmosphere of what Arjun Appadurai (1991) called "the Global Ethnoscape" are not mere subjects of a settled space of unproblematic access and interaction. No, as influential voices such as Dipesh Chakrabarty (2007), Edward Said (1993) and others have argued, they are social actors who are exercising their prerogative to deepen and extend a set of social and institutional relations that have defined the differential locations of power throughout the modern era. These relations are of course elided and made tacit by facile and superficial references to "the global." And the role of systems and circulations of communication in this is profound. Their "double articulation" at the same time seeks to normalize relations of power that wish to describe contexts of communication as broad, democratic, and accessible, and present to us imaginaries of the world that elide boundaries.

The digital age has extended and deepened these capacities of communication, media, and mediation. While it has afforded new channels, networks, connections and communities of reference that horizontally connect once diffuse and disconnected communities of reference and interest, that is not its only effect. At the same time that it has enabled possibilities for resistance, alternative voices, and diverse communities of articulation, it also extends the ideological project of media in modernity. Many of the ideologies and formations that have been typical of global media since the advent of print (the centrality of economic, state, and clerical power, for instance) have simply found new force and presence in the digital age. But there is a more material and practical side to our media era. We have come to call this contemporary condition "hypermediation." Echchaibi (2020) has described the source of the idea this way:

> What marks our current media moment is not simply the newness of its technological artifacts, but the velocity, ubiquity, aesthetics and ethics of these artifacts and the intimate place they hold in everyday life. This context of deep mediation we refer to as "hypermediation" not as a pathological and staged condition of an impoverished sociality á la Baudrillard or an oversaturated space of dizzying media infrastructures and devices ordering our lives beyond control. Rather, we use "hypermediation" as a conceptual shorthand and a material space to account for and interrogate the speed, superabundance, intensity, and ubiquity of media and their (in)ability to address the limitations and deficits of our social life.

This describes well the new media and communication moment. In the past we could think of media in terms of their sources, their means of transmission, and their reception. The essentially static nature of this model was not obvious until we entered a period (that is, the past two decades) where the technical, political and social economies of mediation have centered its materialities and practices as settled facts of social life, deeply embedded in our communities, identities, and subjectivities as contemporary social actors. Communication and media are not distinct from our social experience and consciousness. They are increasingly part of their fabric. And the dimensions of hypermediation described by Echchaibi point to a set of social anxieties or even moral panics over contemporary digital media. These trends are even more deeply embedded and problematic in that they are so extensively articulated into the processes of emerging neo-liberal cultural markets with their projects of commodification and "branding." As critics such as Sarah Banet-Weiser (2012) and Katherine Sender (2012) have demonstrated, these processes are far from inert. Instead, they aspire to bind audiences and circulations into new systems and networks of social conditioning and control through the opacity of seemingly benign processes of consumption and distribution. As contemporary social actors, we are thus subject to a media environment that often seems more like a whirlwind than a coherent flow.

The discrete elements of this whirlwind include, of course, an ever-expanding range of sources and channels, an accelerating range of modes of engagement and circulation, new and emergent locations of production and consumption typified by their merger into one set of practices, an assumption of interactivity and "public-ness," and an ideological apparatus that conditions subjectivity in relation to these elements. That ideology, as we all know, is one that celebrates each of these conditions, suggesting that our embedment in hypermediated spaces is necessarily a good thing. After all, what could be wrong with nearly unlimited access to knowledge and to locations of discourse, or with unlimited potentials of new relationships and networks, or with a media practice that centers and empowers individuals? This appeals to a kind of enlightenment humanism provides significant cover for whatever underlying processes and dynamics may reside at the heart of the hypermediated moment. It also goes without saying that both hypermediation and the way we talk about hypermediation are affordances that are not equally distributed geographically, politically, or in class, racial, and gendered terms. To put it bluntly, only certain populations have the luxury of availing themselves of the full fruits of the media moment.

Religion has taken new and multivariate meanings and locations in the context of the contemporary "global." As we have said, it has not "gone away," but instead has endured, even persisted, in the first decades of the new century. But discourses of politics, of social change, of journalism, and of cultural formation have struggled to account for it. Part of this is due to the inadequacy of the languages and conceptual tools that intellectual elites in the North Atlantic West have used to address and interpret it. This is itself a legacy of the theories of "secularization" that have dominated these discourses for decades (Calhoun, et al., 2011). The idea that secularization might be an inevitable process that would yield universal results (that in all places, modernity would undermine essentialized religion as we have understood it) was another legacy of the consensual modernity narrative of the West. The fact that it is at best uneven in its consequences and that religion has come to insert itself in real and deep ways in contemporary politics contradicts much of this thinking.

That religion is articulated into a broad range of contemporary social and cultural flows and struggles suggests that it has been too narrowly defined and misunderstood for too long. And, the fact that it is increasingly surfacing in problematic ways – ways that defy received public and modernist Anglo-American principles (chiefly that it should necessarily be about good and positive things to be "legitimate") makes our received categories of understanding and evaluation inadequate.

The received view of religion is of course also a universalist view. All religions are all essentially the same, and about the same sorts of things. And this universalism and essentialism necessarily complicates our ability to understand religion in a period where it no longer sits on a shelf but instead confronts us in the middle of deeply challenging social and political conflicts (for a discussion, see Quirk, 2015).

As we begin to re-think how the mediation of religion may play a role in contemporary politics and discourses, then, we must confront some truisms. Religion confronts us in public discourse in both universal and in particular guises. There are the large categories of "the religious," such as the historic "major faiths." But then there are the smaller categories of "fringe" or "marginal" or "emergent" religious traditions, including those religion scholars like to call "new religious movements." There are also ways that religion is particularly and differentially integrated into other social and cultural formations, such as its articulation into the emergent politics of post-Brexit, post-Trump nationalism and populism. So, do we think of these things as variations on the universalist or essentialist theme or do we think of them as entirely novel? We see examples of both approaches in contemporary journalism.

Since our purpose here is to engage a conversation about how we know what we know, the larger question is whether things are better understood as universals or as distinctions. Is a given formation *sui generis* or merely a variation on a larger theme? It should be obvious that, in our view, this is a false distinction, itself rooted in earlier universalist and tacit categories of knowing – legacies of the Enlightenment project's aspiration to broad and summative explanations. Our developing argument here is that we must begin to engage in a process of de-constructing and then re-constructing our sense of what we are doing and how we do it. Yes, religion is problematic and carries with it great potential for struggle and even violence as it interacts with emerging political formations today. But, in the context of public discourse (and then public scholarship), the essential challenge is to understand how and where it becomes problematic. That points to an inquiry focused on the genealogies and trajectories of the relations that bring it to the fore, rather than one focused on perfecting, legitimating, or delegitimating it.

It logically follows that the large frame here is again in the legacy of the Enlightenment and specifically in the particular ways that the intellectual legacies of colonialism have created this moment. As we have said, a process that would resemble Chakrabarty's "provincialization of Europe" repositions many of our questions. It also historicizes them, and places them in dialog with emerging centers of knowledge and power and cultural production. And do we need to add that the context of this dialog is of course a context afforded and conditioned by the institutions and industries of "the media?"

Public and journalistic discourses about the role of religion in these relations present a range of questions or provocations to scholars who wish to extend and deepen knowledge. They ask of religion questions such as whether it is a "first cause" of political struggle or violence; whether it is merely a "marker" for other, deeper values and interests; whether it is a "rationalization" for impulses toward conflict; whether it is no longer "religion" but instead is becoming a political force. These and other ways of framing "the religious" can be seen to be rooted once again in the earlier, secularization-inflected and modernist-universalist understandings. And, of course, we can see here that religion is not any one, or all, of these things. It can be seen to have functioned in these ways in specific cases, but can we draw universal learnings from any of these?

We are helped in our project by emerging trends in the scholarships devoted to the study of media and of religion. In the case of religion, scholars have long since moved beyond essentialist and universalist questions to questions of how and where religion and religious meaning are being generated today. There is a new focus on practice and on materiality in religion. The questions move beyond received understandings of the true or authentic in religion and toward how religion is integrated into the larger social and cultural trends we are observing. The real question then is "what is produced" by a given set of relations. Looking at religion this way frees us to a broader and yet more dynamic and tensile approach to religion and to the mediation of religion in contemporary culture and politics.

The Challenges

We have begun outlining a view that in fact presents itself as a set of challenges to inquiry and to scholarship. We are at a juncture where many of our received categories, frames, and tools are no longer adequate. We began by suggesting that the contemporary situation cannot be fully apprehended by either scholars or publics without first acknowledging and then somehow accounting for a set of contradictions to our traditional ways of seeing things. Our project here is a large one in that we have sought to think about these things in relation to a "global context." We have suggested that to make progress we need to have theoretical or empirical purchase not just on the role of religion in politics, society or culture, but also in relation to knowledge and understanding – in relation to how we know what we think we know. In contemporary life, that means that we must also have a theory of media and mediation and how the media are articulated into – and articulate – these relations.

The challenges can each be seen to point to a re-thinking. Some of these discourses have been underway for some time. For example, the sense and meaning of "the global" have been subject to sustained debate. We identify with those who hold that ideas of "the global" are necessarily partial and conditional. The grand and universal ideas of the global are clearly rooted in the European sensibilities that emerged out of the Age of Exploration. The way Europe chose to see and to classify the world enabled it to establish its perspective as the universal perspective. Its interests in classifying, understanding, and – need we say – exploiting the world led to certain ways of seeing it and seeing the project that we today call "Globalization." These are of course not necessarily the same ways that people who live in the regions thus classified, understood and exploited see things.

So we need to re-think "the Global," understanding it in the terms of its genealogy and trajectory through Western history and thought. But we also need to re-think both "the religious" and "the mediated" or "the communicational." Everything is more complex, layered, and interactive than in the past, and this means – among other things – that there is at least the potential for the balances of information and knowledge to flow in new directions. We in the West know more about the world as a result of our exposure to media. But "the world" also knows more about "us." And there is also the potential (and evidence) for increasingly deep and persuasive influences and networks of action to form and grow and evolve using contemporary media. This structural reality means that religion today has a much more complex and layered set of ways that it might be "mediated" than in the past. New religious formations have evolved as a result. We've further complicated the picture by pointing out that our received ways of thinking about the nature of communication or mediation are too narrow and limited in the digital age of "hypermediation."

We are arguing then that our sense of "the global" cannot be understood outside of "the colonial" and the global experience of exploration, conquest, and domination that was the foundation of the development of the West. We are all subjects of and subject to this situation and to its means and categories of knowledge and understanding. If we want to understand any sense of "the global" and the narratives of religion in relation to it, then we must ask "whose story is *the* story?" Until now it has been the story of the economic, cultural, and intellectual forces that have controlled the channels through which knowledge is produced and remembered.

We might ask of communication – as we asked of religion earlier – whether we can draw some conclusions about its role in all of this. It has been asked whether communication (in its modern, technological, and mediated forms) binds, universalizes, or divides? Evidence of each of these is present in our modern global experience. Is it about understanding or misunderstanding? Do the new media, with their claims of empowerment, democracy, and interactivity, de-stabilize or merely reinforce global relations of media power?

There are, of course, new ways of entering discourse and exchange afforded by these new media. At the same time, the global media marketplace is increasingly marked by neoliberal globalization and its markets and practices of commodification. What is valued and legitimated in contemporary culture and politics is increasingly that which can be monetized and commodified, and thus survive. And, as we have said, the age is marked not as a "media age," but as a "hyper-mediated age." What were once definable and understandable in one or two dimensions are now circulated in more dimensions. Time and space have been enhanced by ubiquity, universality, acceleration, and immediacy.

Media history in relation to religion is also important to keep in mind. Western modernity was in part a result of an interaction between emergent religion and emergent media. To the extent that the Protestant Reformation was a major contributor, it was itself an affordance of emergent means and networks of communication. It is significant then that both Christianity and Islam emerged in the context of a certain stage of imperialism and domination, but also of communication: the transition from the Roman to the post-Roman eras. The way these two religious movements formed, pursued their goals and interests, and established themselves as the "modern" world religions was a function of the state – and communicational – networks of their times. Their interactions with emergent forms of communication were critical to their development.

We began by suggesting that our whole understanding of the world rests on certain images and icons and imaginaries, things that are today inflected with the technological affordances of modern, public media. The "double articulation" we spoke of earlier describes this situation well. At the same time that we want to engage in social and political discourses about the nature of contemporary global life and the place of religion in it, we are subject to the information about that world that we get from the media. At the same time we need to understand how those same media form the fabric of our evolving understandings.

Conclusion

We might aspire to build knowledge and practice that enables us to untangle some of these complex relations. We might envision a way that "the global" might transcend its colonial roots. We might envision a way that global discourses might create contexts, moments, and possibilities where exchanges and circulations might exist freer of the reins of the received legacies we've considered here.

This of course begins with a process of deconstruction, where we begin to rethink the received definitions and categories and possibilities as we've entered an era increasingly defined as "global." Understanding the complexities of the situation is essential. And the situation is complex and many of the tacit truisms are deserving of re-thinking and re-framing, as we've argued here.

In one sense, we'd argue for a prescription that is rather simple. It is almost tacit that we look at the evidence at hand in contemporary discourses and struggles in society, culture, and politics and then aspire to universal and large explanations. That is the modernist, enlightenment, impulse. It is also the one that seems determined by our received traditions of scholarship. But rather than a scholarship of universal explanation, we would argue that we aspire to inquiries and scholarships that are instead deeply revealing of the genealogies and trajectories of the "facts" we see. Where did this set of formations come from? What do they reveal about the way that "the religious" is working here? What do they tell us about how and where structures and means of communication frame, condition, and afford what we see?

This would seem to be a call for a kind of historicism, and we accept that. It also suggests that the way into a quest for knowledge and understanding here is through deep description of phenomena and cases. By looking at and thinking of cases in their historical and cultural histories and contexts, it becomes possible to re-think and contextualize both these cases and our own implicit framings of the essential questions. It is not about coming up with universal descriptions, taxonomies or explanations that are conceptually "prior," but to understand things as they are evolving in their contexts. A global view is not then a view to an aspired "globalization," but instead a view that understands and assumes the global, but strives for understandings that transcend the easy determinations of the past.

We are thus not arguing against all universals. In a sense, we are not contesting the very idea of universality as much as we are probing its provincialism as in its origins in Western thought and the power relations that were produced as a result of that parochialism. We are against this particular kind of universalism but call for a different deployment of the concept of universalism, one that is more lateral, what Senegalese philosopher Souleymane Bachir Diagne calls a ". . . collective and planetary form of universalism." The challenge here is whether we can truly imagine a planetary order where universality is enunciated from multiple locations without resorting to accusations of relativism, fragmentation, disorientation, or a decline of the West. In this alternative configuration of a truly global and hypermediated (and hyperconnected) world, are we doomed to become simply a multitude of thinking provinces which do not cross borders and circulate for the benefit of change? Circulation and speed are defining logics of a hypermediated existence, but what is the outcome or impact of this circulation?

We are left with the question of what we should or might mean by inquiring into media and religion in a global context. It cannot of course be a simple process of comparison across contexts – an impulse that might have worked in the past. As we've said, it cannot ignore the complicated and problematic ways that "the global" has been deployed. It must understand the sources and the implications of its terms and its aspirations. It is in one way necessarily partial, yet in another way must attempt some kinds of applicable languages and terms of reference. In positing a "global view" we find ourselves contesting the very terms and basis of such an inquiry. This self-criticism may well be best understood as a further contribution to ongoing scholarly consideration of the critical questions that arise when we understand that religion persists in national and regional contexts and in the relations between them and that media and mediations are fundamental to this condition. We must understand it as a start, not as the conclusion, of inquiry.

Works Cited

Appadurai, A. 1991. "Global ethnoscapes: Notes and Queries for a Transnational Anthropology," in R. Fox (Ed), *Recapturing Anthropology: Working to the present*. Santa Fe: School of American Research Press.
Banet-Weiser, S. 2012. *Authentic™: The Politics of Ambivalence in a Brand Culture*. New York: NYU Press.
Buskirk, C. 2018. "If There's a Red Wave Election in 2018, Here's Why," *The New York Times*, June 8. https://www.nytimes.com/2018/06/08/opinion/sunday/if-theres-a-red-wave-election-in-2018-this-will-be-why.html. Accessed July 9, 2018.
Calhoun, C., M. Juergensmeyer, and J. van Antwerpen, (eds.) 2011. *Rethinking Secularism*. New York: Oxford.
Chakrabarty, D. 2007. *Provincializing Europe*. Princeton: Princeton University Press.
Echchaibi, N. 2020. "What's the Use of Hypermediation?" Working paper, Center for Media, Religion and Culture, University of Colorado, August 1.
Farinelli, F. 2014. "Faith and the Map: On the Metaphysical Nature of Visual Spatial Representation" in M. George, D. Pezzoli-Olgiati (eds.) *Religious Representation in Place*. New York: Palgrave Macmillan.
Fukuyama, F. 1995. *Trust: The Social Virtues and the Creation of Prosperity*. New York: Simon and Schuster.
The Guardian 2004. "Christianity Bedevils Talks on EU Treaty," May 24. https://www.theguardian.com/world/2004/may/25/eu.religion Accessed July 9, Accessed July 9, 2018.

Gorsky, P. 2017. *American Covenant: A History of Civil Religion from the Puritans to the Present*. Princeton: Princeton University Press.

Hoover, S.M. 2017. "Residual and Resurgent Protestantism in The American Media (and Political) Imaginary," *International Journal of Communication*, Vol. 11.

Ingelhart, R. and Welzel, C. 2005. *Modernization, Cultural Change and Democracy: The Human Development Sequence*. Cambridge: Cambridge University Press.

Lipset, S. M. 1996. *American Exceptionalism: A Double Edge Sword*. New York: W.W. Norton.

Mahmood, S. 1996. "Interview with Talal Asad: Modern Power and The Reconfiguration of Religious Traditions, " *Contested Polities 5(1)*.

McLuhan, M. 1964. *Understanding Media*. Toronto: Gingko Press.

Morone, J.A. 2003. *Hellfire nation: The politics of Sin in American History*. New Haven: Yale University Press.

Pew Research Center (2018). "Being Christian in Western Europe," https://www.pewforum.org/2018/05/29/being-christian-in-western-europe/?utm_source=AdaptiveMailer&utm_medium=email&utm_campaign=18-05-29%20Western%20Europe%20ENG&org=982&lvl=100&ite=2635&lea=593443&ctr=0&par=1&trk= (accessed March 18, 2021).

Posner, S 2020. Unholy: Why White Evangelicals Worship at the Alter of Donald Trump.

Quirk, M 2015. "Religion, Essentialism, and Violence: Cherry Picking on the left, " Public Seminar, June 15. http://www.publicseminar.org/2015/06/religion-essentialism-and-violence/ (Accessed July 8, 2018).

Said, E. 1993. *Culture and imperialism*. New York: Vintage Books.

Sen, A. 2002. "How to Judge Globalism," The American Prospect, 13(1) January, pp. A2–5.

Sender, Katherine 2012. *The makeover: Reality Television and Reflexive Audiences*. New York: NYU Press.

Silverstone, R. 1994 *Television and Everyday Life*. London: Routledge.

Simagine Consortium 2018. "Religion, Community, Borders: Social Imaginaries and the Crisis of Neoliberal Democracy," a discussion paper, Utrecht: University of Humanistic Studies.

Spivak, G. 2003. The Death of a Discipline. New York: Columbia University Press.

Strand, J. Mueller, F. McArthur, J. 2005. "The Essentially Contested Concept of Globalization," *Politics and Ethics Review*, 1(1) 2005, 45–59.

Tomlinson, J. 1999. *Globalization and Culture*. Wiley.

Tomlinson, J. 2007. *The Culture of Speed: The Coming of Immediacy*. London: Sage. ISBN 1412912024.

Weiss, B. 2018. "Why hasn't Trump Lost the Evangelical Vote? Ralph Reed explains," *The New York Times*, June 20. https://www.nytimes.com/2018/06/20/opinion/trump-evangelicals-ralph-reed.html. Accessed July 9, 2018.

Florence Pasche Guignard
High Tech Mediations, Low Tech Lifestyles: The Paradox of Natural Parenting in the Digital Age

"Maybe Baby", "Glow", "Pink Pad Period Tracker", "iCycleBeads", "Sympto" and "FemCal": these are the names of a just few among the many "menstruation", "ovulation" or "fertility calendars" applications available through the App Store. As early as 1990, none other than Carl Djerassi, the chemist whose research contributed to the invention of "the Pill" in the 1950s, fantasized about a "jet-age rhythm method" for a hormone-free, safe, and effective contraception (Djerassi 1990). Different from the software calendar "apps" just mentioned, integrative fertility monitors such as the "Clearblue Fertility Monitor" or the "Persona Contraception Monitor", are now widely available. In contrast with these sophisticated "domesticated health tools" (Childerhose and McDonalds 2013), even the most recently launched fertility tracking apps can only record and interpret data provided by their user. Smartphones cannot (yet) conduct hormonal analysis of a saliva or urine sample. Another digital tool, the thermometer, is still needed to measure body temperature. Users, however, only purchase (or download for free) the app (software), and need not buy a separate device, nor renew their supply of testing materials (such as hormone detecting strips). Along with the devices they run on, such as smartphones, tablets and computers, these apps have become part of the daily (and sexual) life of an increasing number of women and their partners, though other hormonal and mechanical contraceptives still prevail, in particular in the francophone contexts that will be referred to in this chapter.

Fertility awareness is one of the many domains where, in the early 21st century, embodiment and scientific medical knowledge have been brought together with media and communication technologies. Tracking and monitoring one's menstrual cycle is an obvious example of "the quantified self", defined as "any individual engaged in the self-tracking of any kind of biological, physical, behavioral, or environmental information" (Swan 2013:85). The Apple Watch

---

Note: This chapter presents selected aspects of a larger research entitled "Natural Parenting in the Digital Age. Mothering at the Confluence of Religion, Environmentalism and Technology". I am grateful to the Swiss National Science Foundation for funding this project through a fellowship and to the Department for the Study of Religion at the University of Toronto for hosting me as a postdoctoral researcher. I also thank the School of Gender, Sexuality and Women's Studies at York University for granting me access to additional resources.

https://doi.org/10.1515/9783110497878-003

(to be released in 2015), among many other tasks, functions as a pedometer and measures or even replicates a heart beat. It is the most recent example of the digitalization (the use of digital devices to measure and record) and of the increasingly common mediation (the use of several types of media to share one's data or to relate it with that of others) of self-tracking cultures.

A potentially fertile, pregnant or lactating body is a significant site of a particularly feminine type of the quantified self and of its mediation. Women are using (or are subjected to) medical technology now "in conjunction with other technologies, particularly social media, to new ends: to maintain familial and social ties, and to create new connections and communities with other women and couples" (Childerhose McDonalds 2013:4). The mediation of cycle tracking generates a new communal dimension to the practice: social media, in particular, provide a space where fertility awareness can be discussed, with the option of anonymity. As will be explored in this chapter, this is the case with online communities of mothers who engage in natural family living and practice fertility awareness. Posting a ultrasound picture on social media is a new form of pregnancy announcement in line with the tendency to share an increasing amount of data about one's pregnancy online. Mothers will also look up breastfeeding advice online, let alone by searching for the time and place of the next drop-in clinic at their local lactation consultant. Some of them will also use apps, such as the Breast Milk Calculator, to assist them in keeping track of on which breast, when and for how long their baby has nursed. Such instances of "new digitised strategies for self-tracking" are "specifically goal-oriented" (Lupton 2014:3). Health, well-being and family planning are the goals of fertility awareness practitioners at the center of this chapter. Their motivations for engaging into such self-tracking practice, with or without the help of apps and other digital devices, are driven by specific values and worldviews that will in turn be highlighted.

Along with *in vitro* fertilization and surrogate pregnancy, contraception is an instance of the contemporary "total separation between the realisation of human sexual drives and human reproduction" (Blyth and Landau 2009:11). It is often at the center of vivid debates on reproductive health, women's rights, ethics and moral values, often shaped by religious discourses. While one might argue that medical technology has contributed to disconnect sexual intercourse from the risks of reproduction, fertility monitoring apps are an example where technology reconnects fertility and sexuality on the basis of scientific medical evidence (and not ritual purity imperatives, popular belief or mythologies of menstruation). When it comes to directing humans about when –and, sometimes, how– they should or should not have sex, the confluence of Western biomedical knowledge and media constitutes an influence competing with that of normative religious teachings and laws (or whichever persistent remnants of their former influence), at least where diverse type of media make such knowledge accessible.

Scholarship in health research has demonstrated that the use of "Internet-supported fertility-awareness-based methods" of family planning (with electronic hormonal fertility monitors) is more efficient and accepted than methods relying solely on self-observation and recording (Fehring et al. 2013). Debating whether fertility awareness is an effective mode of contraception or, rather, a type of birth spacing method exceeds both my competence and the scope of this chapter. Whichever the perspective on fertility awareness, it cannot be denied that its conscientious (if not always successful) application for contraceptive purposes requires a good knowledge and an accurate recording of the menstrual cycle, as well as an informed interpretation of the biological data thus gathered. More frequently, two or more among several "methods" are combined for a greater efficiency: calendar (counting the days), symptoms (changes in the consistency of the cervix and the cervical mucus), and bodily temperature usually are paid attention to. Fertility awareness is an umbrella term for different combinations of such methods, with a certain confusion about them among non-specialists. In the francophone contexts in question in this chapter, the method based on monitoring symptoms and basal body temperature is known as *"la méthode symptothermique"* (the sympto-thermic method) or simply *"la symptothermie"*. Its promoters refer to it as the *modern* sympto-thermic method in order to distinguish it from earlier (and proven less effective) methods known in English as "the Billings method" or "the Ogino-Knaus method". The basic principle of fertility awareness is to identify and distinguish the infertile, potentially fertile and fertile days of the menstrual cycle. On certain days, the couple will engage in or abstain from intercourse, depending if they wish to achieve or avoid conception. Fertility awareness can be used both to foster or to prevent pregnancy. It is particularly popular among parents who engage into natural family living, even if couples also use mechanical barrier methods (condoms, diaphragm) during the days identified as fertile, when their religious convictions do not forbid this.

The material presented in this chapter also aims at challenging the traditional association of fertility awareness with religious imperatives. Personal analytics are not a new phenomenon and neither is fertility monitoring in its earlier, low-tech versions. Contemporary cycle tracking apps confer them both a new digital aesthetic and a practicality that retain little in common with the stern circling of calendar days or charting on a piece of paper already done by our great-grandmothers. The brightly colored interface designs of these apps on mobile devices do not convey an idea of sexual asceticism. Pink and purple suggest neither bodily discipline nor the disciplining of bodies, in a Foucauldian sense, imposed on women and their partners, for a concrete and successful implementation of the practice. Even the "beads" of the iCycleBeads app are more reminiscent visually of a pill's packaging than of those of a rosary's prayer beads. The designs of these apps generally does not allude to religious obligation, nor to notions of non-procreative sexual practices (albeit normative heterosexual monogamic ones) as "sinful". Such notions are often instilled by religious teachings that are also still widely circulated, both online and offline, and that are frequently considered as primary motives for turning to fertility awareness as a method of family planning. The generally playful user's interfaces of fertility tracking apps contrast with the seriousness of what is at stake with family planning and masks the complexity of the medical research and technological expertise needed to produce the digital tools necessary for its implementation.

A balanced feminist critique of the wide range of discourses about fertility awareness cannot be fully developed in this chapter, but two distinct feminist perspectives on this issue can be briefly outlined here and put in relation with the experience one of my informants named Félicie (34 years old, originally from France and living in Ontario when I interviewed her), whose considerations about contraceptive options reflect typical values of natural parenting. The first strand of feminist discourse about fertility awareness revolves around the concern that such methods not only depend from the male partner's cooperation and discipline, but that they also place the burden of implementation, observation and recording primarily or only on women (just like remembering to take the pill everyday). In case of failure, who is to be blamed? The new generation of fertility tracking apps and monitors might minimize this objection. Even if data collection probably still falls to women, the task of archiving and analyzing is transferred to apps and computing programs that are sometimes built in the devices themselves and rather easy to use. Technology then tends to be viewed as a third party in the responsibility for contraception. Another strand of feminist discourse emphasizes the empowering aspect of fertility awareness: through education and experience, women reclaim basic knowledge about and control over their own body. Technology enables them to reclaim a form of "authoritative knowledge" (Davis-Floyd and Sargent 1997). Moreover, they free themselves from dependence on the medical system and on the doctor and they no longer have to consume the products of "BigPharma" (pharmaceutical firms that dominate the market). This argument had much appeal among those of my informants attracted to lifestyles of voluntary simplicity. Autonomy and independence from the medical establishment in the management her own fertility is one of the motivations that drove Félicie into fertility awareness. Her discourse is representative of questions and objections raised by many natural mothers (and fathers, too) and vehemently debated online. When Félicie stopped taking the pill in order to conceive her first child, she clearly felt the difference in her body, mood, general health and "level of energy". She "never again wanted to go back to the pill".

After their second child was born, in Canada, she and her husband felt that they did not want a third pregnancy in the near future. Félicie had already consulted a gynecologist and was ready to have a copper intra-uterine (IUD) device inserted, another popular hormone-free contraceptive among the natural mothers. She even had a prescription for buying the IUD and her next appointment booked with the specialist. She then changed her mind after realizing that she would need to *wait*, again, in order to have the device removed by a professional, in case she and her husband would decide that this was the right moment to plan another pregnancy. It did not matter to her whether the waiting period to get the appointment was three days, three weeks or, more likely, three months. Having an instantaneous and independent possibility for reversing her contraception proved a determining factor for Félicie in choosing fertility awareness as her method of contraception.

Natural Parenting, Mediated Technologies and Fertility Awareness

Taking fertility awareness as a case study, this chapter explores how religion, gender, and sexuality intersect with media and technology in the particular milieu of "natural parenting" practitioners in francophone contexts. It looks at how the desire to engage in the embodied and mediated feminine experience of menstrual cycle monitoring and its actual practice are accounted for in terms of lifestyle choices coherent with moral and ethical values such as respect, autonomy and sustainability. These may not necessarily be linked to established religious traditions, even if practitioners sometimes describe in religious terms some key aspects of their experimenting with what is an integral part of wider lifestyles of health and sustainability (LOHAS) in the domains of fertility and parenting.

In line with LOHAS and their contemporary mediations (Emerich 2011), natural parenting is better understood as a cluster of representations, discourses and practices that value "Nature" or "the natural" under different forms and expressions, in particular as "the environment" or "the planet" (Earth), and as the maternal body or as idealistic representations of healthy human bodies in general. The "sacred space of the home as a refuge worth of protection" (Bobel 2002:111) constitutes another strongly valued site in natural parenting (that of *home*birth, *home*schooling, *home*cooked meals or *home*made remedies, among other things). Fertility awareness and natural family planning are examples of domestic practices that media have recently given a greater visibility to, along with their discursive strategies, at least in the francophone contexts in question here.

More specifically, the following analysis highlights paradoxes in the ways in which natural parents inform themselves about, implement and promote fertility awareness as a natural family planning method. One paradox is that high-tech mediations that rely on the use of computer mediated communication tools have become the chief mean through which lifestyle choices and practices that tend to be rather "low-tech" are promoted. Labeled as *"mamans nature"* ("nature moms"), or self-identifying as such in the online and offline contexts I surveyed, some mothers tend to be rather critical of a range of technologies developed at the end of the 20th and in the early 21st century. They are particularly concerned about potential damages that may result from an indiscriminate use and abuse of such technologies, for themselves, for their children and for the environment. An increased surveillance during pregnancy and childbirth through medical examinations (ultrasound imaging, etc.), human genetic testing (including *in utero*), governmental programs for systematic child immunization, the effects of climate change, genetically modified foods, or potentially toxic cosmetics are a few elements of their "mothering in fear" (Villalobos 2010). Wi-Fi waves are also frequently part of their list of concerns. Simultaneously, both natural parenting in general and the computer-assisted practice of fertility awareness require the use of electronic devices whose manufacturing and use consume resources and energy and that, finally, generate e-waste. This intensive and rather uncritical use of media and communication technology might be viewed as contradictory for persons who, otherwise, claim to engage in ecofriendly lifestyles dubbed "voluntary simplicity" or, in French, *"sobriété heureuse"*. Voluntary simplicity "derives meaning from relative austerity and minimized consumption" (Bobel 2002:49). For most of my informants, living frugally implies different degrees of awareness about consumption, rather than a rejection of consumerism altogether. These degrees range from ethical consumption (purchasing fair-trade or certified organic goods without deeply questioning one's consumption nor the foundations of consumerist society) to an engagement with the more radical positions of the movement known as *"la décroissance"* ("de-growth" or "curtail").

In spite of their efforts to become "conscious consumers", many of my informants admit to being "great consumers of technology", as one of them puts it. Furthermore, a vast majority of the thirty parents whom I interviewed so far was critical against mass media and, in particular, television. Less than half of their families had cable TV in their home, but all had access to the Internet. In addition to devices used by their partners and children and at their workplace, most mothers owned their own smartphone, and, very often, their own computer or a tablet as well. Intriguingly, about one third of the mothers either were or had been working for information and communication technologies companies or services, had a professional formation related to them (like webmaster), or had a partner who worked in such professions. The most professionally engaged with ICT technologies among my informants were also often those who most vehemently questioned their own consumption of electronic devices. This questioning, however, was not widespread.

Natural Parenting and Media Misrepresentations in Francophone Contexts

Rather than a fixed list of mandatory or exclusive practices, natural parenting is better understood as an array of representations and discourses about practices that are more likely to be found in "natural family living" than in other styles of parenting. Among these are: natural family planning and hormone-free fertility awareness methods; a preference for a midwifery model of care during pregnancy, childbirth and postpartum; a preference for alternative medicine in general; a preference for second-hand items or reusable items (typically washable diapers); and a preference for specific diets (often flexitarian and vegetarian ones, along with growing or buying organic food). Both in Europe and in North America, contemporary natural parenting draws a lot from attachment parenting and its privileged practices such as bonding after birth, breastfeeding, babywearing, and family bed sharing. However, natural parenting does not completely coincide with attachment parenting, in spite of how media tend to picture together and thus confuse both trends. One can have an elective C-section, use disposable diapers, buy (too many) toys that potentially contain harmful chemicals, and eat large quantities of meat from conventional agriculture and still be an "attachment parent". Natural parenting adds to attachment parenting an environmentalist agenda which was not a preoccupation for the its early theorists such as John Bowlby or William Sears and his wife Martha. Not only must parents raise happy, healthy and well-adjusted children, but they also must do so without harming their own health, that of their children, and the environment.

In recent years, media have played an increasingly important role in the representation of natural parenting and in its international dissemination. The following inquiry into some of the technological and mediatized dimensions of fertility awareness among natural parents is based principally on material gathered for a broader study conducted mostly on European francophone contexts. My methodology for accessing and gathering material for this research aims at reflecting the contemporary location of natural parenting discourses. When Chris Bobel conducted the only extensive study on what she coined *The Paradox of Natural Mothering* (2002) in the mid-1990s USA, she had to physically visit places such as natural food stores and farmers markets. Among others, she attended natural childbirth classes, breastfeeding advocacy meetings, or those of homeschooling organizations (Bobel 2002:181). During the completion of my research project, started in 2012, I met in such places with "natural parents" and I already knew personally a few or them, referred to me by relatives and friends. Although I had already engaged in casual conversations about parenting with many of them, I choose to focus instead on materials from the online platforms that they and I were visiting (mostly specialized forums and Facebook open group pages). In addition to conducting cyberethnography on these platforms, I conducted 26semi-structured interviews, most of them with mothers and through Skype or by phone. However, during a research stay in Switzerland, I also interviewed six of my informants in their own homes, when I was invited to do so, and three in public venues (cafeterias and parks). In addition, I visited events and places such as booths at festivals promoting sustainability, baby wearing workshops, and boutiques where the gear necessary to alternative parenting was sold. In conformity with standard ethical procedures for this type of research, discourse and conversation analysis were applied on online material publicly available and I secured informed consent from my informants before recording the interviews.

According to Bobel (2002:48–49), the American "natural mothering" of the 1990s was situated at the intersection of attachment parenting, voluntary simplicity and cultural feminism. Even if the core practices of my francophone informants remain similar to those of the mothers interviewed by Bobel, significant changes in context and purpose have occurred. The contemporary reception of natural family living in francophone contexts brings a twist to the predominantly child-centered discourses by North American advocates of attachment parenting, in which the claimed "parent-centeredness is somewhat more difficult to locate" (see Friedman 2008:136). Other transformations in the perception of environmentalism or feminism, as social movements or social forces, cannot be acknowledged fully in the limited scope of this chapter. Instead, it is necessary to draw attention to how the rise of communication technologies and their now widespread accessibility directly impacts the ways in which natural parenting is mediated and mediatized. "Being online" is not a special or separate part of the lives of the "natural parents" I interviewed. Now in their late twenties to their mid-forties, most of them have known "the Internet" as an accessible resource for most of their adult lives. Even if they are too old to really be digital natives, they are proficient users of computer mediated communication tools and of the websites they spend time on, at least. Moreover, not only "natural family living" but many different trends in parenting styles have received media attention in recent years. For a parenting style that often offers alternatives to dominant norms, however, this mediatization adds an enhanced and essential social component: a particular online mamasphere that is generally created and contributed to by its users rather than by medical experts or by companies. This in turn "created a whole new conception of support and community" (Friedman 2013:151). These "aesthetic formations" (Meyer 2009:6–11) of natural mothers (and, more rarely, fathers) are the online places where imaginations and ideals of "natural motherhood" are materialized through media. Such communities, as permeable as their boundaries might be, are centered around a distinct maternal identity and style of parenting based on certain values. They are privileged and usually safe spaces where mothers can seek unconventional information and meet other like-minded mothers.

The global dimension that natural parenting has grown to in recent years is reflected in its online mediation. Web-based media, in particular social media, contents sharing platforms and forums, made it possible for parents to discuss the variety of the parenting experience, often under cover of anonymity, without regards for national borders. My informants lived for the most part in France, but also in Switzerland, Belgium and in the French-speaking part of Canada. With the exception of the latter area, mainstream francophone media, just like North American ones, tend to construct a stereotypical image of the "crunchy" or "granola mom". Francophone media tend to portray natural parenting in a more negative light than North American media do. They convey an image of an essentially non-conformist, anti-social mode of parenting bound to fail children themselves, their parents, especially mothers, and society. While natural parenting does not constitute a dominant norm either in North America, practices such as homebirth or breastfeeding for over six months, are seen as acceptable (though uncommon) choices among a range of diverse expert-guided styles of parenting, among certain social classes at least. The "ideology of intensive mothering" (Hays 1996) is pervasive, whereas it is still contested –though gaining ground– in francophone contexts, and in particular in France. Because the *mamans nature* go against the grain of conventional child-rearing in their own contexts, they generally are subject to criticism.

Religion Toned down, Health and Sustainability Played up

In contrast with the dominant "ideology of technology" that produces "technocratic models" of fertility, pregnancy and childbirth management, natural parenting discourses refer to Nature as a guiding and ethical principle for one's lifestyle choices. As previous scholarship has shown (see for instance Klassen 2005:71), the implicit or outward critique of technology frequently draws from religious and spiritual resources. Several typical practices of natural parenting indeed have historically religious roots in their North American context of emergence, or are still associated with institutionalized religious groups whose views on gender roles within the family and society are rather conservative. The leading and now international breastfeeding advocacy group La Leche League was initially funded in 1956 by a group of Catholic mothers. Though La Leche League is now a secular organization, breastfeeding advocacy is another example at the "crossroads of medicine, feminism, and religion" (Ward 2000) and of their respective influences on breastfeeding. Homebirth is another example (see Klassen 2001). The midwife Ina May Gaskin, one of the leading figures of the homebirth or "natural childbirth" movement and author of *Spiritual Midwifery* (originally published in 1975) was the wife of a Christian hippy pastor.

Restrictions about contraception on ethical or moral grounds commonly are associated with religion, even if not *all* religious institutions and traditional teachings ban *all* forms of contraception (see Blyth and Landau 2009). Fertility awareness is thus often attributed to religious motivations because it is the only licit family planning option for couples following teachings that forbid the use of mechanical and hormonal contraception. As for other practices typical of natural parenting, fertility awareness is situated in that circle of overlapping practices implemented *both* (1) on religious grounds by religiously observant couples and (2) by those who engage in natural family living, though for different reasons, as will become clear from the examples below. One set of discourses is based moral and ethical teachings by religious institutions, while the other focuses mostly on health and sustainability. Although their juxtaposition is not systematical, this overlap is sufficient to make natural parenting appear as religiously motivated in mainstream media representations and in the general public.

Notwithstanding this portraying of natural parenting as religious in many francophone media, only a few of my informants and among the participants to the online forums I surveyed do self-identify explicitly as "religious" or even as "spiritual". In fact, among the mothers I interviewed, few said that they saw a spiritual dimension in their mothering. This dimension sometimes pervades their online identity (for instance, when they made their religious commitment visible through the inclusion of religious imagery, prayers, inspirational quotes or excerpts from the Bible or the Quran in their forum signature line or user's profile). The subsections of one of the forums where I engaged with natural parents are organized thematically. Even if everyone could publicly access and participate in them, several subsections are spaces clearly aimed at mothers of specific traditions, even though religion is not a dominant topic of their conversations (e.g. Muslim mothers meet in a section called *les Ramadanettes* and Jewish mothers in *les Cacherettes* section; there also are sections for Christian, Buddhist and atheist mothers). Some mothers participate both in one of the religious subsections and in the section specifically dedicated to natural parenting.

The links between natural parenting, religion and mediation are not as apparent as they are in other mediated trends more commonly identified as "religious". The explicitly faith-based sections of the forum (just mentioned above), or a list-serv for Catholic or Muslim mothers, for instance, would be easier to label as "religious" than a natural parenting forum, even if conversational analysis would reveal that most topics discussed do not directly relate to what neither participants nor the researcher would define as religious. In spite of this, religion remains a useful category of analysis for any inquiry into the contemporary reception of natural parenting. Most components of natural parenting precede the recent rise of its mediation through social media and other online platforms. As noted above, specific religious group might have practiced or promoted some particular practices (homebirth, breastfeeding, homeschooling, etc.). New forms of mediation by parents themselves have infused these same practices with new symbolic meanings. They have given shape to new online communities (if not to active or activist social movements with "personal *and* political" feminist overtones). Scholars of religion might want to know to which extent the original religious component is still part of this particular and mediated reception of natural family living in the mostly European francophone online and offline. Do natural parenting practitioners, advocates and critics hold on to this religious element, or do they erase it? Alternatively, do they transform it into a "spiritual" one, detached from any particular historical institution?

The general tendency is that the religious connections and historical roots mentioned above are toned down. In these contexts, especially where *laïcité*, a French acceptation of secularism, prevails, the tendency is to restrict the public visibility of religious practice and to confine religion to the private, domestic or even the intimate sphere, while public debates *about* religion are raging in the media, both in print and online. This sphere coincides with the space where fertility awareness is taking place, with a further impact on the family and on society as a whole (birth rate and general demographics).

Another element that should prompt researchers to look at natural parenting through the interdisciplinary lenses of the study of religions is that when they discuss choices that are still marginal and frowned upon by a majority (in this context), both advocates and detractors of natural family living resort to using a vocabulary reminiscent of religion. The breastfeeding advocacy website "*Je suis une seinte*" ("I am a saint/breast"; with a pun on the word *sein* meaning breast and *sainte*, meaning saint) is an example of such borrowing. Particular experiences of mothering are described as mystical ones even by mothers who do not self-identify as religious. On the other hand, on their own mamasphere, "natural moms" criticize media for presenting them in a rather negative light, caricaturing them with a vocabulary similar to that used to qualify fundamentalist and extremist religious movements and practice, as backward, irresponsible, fanatic or indoctrinated. These mothers are wary of calls from journalists visiting their forums just to post calls for "testimonies" about their unconventional practices, for instance requests for filming a homebirth, a most intimate experience for most of them. Because of this general suspicion against journalists, when I first approached my informants through online communication, I had to reiterate my status as a researcher aiming at an in-depth analysis of natural parenting rather than at a sensationalizing report about them. I could gain the confidence of my informants also because, as a mother myself, I had regularly –though not intensively– participated in several of these platforms before this interest for natural parenting turned into an academic inquiry. I then was able to discuss very intimate and personal issues regarding personal religious convictions or the absence thereof, contraception and fertility awareness, on the forums and through private messages, and then during the interviews.

In addition to those who identify as "atheists" or "agnostics", a significant portion of interviewees considered themselves as "non practicing Catholics" (*catholiques non-pratiquantes*, especially among the French parents) or as "Sunday Christians" ("*des chrétiens du dimanche*", as one Swiss couple put it, attending church occasionally for family celebrations such as weddings, baptisms and funerals). Using hormonal and mechanical contraception has never constituted a religious or ethical dilemma for them. Some of them still use them as their primary mean of contraception. Those who no longer do made it clear that their reasons for switching to fertility awareness based methods of contraception (sometimes coupled with barrier methods) never were primarily religious. Rather, they accounted for such changes in terms of deeply held environmentalist values that informed other lifestyles choices, in particular those relating to parenting and healthcare. Julien[1] (29 years old, France), the only father whom I interviewed without his partner present, said that he "did not really like religions *as institutions*" (his emphasis), but was "open to spirituality" (he practiced yoga, for instance). When asked about contraception, he told me that his partner had already turned away from hormonal contraceptives before she met him. At the time of our interview, they had two children and were open to the idea of eventually having a third one. After trying the range of available mechanical contraceptives, they learned about the symptothermic method and wanted to

---

[1] I have given pseudonyms unrelated to their online names to all of my informants. Other identifying details have been modified or omitted.

implement it: "In theory, we are very well informed, but in practice, it is difficult because Laurence is still breastfeeding, so she does not have her period and does not ovulate". When I asked Julien if this consensual choice was a morally, ethically or religiously informed one, he replied:

This is a health choice (*c'est un choix de santé*), even though we could also say that it is a moral one in the measure that it is respect for one's own body, or respect for the other's body, from my side (*le respect du corps de l'autre de ma part*). [. . .] But in a sense, respect for one's body is health (*le respect de son corps, c'est la santé*), so it is both [a health and a moral choice].

Although my informants generally denied any specifically religious motivation in their search for other family planning options, their discourses still conveyed a sense of following strong values articulated around respect for the self and for other, for future generations and for the environment. Like Julien and Laurence, most of the couples I interviewed did not reject contraception altogether, but were also open to the idea of having another child eventually. They were in stable social, emotional and financial positions that would easily allows them to carry to term an accidental pregnancy (or would be able and ready to access abortion services legally). They could afford to take the risk of contraceptive failure because of their situation of privilege, which they rarely acknowledged.

High-Tech Mediations and Environmentalist Fertility

In addition to the series of apps mentioned in the opening of this chapter, a variety of online and social media, for instance group pages on Facebook or specific channels on video sharing websites, are used to promote fertility awareness and are available in different languages. Feedback from real practitioners, along with advice from "trained instructors" can also be found online. Several of the mothers whose interviews I quote from in the following section, reported researching practical information about fertility awareness not only in the natural parentingon which I first met them, but also on other websites, including those of associations that offer training sessions, face-to-face consultations with couples who are experimented users, and personalized coaching. For instance, Symptotherm is a private foundation, based in Switzerland, that promotes "the modern symptothermic method" and markets their own paying fertility tracking app named "Sympto". On the homepage of the Sympto app, distinct from that of the association, Sympto's slogan is reminiscent both of media and technology: "I *reconnect* with my body". Sympto invites users to "enter the universe of environmental fertility" ("*Entrez dans l'univers de la fertilité écologique!*"). Even if help is available offline through instructors and associations like Sympto, online anonymous discussions about practical issues and doubts are common. Although most of the online platforms where conversations about fertility awareness take place offer the possibility to include images, discussions usually remain textual and not visual. With the exception of temperature graphs, users rarely share pictures of their own observation of bodily symptoms. In contrast, the websites where these methods are explained feature pictures representing the consistence of cervical mucus like egg white spread between the thumb and forefinger. Forum users do not post such pictures but, instead, go at great length expressing their doubts and confusion about their symptoms.

Fertility awareness is one example among several other practices that have a low degree of technological intervention and intrusiveness on the female body, but nevertheless rely on the availability of "high-tech" devices, in particular medical ones, to be implemented. The extended breastfeeding in which my informants engaged is possible thanks to the use of breast pumps, fridges and freezers that makes it possible for some mothers to create and safely store a sufficient supply of milk for their baby, usually for after they return to paid positions in the workforce. Similarly, most contemporary midwife supervised homebirths (an option for some of my informants) rely on the *availability*, before, throughout and after the birth itself, of specific medical appliances and technology, like intermittent electronic monitoring of fetal heart. Although a homebirth midwife follows protocols different and more flexible than those of a hospital, and although she *uses* her medical-technological gear differently –when at all–, she comes to her patient's house with a medical equipment that is very similar to that prepared in a standard hospital birthing room for a low-risk mother. Contrary to prevalent misrepresentations in francophone media, homebirth is in fact subject to specific restrictions implemented through a variety of tests and examinations that depend on medical technology. For instance, a ultrasound might be necessary to confirm that the fetus is in the right position for birth.

A Matter of (Dis)Trust and Respect

Religious perspectives rarely informed decisions and opinions about contraception among the francophone natural parents whom I interviewed. Even so, their discourses about contraception borrowed from the lexical field of religious experience. Several women talked about the period of time following the moment they stopped taking the pill as "a liberation", "a revelation" or a "consciousness awakening" (*une prise de conscience*). One of my informants, Gisèle (33 years old, Switzerland, mother of one child), took the pill for four years and decided to stop: "There is no reason for me to pollute my body. This is an issue of respect. And why should only women care about this?". Stéphanie (42 years old, originally from France and living in the USA, mother of one child) spontaneously mentioned how much better she felt while "off the pill". She also expressed her refusal to "pollute [her] own body again with hormones". More than just her own body, Stéphanie was also worried about "hormones that cannot be filtered out by the wastewater treatment plans and end up polluting the Earth, too". "Respect for oneself", "for the Earth" or "for Nature" and a reclaiming a better health were frequently alluded to as prime motivators.

In addition to health and environmental concerns, harmonious sexual relationships in the couple and increased libido were mentioned as secondary motives for turning to fertility awareness, while my questions about an hypothetical obedience to religious teachings were strongly swept aside. During a joint interview with both Manon (26 years old, Belgium) and her husband, Marc (originally from Québec), Manon identified as "Catholic socially and culturally" and raised up her "Catholic education" several times during our conversation. Before becoming a mother, she even regularly attended mass for a time, in a church with an "alternative priest" (*un curé alternatif*). Manon said that Marc, who worked a teacher of secular morals (*professeur de morale laïque*) in a public school, was an atheist. During most of our conversation, Marc was busy taking care of their child, in the background, but he intervened in our Skype conversation, whenever either I or Manon prompted him to do so, or spontaneously. I asked Manon which type of contraception –if any– they were using after the birth of their first child, who was 16 months old and still breastfed at the time of our interview. Manon had just stopped taking a progestative based pill (named Cérazette), compatible with breastfeeding. Prior to her pregnancy, she had taken the pill, as well as the patch and the contraceptive ring, all with unpleasant side-effects. Manon said that she and Marc planned to turn to a "better knowledge of [her menstrual] cycles or, in the meanwhile, use condoms. (. . .) I feel like I want to see if I feel better when stopping [this pill]". Then, from the background, Marc added loudly,: "Yep, the Cézarette [sic] is *not* good!" ("*ouais, la cézarette* [he mispronounced the name of her pill], *c'est pas bien!*"). Manon then listed some of its side effects, on her general health and libido. She also mentioned that taking the pill was "really a constraint", which she eased a bit through technology: "I had two alarms set on my phone in order to remember to take it at the right time". Manon insisted that, for her, taking the pill was just a practical issue and she had not engaged into the ethical nor the "feminist dimensions" of this debate about whether or not "taking the pill was a liberation or a domination". In any case, this was not a matter of obeying particular teachings of the Roman Catholic Church. She and Marc considered fertility awareness as an option because they did not know yet when they would have another child. Manon needed almost two years to be pregnant with their first child and was worried that taking the pill would further deteriorate her reproductive capacity when the time for another pregnancy would have come.

From the perspective of natural parenting, the choice of an adapted contraception is a matter of trust and distrust. It is also one of "experience", sometimes expressed in religious terms even by those who self-identify as atheists or agnostics. The regularity of the "natural", undistorted, menstrual cycle is to be trusted and women ought to have faith their capacity to observe, detect, monitor, record and interpret changes in their bodies. On websites promoting fertility awareness, this faith in natural family planning is backed up by an efficient mediation of scientific studies that prove the relatively high success rate (in case of a perfect application) of the specific symptothermic method (and the lower ones of older types of "temperature" or "calendar" or "symptoms" only methods, according ot the Pearl index). This faith is reinforced through the reading of many "testimonies" (*témoignages*) of experienced users.

The other side of the coin of this trust placed into fertility awareness methods, and in particular those that are digitalized and mediated, is an increasing distrust in hormonal contraceptive. Recent "pill scares" have received a high media coverage in francophone contexts, both in the feminine press, in specialized health magazines and in mainstream newspapers. Media reported, for instance, on several cases of young women left handicapped by strokes (attributed to their taking the pill) and suing pharmaceutical firms. In this recent wake of health scandals involving 3rd and 4th generation pills, a distrust of "BigPharma" is often given as a primary motive for "*not* taking the pill", along with the will to "respect one's body and the earth", already mentioned above. Against the backdrop of a contraceptive model that stakes it all on the pill, media might play a role in increasing the general public's awareness about alternatives that now are considered uncommon choices. Recent statistics show that these might indeed become more prevalent. The association of fertility awareness with new media technologies and with the wider availability of information about it online, free of cost and anonymously, certainly contribute to popularizing it also among women who already are familiar with other forms of self-tracking and already use electronic devices and similar software on a daily basis. Its emphasis on being "natural" appeals, in turn, to parents engaged in natural family living.

Suspicion extends to Western bio-medicine and in general and to its practitioners who deal with women's and children's bodies. Some of the mothers who use or plan to use fertility awareness specifically for contraceptive purposes avoid mentioning this option to their regular healthcare practitioner. In their opinion, their doctors would not recommend this method anyway, even to couples in stable relationships. In contrast, my informants did not push it aside as ineffective or infeasible, but considered fertility awareness as a serious option. Because of bad experience with mainstream medicine in the past, and in particular during pregnancy and childbirth, these mothers did not perceive medical professionals as able to provide clear information about fertility awareness based methods of contraception. During the interviews, I have often heard that regular healthcare practitioners are "sold to pharmaceuticals" and thus "not really objective about the risks of the pill" and of other medical interventions on female bodies. The inability to find a healthcare provider who would take their (holistic or more conventional) perspectives about health seriously is another factor that drives many to "consult Dr. Google" or "ask the Internet", whether about fertility awareness or other issues such as immunizations. Within these specific online communities of natural mothers, maternal experience is trusted more than the authoritative expertise of doctors. Online media and social media are powerful tools through which they access and disseminate trusted knowledge.

I contacted Johanne, (31 years old, Switzerland) mother of two children (aged 1 and 3) through a private message on a forum in which she participated in the specific sections related to attachment parenting and environmental and sustainability. At the time of our interview, both she and her husband were working in academic research. In addition, Johanne had a home-based online business. She defined her family's lifestyle as one of voluntary simplicity. Johanne relies on naturopathic medicine, homeopathy and aromatherapy for treating common illnesses, and she insisted that even though she tries to "solve problems" by herself, she would be ready to consult with a regular physician if needed, in spite of bad experiences with conventional medicine during her pregnancy and first childbirth. So far, she had avoided vaccination for her children. Johanne told me that she had taken a hormonal contraception for "only three years" before her first (planned) pregnancy. She mentioned that her own mother, a naturopathic doctor, had made her aware of issues like "thrombosis (. . .) and phases of sterility" and "other health related issues" allegedly related to taking the pill over an extended period of time. The issue of contraception was brought up again after the first birth of her first child:

> Johanne: I knew that I wanted to breastfeed her. I bought the prescribed pill, [compatible with] breastfeeding, but I never took it. I did not want her to gulp down synthetic hormones (*ingurgiter des hormones de synthèse*). This would not have been logical for me, in my mind. At first, [my husband and I] had no problem, we used condoms. But now . . . well, I am still breastfeeding [my second child], so we are still using condoms. I still do not want to take the pill. Moreover the strongest supporter (*partisan*) in favor of *not* taking

the pill or synthetic hormones is my husband. So we are directing ourselves towards a natural, symptothermic contraception or something like that.

Me: So how are you or will you be learning *symptothermie*? Where will you find information in order to implement this?

Johanne: In part, I will learn by myself. There are many websites on this topic, on this issue of family planning (*la gestion familiale*). I also have found out about the [method of using the] thermometer through these websites, but I will also simply rely on my network. I know many women who have practiced this for many years and who give information and training . . . training [sessions] for free, where they share information. They even have Facebook groups and similar things where advice can be shared. So far, I never could practice this seriously, as I am still breastfeeding. So, we will see this later (*on verra plus tard*).

Whereas previously women had to physically attend classes taught by qualified instructors, it is know possible to learn "as an autodidact" online, as Johanne was already doing. For her, learning online does not exclude taking advice from "many women who have practiced this for many years", and meeting in person with such experts does not preclude her participation in a Facebook group for collective support.

The compatibility of contraception with breastfeeding was a crucial criteria for both Manon and Johanne. Whereas Manon found it acceptable to take a pill that did not interfere with her milk production (though detrimental to her general health and sexual drive), Johanne could not at all tolerate that her baby would have to ingest "synthetic hormones" through her milk. This went against her values and her ideal of preserving her child's body from any form of pollution or toxicity. Both Manon and Johanne said that they would primarily turn to information found online rather than to their gynecologist. Though neither Manon nor Johanne mentioned specific fertility tracking apps that they would use, a few mothers whom I interviewed did, but they were reluctant to discuss this issue further. A few of my informants did mention other integrative fertility monitors (available in France). Moreover, they also seemed unable to remember exactly how they had first heard about fertility awareness: vaguely through "friends", "on the Internet" or "through a forum friend", but certainly not from their regular healthcare practitioners.

In Julien's case (mentioned above) and in both Marion and Johanne's statements just discussed, male partners positioned themselves clearly against hormonal contraception and in favor of "using other methods", even if these require from them a greater discipline and participation (condoms, fertility awareness or a combination of both). A major issue with hormonal contraception for my informants was that its side effects interfered with harmonious sexual intercourse, something that they valued and considered as essential to their couple. Fabienne (32 years old), another of my informants, spelled out these effects rather explicitly and without my prompting. I recruited her for an interview through the specific natural parenting section a popular health and well-being forum, even though she was more active on another forum for teachers that was not focused on natural parenting issues, as she told me later. At the time of our conversation, Fabienne was living and working part time in France as a teacher in primary education. She was the mother of a three years old. Fabienne had taken the pill "since [she] was 17 years old, so at least for eleven years". She stopped intentionally just before "starting the baby-tryouts" (*avant de commencer les essais-bébé*). Telling me more about the few months that followed, before she achieved pregnancy, Fabienne said that she had never "seen so many changes in [her] body (. . .) for instance on (. . .), vaginal dryness, libido, mood swings". She had "seen so many negative effects of the pill that (. . .) [she] never took the pill again". Fabienne was not only "surprised" but also rather irritated at the thought of experiencing such a dramatic difference. Without blaming the pill itself, Fabienne felt resentful towards the medical system and its specialists: "I am angry at gynecologists who do not at all warn us about these effects". This also further undermined her trust in conventional medicine and drugs, and prompted her to research more information about contraception online. Fertility awareness is one among several options which she is considering because she and her husband do not know yet if or when they will have a second child. In contrast with Manon and Johanne, Fabienne planned to turn not only to online autodidact learning, but to the midwife who accompanied her homebirth in order to implement what she labeled as "exploring the natural cycles of the woman" (*l'exploration des cycles naturels de la femme*).

Conclusion

New forms of technology and media and their interconnections constitute 21st century variables that complicate an old and dynamic equation featuring feminism, medical knowledge, and secular or religious discourses about values and ethics. Historically, female bodies have for a long time been sites for a specifically feminine practice of the quantified self, sometimes prompted by religious observance (ritual purity laws for instance): the monitoring of the menstrual cycle or, better yet, the tracking of its fertile and infertile phases. This chapter has highlighted only some of the current debates and new dimensions of the influence of media over fertility awareness and its representation in the 21st century. Shifting from a formerly very private, domestic and even intimate practice, it has entered the mediated and public mamasphere. In a mostly benevolent and safe space, mothers who follow alternative practices find information and support that their immediate offline environment and their regular health practitioners for the most part fail to offer. Now that both reliable information about fertility awareness based methods of family planning and (some of the digital) tools necessary to its practice are easily available online, this has become a frequent topic of discussion among parents engaged in natural family living and among larger circles that are not necessarily religious.

Fertility awareness is not a mainstream practice in the francophone contexts in question in this chapter, not even among couples already drawn to lifestyles of health and sustainability that value whatever is "natural" over what is "synthetic" and wary about an indiscriminate use of technology. The contemporary digitalization and mediation of fertility awareness, and in particular that of the "modern symptothermic method", contribute to making this option attractive for women wanting to avoid hormonal or mechanical contraception. Just like any other mode of contraception, it comes with a cost: that of taking one's body as a ground for the quantified self. This cost is further associated with the discipline of collecting data, a task that still falls primarily to women. This still constitutes a ground for feminist objections. However, the archiving and analyzing of such data is now transferred to fertility tracking apps or monitors. Echoing the notion of "third space" (Hoover and Echchaibi 2012) of digital religion, technology becomes a "third party" in the responsibility for contraception, in addition to that of the two partners.

Religion is often thought of as a primary motive for turning to fertility awareness based methods, but these are now becoming popular for many other reasons, including considerations for one's health and for the environment. The data that they collect is used for practical purposes, and not to fulfill requirements imposed by religious traditions. Media and technology have contributed to making it easy and practical, transforming the practice into an almost fun and playful path of self-exploration, health and well-being for women.

Religious elements nonetheless still surface in discourses about fertility awareness because of their moral and ethical overtones. Natural parents are attached to distinct ethical principles clearly linked to the worldviews and values that shape their general philosophy of natural parenting and inform other lifestyle. Respect for oneself, one's body and one's own health, respect for one's partner and child/ren, respect for the environment, trust in an ideally constructed notion of Nature as a guiding principle, and altruistic sharing with others constitute just some of these values. Online platforms are the privileged space for such form of sharing, which is in turn an essential component of community building. By sharing in a variety of online platforms their mostly authentic experience of their engagement with natural parenting, including its most intimate practices such as fertility awareness, mothers gain the agency to shape their own self-representation, in sharp contrast with the negative caricature found in most mainstream francophone media.

Works Cited

Bajos, N. et al. 2014. The French Pill Scare: Towards A New Contraceptive Model? *Population & Societies. Monthly bulletin of the French National Institute for Demographic Studies* 511/May, 1–4.
Blyth, E. and Landau, R. 2009. *Faith and Fertility: Attitudes Towards Reproductive Practices in Different Religions from Ancient to Modern Times*. Philadelphia: Jessica Kingsley Publishers.
Bobel, C. 2002. *The Paradox of Natural Mothering*. Philadelphia: Temple University Press.
Bobel, C. 2007. "Resisting, But Not Too Much: Interrogating the Paradox of Natural Mothering." in A. O'Reilly (ed). *Maternal Theory. Essential Readings*, 782–91. Toronto: Demeter Press.
Childerhose, J. and Macdonald, M. 2013. Health Consumption as Work: The Home Pregnancy Test as a Domesticated Health Tool. *Social Science and Medicine* 86: 1–8.
Davis-Floyd, R. and Fischel Sargent, C. (eds). 1997. *Childbirth and Authoritative Knowledge: Cross-Cultural Perspectives*. Berkeley: University of California Press.
Djerassi, C. 1990. Fertility Awareness: Jet-Age Rhythm Method? *Science* 248:1061–2.
Fehring, R. et al. 2013. Randomized Comparison of Two Internet-Supported Fertility-Awareness-Based Methods of Family Planning. *Contraception* 88/1:24–30.
Emerich, M. 2011. The Gospel of Sustainability: Media, Market and LOHAS. Urbana: University of Illinois Press.
Friedman, M. 2008. "'Everything You Need to Know about Your Baby". Feminism and Attachment Parenting", in J. Nathanson and L. C. Tuley (eds), *Mother Knows Best: Talking Back To The "Experts"*. Toronto: Demeter Press, pp. 135–147.
Friedman, M. 2013. *Mommyblogs and the Changing Face of Motherhood*. Toronto: University of Toronto Press.
Gaskin, I. 2002. *Spiritual Midwifery*. (4th edition). Summertown: Book Publishing Company.
Hays, S. 1996. *The Cultural Contradictions of Motherhood*. New Haven: Yale University Press.
Hoover, S. and Echchaibi, N. 2012. "The 'Third Spaces' of Digital Religion. A Discussion Paper." Available at: http://cmrc.colorado.edu/wp-content/uploads/2012/06/Hoover-Echchaibi-paper.pdf (accessed October 3, 2014).
Klassen, P. 2001. *Blessed Events: Religion and Home Birth in America*. Princeton University Press.
Klassen, P. 2005. "Procreating Women and Religion: The Politics of Spirituality, Religion and Childbirth in America." In *Religion and Healing in America*, edited by Linda L. Barnes and Susan Starr Sered, 71–88. Oxford – New York: Oxford University Press.

Lupton, D. 2014. Self-Tracking Modes: Reflexive Self-Monitoring and Data Practices Available at Social Science Research Network: http://ssrn.com/abstract=2483549 or http://dx.doi.org/10.2139/ssrn.2483549 (acessed October 3, 2014).

Meyer, B. (ed). 2009. *Aesthetic Formations: Media, Religion, and the Senses.* New York: Palgrave Macmillan.

Swan, M. 2013. The Quantified Self: Fundamental Disruption in Big Data Science and Biological Discovery. *Big Data*, June, 1(2): 85–99. doi:10.1089/big.2012.0002

Villalobos, A. 2010. "Mothering in Fear: How Living in an Insecure-Feeling World Affects Parenting." In *21st Century Motherhood: Experience, Identity, Policy, Agency*. New York: Columbia University Press. 67–81.

Ward, J. 2000. *La Leche League : at the Crossroads of Medicine, Feminism, and Religion.* Chapel Hill: University of North Carolina Press.

Deborah Justice
Multi-site Mediated Worship: Why Simulcast Sermons Need Live Local Praise Bands

Picture this: You are standing in a darkened auditorium-style space. A rock band is playing music, supported by lighting effects and loud sound system. But this is music for worship and the people around you are singing along enthusiastically, "God is greater . . ." Giant projection screens with the lyrics, graphics, and the occasional close up of the musicians surround the band. Some congregants raise their hands in the air as the chorus repeats. On cue, the band modulates, ratcheting the tone and the vibe up. Even more people reach their hands in the air and sway as collective energy pulses through the room.

After a dynamic set of songs, as the last strains of sound die away. Rather that dissipating, the energy almost seems to quietly concentrate the lead guitarist centers and closes his eyes and prays. With emotion in his voice, he thanks God, Jesus, and the Holy Spirit for being present through the music. "Everyone came together to worship you here, Lord," he closes, "And now we're prepared to keep worshipping through the sermon that is coming next."

Congregants blink their eyes as the house lights come up and the campus pastor comes front and center and invites everyone to be seated. "Thanks so much for coming to this place to worship with each other," says the pastor, "We've got a great sermon today . . . let it bless you." Then, he turns and walks off the stage.

The lights dim again and video rolls on the big projection screens. A brief film clip featuring a logo and catchy theme music rolls to introduce the sermon series. Then the feed switches to live video of the church's senior pastor preaching in a service at a different location. Although he is not physically present in the space, people around you respond both verbally and non-verbally to the pastor's delivery, making comments like "Mmhmm" and affirmatively shaking their heads.

After the sermon and a brief blessing from the pastor's video feed, the lights go up and the service is over.

People start chatting as they walk out into the lobby and parking lot. A woman notices that you are new to the congregation and introduces herself and asks you how you liked the service. You tell her that you liked it a lot, but that you wished there was a service closer to your house and later in the day because of your work schedule. She smiles and says, "That's no problem! Lots of people prefer an evening service. Try our other location – they meet tonight at 6pm. You should check it out."

So you decide to go ahead and see. Later that day, you attend a service in the slightly smaller, but more conveniently timed and located site. It is quite similar to the morning service at the other campus. In the darkened auditorium worship space, this site's praise team leads the same songs that you sang earlier this morning in the other location. This new guitarist leads a very similar prayer following the music. The site pastor introduces the sermon video and you quickly realize that what you are watching now at 6:30pm is exactly the same sermon that you had seen live-streamed at 10:30am. The message had been recorded in the morning as pastor preached it live from the main location and now this evening worshippers were watching it. But, as you look around, you notice that people are interacting with the recorded video as if it was a live stream. This Sunday night congregation laughs at the pastor's jokes and prays along with his video-delivered closing prayer. The service ends, the lights come up, and you walk out into the moonlit parking lot as you mull questions about liveness, media, music, and the divine.

Churches and live music intertwine heavily the American religious experience. Churches are, in fact, a one of the main venues in which most people hear live music According to sociologist of religion Mark Chaves' landmark study:

> It becomes clear that worship services constitute the vast majority of the live musical events experienced by people in American society. Congregations' worship services, where 60 percent of the population hear live music in a given year, are the single most common type of event at which live music is heard in American society. (2004:188)

Live music has remained central in multi-site churches in recent years as these congregations full of media and technology have been proliferating across the United States. In contrast, presenting digital sermons from the main worship site to unite "satellite campuses" has become common. Overall, most congregants report that they would prefer live preaching, with surveys finding that two thirds of American adults would prefer an in-person sermon to a video sermon. 35% report that they would only visit churches with a live sermon. Three out of 10 people say that they are equally satisfied with either live or video sermons. The same number of people (3 out of 10) say a video sermon won't keep them from a church, but they still prefer live preaching (Lifeway Research 2013). Digital sermons are grudgingly accepted, but music is non-negotiable.

This chapter asks a fundamental question: Why do heavily mediatized multi-site churches cling to keeping music live? What does this musical presence do, particularly in contrast to video preaching? While sociological scholarship of multi-sited churches often mentions live music as crucial to the congregation's success (cf. Ingalls, Landau, and Wagner 2013; Ingalls Reigersberg, and Sherinian 2018), this research does not focus on the ways in which live music interacts with the media-centric message of multi-sited congregations. My research explores these issues by engaging with ethnomusicologist Thomas Turino's (2008) work on live vs. recorded sound and Auslander's (1998, 2008) conclusions regarding "liveness." Based on multi-sited ethnographic fieldwork, this chapter explores the interactions of belief, spiritual power, live music and mediatized praise in the most rapidly-expanding worship formats in the United States.

Multi-Sited Churches

In 2006, research predicted that roughly 30,000 American congregations, or 10% of American congregations, will become multi-sited over the next few decades (Surratt, Ligon, and Bird 2006). Nearly a decade later, conservative definitions of multi-sited churches estimated at least 1,500 such congregations in the United States in 2012 (Bird 2013), with those number rising to around 5,000 in 2018 (Leadership Network 2019). Broader definitions, such as those used by the National Congregations Study out of Duke University find roughly 9,000 multi-sited churches serving 5.5 million worshipers. Multi-sited congregations may not be the norm (yet), but they are among the fastest growing religious configurations in American Christianity.

Faith communities typically turn to a multi-site format when they reach a membership of just over 1,000, although smaller churches have been increasingly turning to the multi-site option (Bird 2016, 2013). According to Duke University's National Congregational Survey, the median congregation size in the United States is 75 regular attenders. However, according to the most recent US Congregational Life survey, the average congregational size is 186, due to the influence of very large churches. When the Hartford Institute of Religious Research considers these survey results together and analyzes the Protestant segments of the data, they find that smaller churches serve only 11% of church-goers. Meanwhile, 50% of Protestant church-goers attended the largest 10% of congregations (350 regular participants and up). 23% of American church-goers worship in congregations with 1,000 or more members. These numbers indicate that nearly one quarter of church-going American Protestants worship in institutions that are increasingly turning to a multi-sited format. As the church consultancy website *Portable Church* explains, "The idea of launching a multisite campus was a radical one in the 1990s! Today, the tide has changed and multisite churches have become the norm, rather than the exception" (Portable Church Industries 2018).

The majority of megachurches in the United States – from 14,000-member Lives Changed by Christ (LCBC) in Pennsylvania Joel Osteen's 44,000-member Lakewood Church in Houston, Texas to 22,000-member Saddleback Church in California and hundreds in between – operate on variations of the multi-sited model. In 2006, church consultants Surratt, Ligon, and Bird described five general styles of multi-sited existence that continue to provide a solid paradigm for analyzing multi-sited churches today. In the Video-Venue Model, churches have multiple worship environments (either different rooms in one facility or in multiple locations) that use either live-streamed or previously recorded video. The sermon may be the only identical part of the different worship services, while the worship styles – from music to décor to liturgical elements – may vary. In the Regional-Campus Model, the church tries to duplicate the worship experience of the main campus at branch locations. Simulcast or pre-recorded video sermons play a key role in all of the parishioners relating to the same central teaching pastor. In the Teaching-Team Model, the main campus' style and message is relayed to campus locations by a live "teaching team" of campus ministers and preachers. The Partnership Model allows churches and community organizations or businesses to share space and resources. Finally, the Low-Risk Model involves less programming and centralized control than the others, but allows for rapid proliferation of small sites loosely bonded through staff, style, and theology.

This study focuses on issues of liveness, spontaneity, and divinity within the Video-Venue and Regional-Campus approaches that combine digital preaching with live music. Specifically, I target situations in which a live band plays for every worship service in every venue, but a senior pastor preaches a sermon live in one venue, while branch locations of the multi-site church receive this sermon via video (either live-streamed or recorded). Surratt, Ligon, and Bird's study found that, in these churches, only 31% live-stream the sermon to multiple locations. The vast majority, 69%, use a pre-recorded sermon (perhaps even recorded prior to the weekend during a "low-traffic" time for the pastor). But, all of the congregations feature live music in every venue.

This configuration of digital preaching and live music is rapidly becoming one of the largest, fastest-growing approaches to Christianity in America. New campuses within multi-site churches grow on average by 28% the first year and then by 25% the second year (Portable Church Industries 2018). Whereas traditional Protestant denominations have been losing members steadily for decades, overall, multi-sited congregations are growing at an average rate of 14%

annually. In other words, multi-sited churches are outpacing their religious neighbors in leaps and bounds.

This type of church-going experience presents a dramatic departure from traditional models of American religious participation. The term "parishioner" has long been synonymous with "church-goer" because, historically, people would worship in their neighborhood church, or parish. By the 1990s, sociologist Nancy Ammerman had chronicled a shift from parish-based Christianity in the United States to an affinity-driven niche model (1997). With an increasingly mobile public and decreasing stigma against transferring denominational allegiance, churches could no longer rely on geographic proximity to fill their pews (Wuthnow 1998, 1990). They began to carve out unique identities to cater to certain niches of the worshipping public. By the turn of the millennium, however, continued decreases in church attendance across the United States were prompting churches to reconfigure their strategies. Cultural geographer Justin Willford demonstrates how the shift to decentralized post-suburban lifestyles – with chain stores offering identical products and services around the clock at different locations – prompted a parallel shift in religious consumption (2012). Rather than gathering in one central location at one given time for worship, America's congregations were increasingly wanting a similarly flexible worship experience in which they could chose to worship in a variety of locations at a variety of times. As Erwin McManus, pastor of multi-sited Mosaic church in California explains, "Multi-site is not simply about space; it's about place. Our multi-site strategy is more of cultural acupuncture . . . .about being a finely tuned instrument positioned exactly where it can have the greatest impact" (2006:8).

Multi-sited churches present a uniquely 21st century response to pressures of society and technology. In his 2013 study, Bird analyzed the role of music and media in multi-site expansion. He found that when churches launch new campuses, over 80% of participants feel that musicians are central to successful growth. He also found that *all* 535 multi-sited churches in the survey were using "video teaching." Statistics like these show how the interaction between live music and digital sermons is becoming increasingly central to the study of American religious practice. Rather than depending on physical proximity, multisite churches use a combination of media to create a sense of congregational unity and place. These geographically-dispersed churches pair live music with a mix of live preaching and digitally-delivered video sermons. The resulting religious product encompasses multiple locations in a quality controlled, consistently branded worship experience.

Media in Multi-Sited Churches

Augmenting the new physical reality of multi-site congregations, many churches have also moved toward using media to occupying virtual spaces, as well. These growing churches tend to have substantial presence online and via social media (Justice 2014). Sermons can be streamed or downloaded and footage of music and worship is often available. The virtual world also comes into the worship space, with viral videos as touch points in sermons, congregants tweeting questions to a pastor during interactive times, or music videos being made and uploaded during worship. At the same time that sermons are incorporating film, television, and digital media, sermons and music videos of church praise teams are becoming digital media in their own right.

As a result, Sunday morning messages often create feedback loops between the local religious experience and contemporary globalized media. Clergy, musicians, and laity are aware of their immediate experience in the worship space, but they are also experiencing overlapping levels of mediated reality. This dynamic changes the worship experience in way that resonates with what scholars describe as mediatization. The transformation beyond purely live delivery transforms the messages by means of their medium, and the process also creates a relationship between participants, environment, morals, and media that influences both the message and the sociopolitical context producing it. Writing before the onset of the internet and social media, semiotic philosopher Mikhail Bakhtin noted that in communication of any sort, "orientation toward the listener is an orientation toward a specific conceptual horizon, toward the specific world of the listener; it introduces totally new elements into his discourse" (1982:282). Mediatization creates a complex of layer of events through which participants focus not only upon the content, but also on the media packaging and potential usage, which thereby transforms the content.

An accessible example of mediatization outside of a church context would be the phenomenon of selfies (self-portraits taken via cell phone, generally with the intent of posting them on social media). Selfies are taken as photos, but not with the intention of printing them and framing them. Rather, selfies are most often taken with the explicit purpose of sharing on social media, which will result in comments on the photo. As media scholar Lynn Schofield Clark notes, selfies demonstrate "awareness of our own self-awareness" (2013). This awareness of "performing" for a virtual audience transforms the simple act of taking a picture into a multi-layered event of self-representation.

Theories about mediatization help analyze the dynamics of multi-sited worship in the digital age. When the sermons are preached, recorded, and disseminated among branch locations throughout the weekend, the pastors knows that they are preaching both to live listeners and to the broader congregation. They are also aware that the sermon will be posted to the church's website, Facebook, YouTube, and other social media. The intended audience is no longer the physical congregation alone; the people physically present to hear the sermon in a multi-sited church often comprise the minority of those who will hear the message.

This sense of leading worship for a non-present congregation is not entirely new. Each generation of technological development has seen new levels of mediated congregations, dating back to early recordings of sermons at the turn of the 20th century, to early radio broadcasts, and televangelism. The scale and vivid quality of today's multi-sited mediatization is, however, remarkable. For example, LCBC both live-streams their sacramental baptisms and makes videos. At one service during my fieldwork, moments after about ten adults and teenagers were baptized, the church's media team had already edited the footage – complete with a soundtrack from the band – into a touching video montage with close-up shots of the faithful giving their testimonies, being submerged in the baptismal tank, and then emerging. The participants know that this video was part of the service that was being livecast, as well as being posted to social media. Just like the case of the selfie and the sermon, awareness of live actions and their future digital manifestations intermingle. People live in the moment, but simultaneously occupy anticipated digital space.

Yet, even within the heavily mediatized environment of today's multi-sited megachurch with video sermons and social media presence, music must be live. In the standard model of a multi-sited megachurch, although the sermons may be digitally delivered to most worshipers, live music anchors the services at each location. Technologically speaking, it would be easy to broadcast the music as well as well as the sermon for a type of congregational karaoke. Many larger churches already use video-close ups of the band during the service while they are playing. The moving images on large projection screens in the front of sanctuaries capture worshipers' attention by zooming in on the guitar player's picking or the drummer's flying sticks.

Performance scholar Philip Auslander finds (1998, 2008) that when given a choice between looking at a close-up screen or watching an actual musician at a concert or an athlete at sports game, modern human attention tunes in to the mediated digital feed. In other words, digital trumps live: live + digital = digital (38). In his seminal book *Liveness*, Auslander argues that 20th century audience members often prefer the clarity of recorded media. In events with many participants, digital images can bring people closer to the action. For example, watching the big screen at the football game allows you to see despite your economy-priced seats that require binoculars with 20/20 vision (and you get close-ups and re-plays). In a rock concert, when the camera pans to the drummer from the back, you feel like you are on stage. The mediated experience brings you closer to the action and helps you tune out distractions around you. Plugging your headphones into a live feed may filter out the annoying toddler or candy-wrapper crinkling from the elderly lady next to you. People want a live experience, but they also want to be able to mediate *how* they experience that liveness.

Churches like LCBC are aware of these dynamics and have chosen to embrace and utilize media. This use of media during the service – with large screens zooming in on action on stage – becomes a mediatization introducing a domino effect that has transformed how churches like LCBC present worship. When LCBC's lead guitarist plays a riff, most congregants present during worship watch his fingers on the video screen. And indeed, as the band plays, a music video is often being filmed on the spot. LCBC technicians rapidly edit video and audio to create professional quality music videos of the worship teams during the service.

Given the choice, worshipers at least split, it not devote, their attention to the images on the screen. Yet live praise bands open for simulcast sermons across the country every Sunday. No multi-sited megachurch in the United States regularly relies heavily on recorded music. Instead, following the prevailing models of multi-sited worship, while the sermon is often digitally-delivered, live bands play at each satellite congregations within conglomerate multi-site churches.

A Case Study in Live Bands and Recorded Sermons

In order to engage the implications of the internationally growing phenomenon of worship as both live and mediatized, this chapter centers on one multi-sited megachurch, Lives Changed by Christ. According to the Hartford Institute for Religious Research, this faith community is currently the 33rd largest megachurch in the United States (2019). The church's story of transition from a tiny, locally-oriented Bible study group to a multi-sited worship conglomerate presents a strong case study for analyzing elements of live music, media, and religious community growth.

> Lives Changed by Christ began in 1986 when a handful of Christians felt called to begin a new faith community in Lancaster County, Pennsylvania. Despite competing for members with many established traditional churches, the venture grew quickly through interpersonal relationships and word-of-mouth outreach. The small group soon developed into Lancaster County Bible Church, or LCBC. The current senior pastor, David Ashcraft, began serving the church in 1991. As the congregation grew, leadership decided that they wanted

to expand geographically as well. They planted four branch campuses in Lancaster County and then moved into neighboring counties. The church has expanded rapidly across the rolling hills, farm country, and suburban sprawl of Pennsylvania's Susquehanna Valley, most recently developing three new sites in the West Shore of Harrisburg, Lebanon, and Berks (LCBC 2018). Keeping their LCBC acronym while moving beyond the limits of Lancaster County, the congregation changed its name from "Lancaster County Bible Church" to "Lives Changed by Christ." Since most people connected with the church simply refer to it as LCBC, the name did not functionally change. Within twenty-four years, LCBC has grown massively. From a single location with 150 people attending weekly services, the entity is now a multi-site church with 14 campus locations, 48 weekly services, over one hundred and fifty staff, and a weekly attendance of over 14,000 people.

LCBC's campuses are united under the principle of "One Church, Multiple Locations." The website and other promotional materials emphasize how "one look, one voice and one message" connect the church's different sites. LCBC strives for similarities in production values and worship content across its locations, and the level of reproducible sameness that the church aims for includes the physical setting of worship (See Figures 1–3). According to ethnomusicologist Tom Wagner, religious communities turning to this type of branding – similar to advertising strategies used for well-known, brand-name products like Coke, Nike, or Starbucks – but focusing on worship music, media, and setting has become increasingly popular (Wagner 2013). LCBC utilizes this strategy enthusiastically in worship and in promotional materials. In a video explaining "one church, multiple locations" on their website, the video and audio shifts seamlessly between footage of different branch campuses performing the same worship song. The campus' name, displayed in the upper right-hand corner of the screen, moves from "Manheim" to "Ephrata" to "Branch Creek" to other locations. The bands have different members and slightly varied instrumentation (one does not feature a keyboard), but the similar sound and look of worship across the different sites is striking. Just as much as the logo brands the church's activities as falling under one centralized umbrella, the video shows how each campus aims to provide a continuity that clergy, staff, musicians, and members talk about as "the LCBC experience."

Layers of media combine at LCBC and similar multi-site churches. On any given weekend LCBC uses a combination of live preaching and sermons delivered via video. At the church's auditorium-style main campus, senior pastor David Ashcraft and teaching pastor Jason Mitchell preach most of the services live. The satellite campuses, however, receive the sermon via video. Campuses do have pastoral staff, but they concentrate on congregational care and rarely preach. On their website, the church describes the preaching across all the campuses similarly: "Each location features the same unified experience of music

Figure 1: LCBC main campus.
Photograph by Deborah Justice

Figure 2: LCBC Ephrata.
Photograph by Deborah Justice

Figure 3: LCBC York.
Photograph by Deborah Justice

and one message from a communicator that is broadcasted to each location" ("About" LCBC). Video technology allows this centralized leadership to happen.

As well as being the predominant method of sermon delivery, video also plays a key role *within* the preaching itself. While pastors have long told stories referencing plots of books or films to illustrate their points, they are increasingly using video clips as teaching tools within their sermons. Instead of only hearing a Biblical story such as Jesus resisting in the wilderness to address the theme of temptation, the pastor might use a clip of super-spy James Bond resisting a sexy double-agent. To augment Jesus' parable of the prodigal son receiving parental love and forgiveness, the sermon may include Disney's happy scene when the young cartoon fish Nemo finally swims back into his father's welcoming fins. In addition to incorporating video illustrations like these, LCBC regularly runs sermon series that specifically focus on faith and film (see Figures 4 and 5).

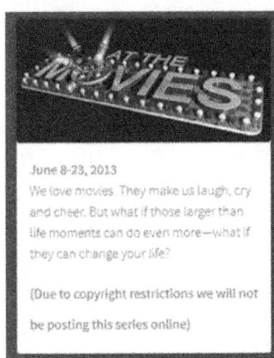

Figure 4

Figure 5

As a result, sermons at churches like LCBC are often layers of video media. For many of the satellite campus locations, the entire sermon is seen via video and then may also use video clips to advance the message. The video clip may be edited into the sermon video, creating a totally digitized experience, but often the clips are shown on a screen "live" next to the pastor as he plays them while delivering the sermon. As a result, sermons at multi-site churches often involve watching a preaching pastor watching a video clip in a taped sermon series about film.

A body of trade resources for churches and pastors has developed to help them integrate film media into their sermons. Books like *God in the Movies: A Guide For Exploring Four Decades Of Film* (2017), *Hearing a Film, Seeing a Sermon: Preaching and Popular Movies* (Cargal 2007) or *Movie-Based Illustrations for Teaching and Preaching* (Larson and Zahn 2003) provide concrete suggestions for pairing film clips with thematic points. Websites such as movieministry.com, worshiphousemedia.com, pastorlinks.com provide the same suggestions, some with links to streaming media and some as subscription services. Need to illustrate Christ's death as a substitute for humanity's sins? Pair appropriate Biblical texts with a clip from Disney's *The Lion King*. For spiritual backsliding? A scene from *The Matrix*. Many tools exist to assist pastors and other worship planners to incorporate film clips into their sermons.

While film clips embedded in digitized sermons present a novel form of religious mediatization, they also stem from a long-standing relationship between churches and media. Video-cast sermons and their cinematic teaching examples belong to a trend of 21st century digital and social media technologies that intensify historical patterns of using popular media to spread the messages of Christianity. From medieval processionals to paraliturgical passion plays, and more, churches have long relied upon theatrical devices and music to attract people and to mediate relationships between humans and the divine.

Whenever technology and media have developed into exciting new forms, changes in church presentation and dissemination of materials have been close behind. Sometimes the new media sparks changes involving worship spaces. During the nineteenth century, for example, as secular theaters with bold new architectural forms proliferated, Western churches began to mirror the success of these gatherings by meeting in similar auditorium-style spaces (Loveland and Wheeler 2003; Kilde 2005). As they did so, these churches adjusted their worship presentations to suit their new environments.

Additionally, sometimes changes in general media technology impact on worship media. By the early twentieth century, for example, production companies found that recordings of popular pastors and sacred music sold successfully. This was true across multiple ethnic subsets of American society, with black preachers such as Reverend E.D. Campbell and Isaiah Shelton being some of the most popular and recording sermons on a series of race records targeting African American buyers on the Victor label during the 1920s. Although these media were not generally played as a substitute for the Sunday morning message during live worship services, they bridged the gap between live preaching and mediatized sermons.

By the 1950s and Jesus People movement the 1960s, segments of American Christianity were fully embracing popular music and media during worship. In his history of the Campus Crusade for Christ organization, historian John Turner suggests that evangelicals have been quicker than other American Christians to embrace popular culture (2008). Work by historian David Stowe contributes further evidence of a strong connection between evangelicals and popular music and media (2011; 2004). In 1955, California pastor Robert Schuller took the evangelical connection to popular culture to new levels. Churches had been meeting in theater-style spaces for decades, but Schuller began holding wildly successful services in a drive-in movie theater. He used the theater's sound system to project the sermon directly into the attendees' private vehicles. Schuller went on to become one of the most prominent televangelists of the twentieth century, founding the Crystal Cathedral ministries. Yet, he was also only one of many pastors who saw increasingly blurred boundaries between sacred and secular media presentations. Churches actually meeting in cinemas began emerging around the world, presenting an innovation in Sunday morning communal devotional practice.

Today's highly mediatized multi-site churches, like LCBC, follow in this legacy. At the same time that they were experimenting with cinematic venues, many churches has also began implementing multimedia presentations that incorporated film during the worship services. By the turn of the millennium, many churches – whether they were meeting in traditional or theater-style spaces or actual cinemas – had come to rely on such video clips in highly mediated presentations during worship. In addition to segments from the silver screen and television, internet videos and social media have made their way into the multimedia experience of many contemporary churches. The relationship between worship services, music, and film developed in parallel to technological advancements in media production during the mid-20th century.

Incorporating familiar popular media draws upon and reinforces a sense of shared cultural background among church-goers. Pastors tend to introduce media clips using language that assumes that the congregation shares familiarity with the media. Phrases like "you've probably seen this show" or "last summer's hit movie that we all loved." Congregants often audibly react with "oh, yeah" or "mmhmm" or similar markers of recognition. The familiarity with the media creates a sense of community and common experience within the assembled group. For people who were unfamiliar with the media, the experience of viewing it together brings them into the community of people who are familiar with it, thus strengthening ties within in the congregation.

With congregations' growing acceptance of at least part of the preaching incorporating a video, having the entire sermon as a piece of media has become a much smaller leap than at any time previously. Outside of church, many people have become accustomed to experiencing connection through virtual interactions on screens of computers, smart phone and tablets. This type of communication has become so pervasive that it is, in some ways, little wonder that faith communities have embraced it along society at large. While not all churches have been equally enthusiastic about video teaching, many congregations rely on it, or even – a topic beyond the scope of this chapter – exist solely online.

The sermon as a video broadcast plays a particularly important role in creating a sense of shared experience and commonality across geographically dispersed multi-site churches. In these sprawling congregations, the digitally delivered sermons do more than only incorporate similarity-emphasizing media. The video sermons connect the dispersed congregants on multiple levels. Video teaching, as many multi-sited churches call it, creates similarity by ensuring that the message and authority structure remains the same across all the campuses. In practice, due to senior pastor David Ashcraft's schedule at LCBC, a mix of senior pastoral staff cover the sermons. Nevertheless, as explained on the website and promotional materials, at LCBC, Ashcraft retains spiritual leadership over the entire temporally and geographically dispersed flock.

In addition to assuring theological continuity and a firm chain of command, mediatization through the video sermons allows Ashcraft's pervasive presence to build a charisma-based continuity across LCBC. Whether worshippers are at a campus location or accessing the church online or via social media, Ashcraft's preaching forms a central thru line of experience. As the central leader featured in the sermon, Ashcraft himself has in fact become part of the LCBC brand. Video sermons are only way that he has been able to achieve this level of reach throughout such a geographically disperse church configuration.

As well as being oriented around one leader, the assumed commonality of sermon experience unites the large congregation across campuses. The fact that the sermons are one of many elements distributed throughout many campuses reinforces the common experience promised in the church's branding. Worshippers know that most other LCBC attendees are literally hearing and seeing the same message on a given weekend. This knowledge helps LCBC church-goers see their experience as shared with the worship experience of the church's over 10,000 other members. As in Anderson's imagined communities (1983), the entire LCBC congregation will never meet together, but individual worshippers are aware of similar experiences and identical preaching across the different campuses. Knowing that they are experiencing the same sermon plays a key role in bonding this imagined congregation.

LCBC's music tries to maintain a similar continuity despite having a different live band, or "praise team," plays at each satellite congregation within the conglomerate multi-site church. While some other churches may allow, and even promote, considerable variation in styles between their sites, LCBC and similar churches have a more tightly controlled continuity.

At LCBC, the actual set lists for worship are fixed and carefully choreographed between locations. Congregants experience a fully-engaged praise team leading them in local worship, whereas the actual multi-site plan is much less spontaneous and much more centralized. While conducting fieldwork, I visited both the main campus on one Sunday morning and the York campus on the same Sunday evening. From the songs to the verbal introductions by the lead guitarists, the services had the same musical content. The bands did differ slightly, with the York campus having a female vocalist and male keyboard player, while the main campus had a woman singing and playing keyboard. But the differences felt largely cosmetic compared to the strong similarities in the sound, repertoire, and overall ambiance. However, since most congregants only attend services once a week, this level of cross-site coordination is not immediately apparent to the average worshipper.

Yet, if musical uniformity was really the goal, a music video of the main campus praise team to accompany congregational singing could be broadcast at each branch campus along with the sermon. This would be an easy, effective method of bringing exactly the same music to the people, but churches do not do it. Instead they choose to spend time and money to hire multiple musical leaders to coordinate various praise teams full of paid and volunteer musicians. Particularly at churches like LCBC where each branch campus sets out to reproduce "the LCBC experience" rather than a unique, local style of worship, why go to the trouble of live music? Why is live music more important than live preaching in America's fastest growing religious configuration?

The Power of Live Music

Approaching the role of live music in worship happens in the broader context of understanding liveness. Live music and recorded music effect participants differently. When and how does liveness matter?

Ethnomusicologist Thomas Turino suggests a four-part typology to investigate music as the politics of participation. First, Turino divides music into two broad categories of live and recorded. Then, he subdivides live music into participatory and presentational and subdivides recorded music into high fidelity and studio audio art (2008). Following this model, participatory live music encourages everyone to be involved in some way. This type of music-making does not encourage a distinction between audience and performers because everyone is actively participating. Varying levels of competence are tolerated and possibly even encouraged. The key is playing together as a community. Campfire singing, old-time jam sessions, or Christmas carol singing provide examples. Presentational music, in contrast, separates audience and musicians. One group creates the music, the other receives it. In a rock show or at a concert orchestra, for example, some people are there to listen but others are there to perform. There is little, if any cross over between the groups. High fidelity recorded music seeks to recreate the experience and ambiance of live music via recording. High fidelity music would use live takes from a session or recordings of a live concert. Finally, studio audio art creates a product through recording technology, using effects, layers, and other mediations that would be impossible in live performance. A single musician singing harmony with herself or other "studio trickery." New technologies – such as recording loops live on stage and then manipulating them or similar interfaces of live and recorded performance – certainly muddy the waters of such a clear typology. Nevertheless, the categories signify basic differences in the ways that people make and experience music together.

In contrast to traditional, non-mediatized churches, the combination of music and media in most multi-sited churches involves all of Turino's categories of music making. At first glance, the band versus congregation may gloss as presentational. In fact, most services are designed to resemble popular music concert. The band remains on a stage, separated from the rest of the people in the room. The music's volume often reaches levels so high congregants can barely hear themselves much less their neighbors singing. The congregation's vocalizations are not miked and broadcast. When the worship tech team makes a music video of the performance, the musicians are also participating in Turino's "high fidelity" recording, and depending on the amount of studio trickery and editing a "studio art" type of product may emerge.

Yet, the congregation *is* supposed to participate in the music making. Lyrics are provided with the expectation that the worshippers will sing. In most multi-sited churches, band members describe their role as "leading worship," "helping people sing," or "supporting the congregation." As the multi-sited Vineyard Church in Syracuse, New York says, the worship team exists to "help bring the congregation into a place of worship"(Vineyard ministries 2014). Whether listening to and meditating on the words the band performs (presentational, according to Turino) or singing along themselves (participatory), the congregants are using the music to interact socially and spiritually. Paralleling Engelke and Tomlinson's anthropological inquiries into the limits of meaning with "preachers whose sermons fall flat, prophets who are marginal, [and] members of the audience who become bored and fall asleep" (2006: 2), a lack of congregational participation would result in the musical interaction being a social and spiritual failure.

Worshippers tend to believe that participating in the music enables both social and spiritual communication. It is the spiritual element here that anchors the participatory nature of this style of worship music – if not worship music in general – and differentiates it from purely presentational music. Participants expect to be interacting not only with each other but with the divine. Analyzing this element of liveness enters nearly uncharted territories; neither Turino's typology nor Philip Auslander's seminal work *Liveness* (2008) focus on people's beliefs about the potential involvement of a deity as an aspect of musical participation. Sociologist Robert Wuthnow's research (2003:141) found that Protestant church-goers reported that both live church music and live sermons resulted in their feeling similar degrees of closeness with God. Participants talk about powerful worship as happening when music brings "the Spirit in this place" or helps people feel "God among us."

The elements of uncertainty and risk in participating in live music-making render it particularly effective. As events unfold in time in front of us, we never truly know the outcome until it has happened. According to ethnomusicologist David VanderHamm, recognizing a musical virtuoso partly affirms their possessing nearly superhuman abilities that allow them to defy risk and perform difficult passages flawlessly (2018). Similarly, congregational musical participation suggests the potential for worshippers to draw on each other to collectively transcend beyond the mundane, or daily life to a "place-out-of-place" and "time-out-of-time" (Falassi, 1987). The embodied act of working toward these experiences together creates a sense of togetherness that practitioners may perceive as social, spiritual, or a combination thereof.

Countless studies have investigated both the affective change in state when people attend a collective musical performance and when they sing in a group. These "secular" benefits remain in faith communities like LCBC, but these churches also have other intentional framing for their music making. Using distinctive language and imagery, LCBC strongly positions their worship music as a way to praise and experience God. The way that evangelical multi-site congregations like LCBC teach congregants to understand music as a means to experience God resonates with anthropologist Tanya Luhrmann's study of American evangelicals: "The church teaches congregants a new theory of mind, in which thoughts they might have ascribed to random musing are now to be interpreted as the presence of this eternal being... Knowing God involves training" (2012: 222). Regardless of deities' existence, these churches help people who want to learn to experience God through music to be able to do that and to become more effective at this practice over time.

For thousands of multi-sited church worshipers, the power of live music has a strong enough effect to compensate for the potential social and spiritual impacts of a multi-site megachurch's recorded sermon. This is a primary reason why, while recorded sermons may be accepted (although not preferred overall), for worship as a whole, screens themselves do not suffice. When the band plays well and the congregation is so involved that nearly everyone has their hands in the air by the second modulation on the chorus, people report feeling that God is active. In the vast majority of cases, live music remains a necessary element in effective multi-site church configurations. The strong national trend among American churches demonstrates the power that the spontaneity of real-time, in-person music-making.

Works Cited

Ammerman, N. 1997. *Congregation & Community*. Rutgers, NJ: Rutgers University Press.
Anderson, B. 1983. *Imagined Communities*. London: Verso.
Bakhtin, M. M. 1982. *The Dialogic Imagination: Four Essays*. Edited by Michael Holquist. Translated by Caryl Emerson. Reprint edition. Austin: University of Texas Press.
Bird, W. 2016. "12 Intriguing Megachurch Trends." *Leadership Network*. Accessed March 18, 2019. (http://leadnet.org/12-intriguing-megachurch-trends/)
Bird W 2013. "Leadership Network/Generis Multisite Church Scorecard," *Leadership Network*.
Cargal, T. 2007. *Hearing a Film, Seeing a Sermon: Preaching and Popular Movies*. Louisville: Westminster John Knox Press.
Chaves, M. 2004. *Congregations in America*. Cambridge: Harvard University Press.
Engelke, M. and Tomlinson, M., eds. 2006. *The Limits of Meaning: Case Studies in the Anthropology of Christianity*. New York and Oxford: Berghahn Books.
Falassi, A. 1987. *Time Out of Time: Essays on the Festival*. Albuquerque: University of New Mexico Press.
Hartford Seminary Megachurch Database. 2014. Accessedm(http://hirr.hartsem.edu/megachurch/database.html).
Ingalls, M. 2012. "Worship on the Web: Building Networked Religious Community through Christian Devotional Music Videos." The International Society for Media, Religion, and Culture Conference, Anadolu University, Eskeshehir, Turkey.
Ingalls, M., Landau, C. and Wagner, T. 2013 *Christian Congregational Music: Performance, Identity and Experience*. London and New York: Routledge.

Ingalls, M., Reigersberg, M. S. and Sherinian, Z. 2018. *Making Congregational Music Local in Christian Communities Worldwide*. London and New York: Routledge.

Justice, D. 2014. "Religion Reinserted: When Church and Cinema Blur Boundaries through Media-Savvy Evangelicalism." *Journal of Religion, Media, and Digital Culture*. Vol. 3, No. 1, 84–119.

Kilde, J. 2005. *When Church Became Theatre: The Transformation of Evangelical Architecture and Worship in Nineteenth-Century America*. New York: Oxford.

Larson, C., and A. Zahn. 2003. "Movie-Based Illustrations for Preaching and Teaching," – Volume 1. Grand Rapids, MI: Zondervan.

Leadership Network 2018. "Multisite Church News." *Leadership Network*. Accessed February 13, 2019. (http://leadnet.org//blog/post/big_news_multisite_churches_now_number_more_than_5000)

LifeWay Research. 2013. "American Views on Video and In-Person Sermons." *LifeWay Research Group*. http://www.lifewayresearch.com/files/2013/12/American-Views-on-Video-Venues.pdf.

Loveland, A., and O. Wheeler. 2003. *From Meetinghouse to Megachurch: A Material and Cultural History*. St. Louis: University of Missouri Press.

Luhrmann, T. M. 2012. *When God Talks Back: Understanding the American Evangelical Relationship with God*. New York: Vintage.

McManus, E. 2006. "Foreword." In *The Multi-Site Church Revolution: Being One Church in Many Locations*. Grand Rapids, MI: Zondervan.

Portable Church Ministries 2018. "8 Statistics Every Multisite Church Leader Should Know." *Portable Church Industries*. Accessed March 10, 2019. (https://www.portablechurch.com/2016/church-planting/multisite-church-statistics/)

Schofield Clark, L. 2013. "Scholarly Reflections on the 'selfie.'" *OUPblog*. http://blog.oup.com/2013/11/scholarly-reflections-on-the-selfie-woty–2013/.

Stowe, D. 2004. *How Sweet the Sound: Music in the Spiritual Lives of Americans*. Cambridge: Harvard University Press.

Stowe, D. 2011. *No Sympathy for the Devil: Christian Pop Music and the Transformation of American Evangelicalism*. Chapel Hill: The University of North Carolina Press.

Surratt, G. Ligon, and W. Bird. 2006. *The Multi-Site Church Revolution: Being One Church in Many Locations*. Grand Rapids, MI: Zondervan.

Turner, J. 2008. Bill Bright and Campus Crusade for Christ. Chapel Hill: University of North Carolina Press.

VanderHamm, D. 2018. Phenomenology in Ethnomusicology 2018: The St. John's Conference, Research Centre for the Study of Music, Media, and Place, Memorial University of Newfoundland.

Vineyard Ministries 2014. "Syracuse Site Ministries – Vineyard Church at Syracuse." Accessed September 29. http://vineyardny.org/ministries/syracuse-site-ministries–2/.

Wagner, T. 2013. "Branding, Music, and Religion: Standardization and Adaptation in the Experience of the 'Hillsong Sound.'" In *Religion as Brands: New Perspectives on the Marketization of Religion and Spirituality*. London: Ashgate.

Wuthnow, R. 1990. *The Restructuring of American Religion*. Princeton: Princeton University Press.

Wuthnow, R. 1998. *After Heaven: Spirituality in America since the 1950s*. Berkeley: University of California Press.

Wuthnow, R. 2003. *All in Sync: How Music and Art are Revitalizing American Religion*. Berkeley: University of California Press.

Kathleen M. Ryan
Silencing the Tongues of Angels? The Aesthetics of Destruction in Environmental Edens

> You shall top a rise and behold creation.
> And you shall need the tongues of angels
> to tell you what you have seen.
>
> Ansel Adams and Nancy Newhall
> *This is the American Earth* (1960)

The epigraph above is but one example of the way early landscape photographers, environmentalists, and curators described the environment, specifically the American West. Visiting these wild lands, seemingly pristine and unmarked by humans, was akin to a religious experience; an experience where only the "tongues of angels" (or the eyes of a talented photographer) were suitable to convey the majesty to others. It comes from the Sierra Club-published monograph *This is the American Earth*, and is positioned in the book to accompany a photograph by Ansel Adams entitled *Winter Storm, Yosemite*. In the image, the sun sneaks out from behind luminous, puffy clouds. Its beams touch the ground below; tendrils of light which caress the valley. It appears luscious, pristine, and, above all, sacred.

Indeed, America's Frontier narrative is rife with this sort of religious allegory: man explores an untamed Eden and preserves it so future generations can have the ability to worship in the same spirit (Salvesen 2010). Environmentalism, is has been argued, *is* a kind of religion (Dunaway, 2005). But 21st century photographers are challenging this notion of environmental religiosity. While *Silent Spring* (Carson 1962) posited that environmental degradation is something akin to hell, a new cohort of landscape photographers (including Robert Adams, Lynn Davis, Andreas Gursky, Richard Misrach, and Camille Seaman) is demonstrating aesthetic beauty and exultant qualities can be found in the human-altered environment. Drawing inspiration from the "New Topographics," who challenged the notion that the human-altered Western landscape was somehow bereft of value (Jenkins, 1975), these photographers look at spaces of environmental destruction and find a strange, otherworldly beauty.

This chapter will position the work of photographer David Maisel within this context. Maisel documents the environmental impacts of American West projects like open-pit mining extraction and large-scale water diversion. The chapter will first trace the American landscape tradition, which established this myth as an evolution of the philosophical notions of Puritanism and Manifest Destiny: not only did Americans have an obligation to "settle" the land, but in so doing they would discover a spiritual revival within those undeveloped spaces. This notion of spirituality found in "undeveloped" nature would be amplified and exploited in photographs used within the environmental movement of the 1960s and '70s, specifically the photographs of Ansel Adams and Eliot Porter. Next the chapter will look at how the photographers of the New Topographics movement exposed the falsity of the human versus wilderness construction, focusing on the work of Robert Adams. Finally, it will explore how photographs of environmental devastation can fit into this tradition of photographic environmental religiosity. I argue that Maisel's photographs demonstrate a revised model of spirituality in photography, which invites humans back into the (recreated) Garden both to asses the damage and to find pleasure within a new environmental aesthetic.

The Landscape Tradition, or Creating the Myth

The narrative about the North American continent is, as Henry Nash Smith (1950) argues, a creation myth, where European settlers came to the "new world" searching for a promised land. Smith compares this to a recreation of the Garden of Eden narrative from Biblical texts. In this case, the white settlers were fleeing a wrecked and devastated Garden (Europe) in favor of a new and pristine land, where they could fix the problems found in the land left behind in a new Garden. The first Pilgrim harvest demonstrates this creation myth in action: man is struggling against a sometimes hostile wilderness, only to eventually persevere and tame it (Smith 1950:141).

This narrative would extend to the American Interior, which even by the late 1700s was "bathed in golden mist of utopian fantasy" (Smith 1950:11). The land was believed to be fertile and productive, a space where the rugged individual could create his (for this was also a historically white male narrative) personal Garden of Eden. As Carolyn Merchant (1995) observes:

> The narrative of frontier expansion is a story of male energy subduing female nature, taming the wild, plowing the land, re-creating the garden lost by Eve. . . . To civilize was to bring the land out of a state of savagery and barbarism into a state of refinement and enlightenment. (146–147)

The problem was that the land didn't necessarily conform to this narrative. The Plains and Mountain West were (and still are) arid landscapes, difficult to farm or ranch when using methods more common in other regions of the world.

Poor land management practices such as deep plowing, the elimination of native grasses in favor of more water-intensive species, and overgrazing by domesticated livestock would have devastating effects on the land (National Drought Mitigation Center, 2014). The Garden of Eden couldn't be conquered, or created as one's own personal Edenic space, because the land didn't cooperate (Smith 1950).

As this was happening, however, a new American landscape narrative began to emerge. What if it *wasn't* an obligation of Americans to recreate the Garden? What if instead the Garden was already there, a place where man (again, this was a historically male domain) could go to contemplate and reflect within land left relatively undisturbed? It was this impulse that led Thoreau to Walden Pond, and John Muir to the Far West.

Thoreau spent two years in his Walden Pond cottage in the forest near Concord, Massachusetts, from 1845 to 1847. In *Walden*, published seven years later, Thoreau (1993:305) explored the personal transformation he found in the woods. He found in the pond "earth's eye" where "the beholder measures the depth of his own nature." As theologian Malcolm Clemens Young (2009:234) notes, inherent in Thoreau's vision of nature was something wild, a nature we cannot control: "The identifying qualities of nature are its vastness, its freedom, and, above all, its wildness; that is, its independence from all the constraints of human society." Thoreau (1993:309) himself said, "I cannot come nearer to God and heaven" than when in the woods of a place like Walden Pond. While Smith warns of the "cultural primitivism" inherent in Thoreau's belief of "a supreme good in the trackless wilderness" (1950:78), Thoreau's experiences would nonetheless strike a chord. His work lay the foundation for the notion that the untamed land was nearer to God than more "civilized" places.

Muir found a similar spiritualism in the Sierra Nevada mountains east of Fresno, specifically Yosemite Valley and the Tuolumne River. Muir (1912) repeatedly described the Valley as "temple" and offered a detailed description of a natural "cathedral" near Tenaya Lake (now known as Cathedral Peak):

> . . . a building of one stone, sewn from the living rock, with sides, roof, gable, spire and ornamental pinnacles, fashioned and finished symmetrically like a work of art, set on a well-graded plateau about 9000 feet high, as if Nature in making so fine a building had also been careful that it should be finely seen.

Muir found other parts of the Sierras equally valuable, and equally awe-inspiring; he called Hetch Hetchy Valley "one of Nature's rarest and most precious mountain temples" with "sublime rocks" that "seem to glow with life, whether lending back in repose or standing erect in thoughtful attitudes" (1912).

Though the frontier was considered the last bastion of rugged individualism (Cronon 1995, 77), it was declared "closed" in 1893. However, it was through the actions of writers and conservationists like Muir (and others) that some of the frontier was preserved, set aside as National Parks. The first would be Yellowstone National Park in 1872. Yosemite, initially managed by the state of California as the Yosemite Land Grant, would receive that National Park designation through Muir's efforts in 1890 (National Park Service 2014). With the establishment of The National Park Service in 1917, the notion of "wilderness" landscape transformed from a "garden" where one lived and worked to an "other": a spot not in one's world. As Sigurd F. Olson (1961) observes, "The real significance of wilderness is a cultural matter. It is far more than hunting, fishing, hiking, camping, or canoeing. It has to do with the human spirit. And what we are trying to conserve is not scenery as much as the human spirit itself" (24).

Implicit in these writings is the notion that nature offers a deep spirituality for humans–a spirituality akin to that found in the original Garden of Eden–but that the land must remain "unspoiled," i.e. without modern human development. Muir (1912) compared the arguments of those who would develop Yosemite and other similar lands as "curiously like the those of the devil, devised for the destruction of the first garden," and praised the restorative qualities he found within "the Range of Light." Thoreau (1993:234) described himself as a "worshipper of Aurora," where the pond offered a type of rebirth or restoration. These healing qualities could only be found in the "wild" landscape.

This transformation, from garden to preserve, entwines the romance of primitivism (a simpler time could serve as an anecdote to ills of modern society) with the myth of the frontier in the United States (Cronon, 1995:76). The land thus has a value beyond the human-created world that is fully naturalized. As Neil Evernden (1992:22) notes, "To be associated with nature is to be placed beyond human caprice or preference, beyond choice or debate. When something is 'natural' it is 'the norm,' 'the way,' 'the given.'" Seemingly undisturbed places found in the natural world were described as sanctuaries, where one could find renewal from the increasing conformity of society (Dunaway 2005: 126–127). Thus the land's value is tied up in its ability to act as an antidote to the consumerism, pollution, and development inherent in the modern world. Its value, in an increasingly secular society, became akin to the value of religion itself (Dunaway 2005), and, in some cases, would replace religion altogether (Turner 1994).

"Sierra Club Religion"

This move for the "pristine" environment to be seen as a sacred space, akin to the high cathedrals of various religions, was aided and abetted by the Sierra

Club and its stable of talented photographers. The conservation organization's mission was to preserve America's natural heritage, and it promoted its mission aggressively through its publications, including calendars and photographic books. The *Exhibit Format* series, published from 1960–1968, in some ways became the biblical texts for the burgeoning environmental religiosity. Finis Dunaway argues:

> The books used the idea of natural beauty as a citizenship right to galvanize support for wilderness legislation. The series depicted wild places as sanctuaries for the spirit, landscapes of therapy that offer physic renewal to postwar Americans, providing them with a temporary escape from the pressures of modernity and the snares of conformity. (210:17)

The books often linked the works of the top Sierra Club landscape photographers (Ansel Adams, Eliot Porter, Phillip Hyde) with texts from key environmental advocates (Muir, Thoreau). Dunaway (2005) says that the books served as a type of propaganda for the Sierra Club Religion.

This is the American Earth would be the first book released in the Exhibit Format series. The 1960 monograph, with photographs by Adams and text by Newhall (Adams and Newhall 1960), presented the American West as the place where "real" nature could be found, a nature that offered profound spiritual experiences. Or, in the language of the book, in wilderness:

> You shall live lifted up in light; you shall move among the clouds. You shall see storms arise, and, drenched and deafened, shall exult in them. You shall top a rise and behold creation. And you shall need the tongues of angels to tell what you have seen.
> (Newhall 1960:84)

Newhall's language is almost biblical, as much in place in the book *Genesis* as in a photographic monograph. And it's typical of that found in the rest of the monograph, which warns that unbridled development can spell "the end of Eden" (1960:23) and that we should instead come to the wilderness "as pilgrims to these sanctuaries" (1960:76). John Szarkowski observes, "Intentionally or otherwise, the book projects a Calvinist insularity. It appears to see most of the world as beyond salvation, and the American West as the last chance for New Jerusalem" (2001:34). The book, and attendant exhibition, featured the work of Adams (more than half the images) as well as twenty other photographers; the vast majority came from the American West.

The image next to the "tongues of angels" text (*Winter Storm, Yosemite* also known as *Clearing Winter Storm, Yosemite Valley*) is black and white and dates from 1942 or earlier. It shows the valley dusted by snow. Slightly to the left of center, sun peeks through the dark storm clouds, basking them and the valley in the foreground in a bright white light. Dunaway (2005) calls this light a "vital agent" (139), drawing and welcoming viewers into the image. The center of the photograph almost glows; the image seems to offer ample evidence that the land should be "saved" for future generations. But as Szarkowski (2001:38) notes, the photographer didn't chose "the landscape as a matter of social service, but [rather] as a form of private worship." The light in *Winter Storm* is an example of how Adams merged this personal religion and aesthetics in his photography: "By drawing on the sublime tradition, he sought to emphasize the emotional power of nature and to glorify the divinity of the wilderness" (Dunaway 2005:141).

Two years later the Sierra Club would publish *In Wilderness is the Preservation of the World*, which featured color photographs by Porter combined with text by Thoreau. Porter combed through Thoreau's writings to find excerpts that complimented his photographs: Porter's images offered insights into Thoreau's words and vice versa (Porter 1962:14). In the book:

> The emphasis on defining nature as a repository of aesthetic value denies the ways that work connects people to the natural world. It suggests that any use of nature is not merely a mistake but a profound moral failing. It means all human-constructed spaces – farms, factories, cities–seem tainted, far removed from the pristine world of wilderness
> (Dunaway 2005:164)

One of the images in the book is *Pool in a Brook, Pond Brook, Near Whiteface, New Hampshire, October 1953*. At the foreground of the image, a scattering of brownish leaves rest on the cool-toned blueish-black water. Moving from bottom to top, the tones in the image grow richer and more varied: purples and reds seep into the frame. At the top of the image, there are few visible leaves on the water and the color palate has shifted to the warmth of orange and yellow. The hues of sunrise (or sunset) kiss the pond.

Alongside the image (Plate 22 in the book) is this quote from Thoreau, drawn from his *Journal*, and written on October 7, 1857:

> I saw, by peculiar intention or dividing of the eye, a very striking subaqueous rainbow-like phenomenon . . . forming sharp pyramids of the several colors, gradually reduced to mere dusky points. The effect of this prolongation of the reflection was a very pleasing softening and blending of the colors.
> (Porter 1962:124)

The words are strikingly less reverential than the "tongues of angels" phrase found alongside Adams' *Winter Storm*. But Young (2009) cautions the reader should not think that the *Journal*'s seemingly prosaic language lacks religious reverence. Instead, he says, *Journal* should be seen as "an outgrowth of Protestant spiritual journals," a reading which allows one to understand Thoreau's focus on nature as a road to salvation (Young, 2009:251). While Thoreau rejected institutionalized religion, at the same time he "longed for intimacy or communion with the force that he believed brought forth all nature" causing "an almost mystical fascination with God . . . [a] sincere conviction that we come nearest to God in nature" (Young, 2009:250). This notion – that within nature one can find a higher power – is echoed in the monograph's introduction, where naturalist Joseph Wood Krutch wrote:

> One cannot begin to "love Nature" in any profitable sense until one has achieved an empathy, a sense of oneness and of participation. 'Appreciation' means an identification, a sort of mystical experience, religious in the most fundamental sense of the terms. (1962:15)

Like *American Earth*, *In Wilderness* is an example of the Sierra Club Religion in action.

Porter was committed to the idea that the natural world in the Americas (he didn't limit himself to the American West) should be considered as sacred as the desert of the Middle East, the birthplace of Judaism, Christianity, and Islam. "Porter tried to infuse his photographs with this religious feeling. By using the camera, he sought to mix his emotions with the machine to express his belief in the spiritual possibilities of the nonhuman world" (Dunaway 2005:151). But unlike Adams, who was politically active with the conservation movement (specifically the Sierra Club), Porter denied that he was trying to promote conservation. Rather, he says, "I photograph for the thing *itself* – for the photograph – without consideration of how it may be used" (Porter, 1979:11, emphasis in original). He photographed for his own aesthetic joys.

Adams and Porter, through their collaborations with the Sierra Club, were able to have an impact unimagined by most photographers. Rebecca Solnit notes that the two:

> functioned in a unique way at a unique time: their aesthetic work had a kind of political impact that is hard to imagine in any other arena . . . It was a rare moment in history when art could achieve political ends so profound, when the mere sight of such images and reminder of such places became a powerful motivating force, when a pair of artists who were much admired in museum circles could do heroic work in environmental ones.
> (2007:251)

But the work the two did with the Sierra Club also shone a spotlight on what may be an uncomfortable truth: nature itself (religious or not) is, to borrow from Cronon (1995:25), "a profoundly human construction." The values and descriptions that we attach to it say more about the values and descriptions of our own society than about the natural world. Which raises the question that has plagued advocates of the undeveloped landscape: if nature is exposed as a human construction, does it then lose its moral and spiritual authority?

Pulling Back the Curtain

Enter *New Topographics: Photographs of a Man-altered Landscape*, a relatively small 1975 exhibit at the George Eastman House in Rochester, New York. Ten photographers made up the group, including Robert Adams (no relation to Ansel Adams). Unlike previous landscape photographs common in the Sierra Club Religion model, where nature was an untouched-by-human-hands place the photographer went to outside of and apart from everyday life, these images pointed out that man and nature were unconditionally linked. For the New Topographics, the trash alongside an otherwise-pristine stream or the housing development in the background behind it were as much a part of the landscape as the stream itself (Rohrbackh 2010:xvii).

The New Topographics' images were in many ways the polar opposites of works like *Winter Storm* or *Pool in a Brook*. Photographs showed excavations for home or office developments, deserted/abandoned downtowns of American West cities, land-use management projects, and suburban sprawl. This was a paradigm shift for landscape photography.

> These photographs of man-altered landscapes forestalled nostalgia and prevented an escape into the past – instead they forced viewers to remain in the present and think about the future. New Topographics had redemptive aspects in its renovation of landscape photography, attention to cultural landscape, and depiction of heedless land use. Its key message was not revelation but responsibility. (Salvesen 2010:55)

Drawing from postmodern ideas of visual art in general, i.e. that art needed to challenge the viewer and could be at times difficult to understand, the New Topographers demonstrated that photographing the land couldn't simply be based in aesthetics, nor could the image maker ignore the presence of human influence (including the presence of the photographer).

In so doing they also laid bare the snobbery and elitism that were inherent within the pristine Sierra Club model, which demands moving off the beaten path, to discover an "unknown" landscape (or "cathedral") and experience redemption, often at the end of a grueling hike through backcountry (Marling 1992). Nature lives in one place and human in another. For the New Topographics, by contrast, the landscape wasn't something to go to, but rather something found in the areas where people lived. The traces of human intervention on the land (buildings, trash, etc.), and in some cases actual people, were the subject matter of the images. Human and nature were one.

Robert Adams said of his own work that he was driven to "include the objects we'd brought to the landscape and which by common consent are most ugly, but also to suggest that light can transform even grotesque, inhuman things into mysteries worthy of attention" (Digrappa 1980:10). In other words, he sought the beauty within human-caused "devastation," be it a suburb plunked down on the Western prairie, a scrawl of graffiti on a scenic overlook, or an exit sign along a desolate Colorado interstate for the town of Eden. Adams' work centered on Colorado, specifically the eastern edge of the Rocky Mountains because "it is overspread with light of such richness that banality is impossible" (Adams, 2010:236).

Alan Berger (2006) argues that the seeming paradox of the beauty found in both the altered and traditional landscapes via the New Topographics demonstrates an awareness of the history of the land. Or, as Evernden (1992:99) observes:

> The dualism cannot actually be resolved, *because it never existed*. The dualism we fret over exists only because of our own decision, not only to constrict the nature-tube into two domains, but to create the container in the first place. One might even say there is no 'nature,' and there never has been. (emphasis in original)

Because, of course, the "untouched" nature we pine for within the Sierra Club Religion ignores the reality of the American West: that it was a land settled by humans long before the first European immigrants made their way westward in their search for Eden. As Raymond Williams (1980:78) observes, even the things we consider natural, even the "wilderness" itself "is the product of human design and human labour, and in admiring it as natural it matters very much whether we suppress that fact of labour or acknowledge it." The Garden found in the West, as pointed out by the work of the New Topographics, was an artifice.

Adams' *Burning Oil Sludge North of Denver* (1973) serves as a useful fulcrum of sorts in the reconceptualization of the Environmental Eden. The image itself is stunning. The black and white photograph, looks west toward the Rocky Mountains. Long's Peak, one of the state's 14,000-plus foot mountains, appears on the far right side of the frame. The natural environment – the flatness of the prairie, the snow-capped mountains on the horizon, the cloud-studded sky – is bathed in washed-out patina of pale grey and white. Four items in the image stand out against this background: a lone cottonwood tree, a split rail and barbed wire fence, an oil derrick, and, most strikingly, a plume of black smoke that billows from the lower left of the photograph to the upper right.

The subject matter is similar to much of what was trod in the original New Topographics exhibition. It largely depicts what was a fairly mundane scene in the rural American west of the late 20th century. Active and dormant oil derricks dot the region, as much a part of the environment as the mountains, prairie and skies. It is part of a series Adams called *What We Bought*, where he consciously avoided Colorado's spectacular mountain vistas in favor of the perspective from the prairies. Man's intervention in the environment is front and center. In the photograph this intervention is highlighted by Adams' high contrast shooting/printing methods, which make the human altered (the fence, the oil derrick, the plume of smoke) more prominent than that which is traditionally defined as "natural."

But one specific element of the image–the dark black smoke plume–moves it from the more banal scenes of the New Topographics to a direct challenge to the previous norms of Environmental Edens found in the Sierra Club Religion. The smoke cuts a scar across the horizon, interjecting toxic fumes into an otherwise-peaceful environment – even the oil derrick, linked to if not the direct cause of the smoke, sits seemingly at one within the land. It is the smoke that is the intrusion, but, at the same time, it is also the source of the unsettling beauty of the image. It offers, in the words of Adams (2010:238), "a tension so exact that it is peace." It points to the active role humans are taking in shaping and changing the land in ways that aren't always positive. But despite this intrusion, within the movement of the smoke are echoes of the natural; in another setting it could be the ink flow from an octopus or squid taking evasive measures when threatened. The land is pushing back in some way, trying to adjust to man's intervention. The aesthetic delight caused by the smoke plume draws us into the land. It's this tension–between the sacred and profane – that adds to the image's appeal.

The machine in the garden: Environmental hell or new religion?

The American West, as historian Patricia Nelson Limerick (1999) reminds us, is an altered landscape. By using the word "altered," one can avoid some of the diametrical, value-laden oppositions often found in descriptions of the land, i.e. that "natural" is good and "man made" is bad. Instead, the West is a land which has been constantly shaped and changed by both human and non-human forces, forces which leave traces behind: the scar on a hill after a landslide, the blackened trees after a forest fire, the abandoned cliff dwellings of an ancient civilization. As Solnit (2007:355) notes: "Ruins stand as reminders. Memory is always incomplete, always imperfect, always falling into ruin; but the ruins themselves, like other traces, are treasures: our links to what came before, our guide to situating ourselves in a landscape of time." Even the damaged landscape can offer a way to see what has happened in the past and use it to come to an understanding about our world.

Merry A. Foresta argues that "nature" in the late 20th century "lies somewhere between the ideals of home and heaven. Echoing the older traditions of Arcadia and Utopia, this double vision of landscape promises either a return to an edenic past or innovation that will make us a paradise in the future" (1992:38). But the ruins found in the altered landscape may demand a reconsideration of aesthetics, especially when contrasted with either the Sierra Club Religion photos or the work of the New Topographics. "The reclamation of these areas demands a new vision of pastoralism–a sweet recognition of a kind of beauty in the transformation of the land, even its slow destruction" (Burnett 2010:155). The ugly or unexpected or even the devastated can transform the notion of beauty.

Limerick herself comes to this conclusion. Using the example of a photograph by Wanda Hammerbeck, which shows a car partially blocking an otherwise-perfect stream, she notes, "Grace coexists with sin. Grace may even be deepened and increased by its proximity to sin" (1999:12). Through this intertwining, a photograph of the damaged landscape peels back another layer of artifice found in the pristine or cathedral-like landscape representations: it demonstrates what Leo Marx (2000) calls the machine in the garden. Not only are the images a physical record of the machine, they also remind the viewer of the machine needed to create the image, i.e., the camera. The falsity and intrusion are always there (Foresta 1992).

Photographer David Maisel points out this falsity. Not only is he bringing the camera into the garden to document the damaged landscape, but the perspective he chooses demands an additional mechanical intrusion: he shoots aerial photographs from a small plane. The resultant photographs wrest a type of "jarring beauty . . . from the toxicity [that] shifts the way we see and think" (Thompson 2013:162). His works have focused on open pit mining (*The Mining Project/American Mine/Black Maps*), deforestation (*The Forest*), urban development (*Oblivion*), and the Great Salt Lake (*Terminal Mirage*).

The square photographs are large, measured in feet rather than inches. They hold an otherworldly beauty, often bearing more resemblance to the abstractions of Mark Rothko or Richard Diebenkorn than traditional landscape photography or even the New Topographics. But as Kazys Varnelis (2013) observes, like the New Topographics, in Maisel's work "photography is not accident, but rather is deliberately composed" (94), referencing each of these past touchstones. In one (*Terminal Mirage 18*, 2003), a patchwork of red-tinged white, kelly green, rusty orange, black, chartreuse, and beige create a bold pattern in the frame. In another (*The Mining Project, Clifton, Arizona 1*, 1989), an almost- black forest green splotch gradually splays toward a beige-tinted land mass; only along the edges of the mass does the darkness fade to a cloudy jade green. A third (*American Mine, Carlin, Nevada 1*, 2007) resembles a crystal-laden geode: a greenish-black, rough-edged, hollowed out, concave half sphere is surrounded by a flat-looking surface of brown, orange, and white.

In *The Lake Project*, Maisel turned his lens on Owens Lake, California; the Owens River feeding the lake was commissioned in the early 20th century to service Los Angeles' growing water needs. As a result, by 1928 Owens Lake all but dried up, and the area was plagued with dust storms and alkali pollution. The series demonstrates "the photographic manifestation of the annihilation of the Western self . . . Confronting such work, we face that self-reflexivity at the heart of art, and by extension, humanity" (Varnelis 2013:94). Three images, in particular, stand out. In *The Lake Project 15*, 2002, shades of blues and grey dominate, ranging from a steely slate grey color at the lower quadrant of the image to a pale azure at the top. Toward the center of the image, several circular splotches of a dark greyish-blue sit next to bright blue swirls that resemble not so much land as the whorls of oil paint on a mixing palette. *The Lake Project 20*, 2002, is awash in shades of blues and grey, ranging from a steely slate grey color in the upper left corner of the image to a bluish-white in the lower right. Dividing the image is a tendril of red, darker toward the bottom of the photograph, lighter toward the top. In *The Lake Project 1*, 2001, a broad gash of blood red divides the photograph in half. To the left of the frame are tones of gold and pale yellow; to the right a column of white and a slash of salmon, cracked and mottled like an aging canvas.

The viewer understands that these images are of a toxic land, a site so devastated that the state of California and the Federal Government required the city of Los Angeles to attempt to mitigate the impacts of the damages its water usage (or water theft, depending upon one's perspective) caused. Maisel shows the devastation upon the land: in each, the red is actually water so polluted that it appears it is infused with blood–the red is the color of the microorganisms that infested the lake when the waters were siphoned to Los Angeles. The blood-red water demonstrates "the contrast between the machine and the pastoral ideal" (Marx 2000:353): a literal manifestation of the machine in the garden.

As Varnelis notes, using language that echoes that found in the Sierra Club Religion, the images can be profoundly unsettling:

> We are led to wonder if we are looking at the future of the Earth, after its destruction by humans. Is the planet's fate to follow that of historical Eden itself, the now-desertified Tigris-Euphrates Valley? Is the Fall really an allegory for the destruction of nature? Pondering *The Lake Project*, we understand this, and as we do, we see that we are not only inseparable from nature but that our destruction of nature is inseparable from nature as well. Gazing at the toxic colors of these landscapes, we see ourselves. (2013:94)

But we also see an echo of our photographic past – of the beauty espoused in the work of Ansel Adams and Eliot Porter, and the oneness with nature found in Robert Adams and the New Topographics.

Consider *The Lake Project 15*: the aerial photograph looks down at land, but the textures harken back to those of the clouds in Adams' *Winter Storm*. In *The Lake Project 1*, it is the tones of the color spectrum that offer an echo, this time of Porter's *Pool in a Brook*. *The Lake Project 20*'s construction (un)intentionally references Adams' *Burning Oil Sludge*. The poisoned red of the river, like the poisoned plume of smoke, pulls the viewer from the left to the right of the frame. Maisel references the past, notions of Environmental Edens, and the unsettling beauty of the New Topographics within his work.

The artistic cross-referencing is similar to that of modern environmental writers who Young (2009) argues build off the work of Thoreau in their writings about the need for conservation and smart land stewardship in an increasingly industrialized world. While they attempt to "love nature in its own terms in a kind of post-mythical, post-Romantic, post-religious way," they can't help themselves (3). Nature beckons, "even in their criticisms of it, these authors reveal a debt to American transcendentalism" (Young, 2009, 4), or the idea that nature is somehow entwined with the holy. Likewise, Maisel can't help himself: even in his representations of environmental horrors, traces of the Environmental Eden still emerge.

However, it's within this tension that the framework for a new Environmental Eden can also be found. It lies in the aesthetic pleasure of the photographs. Because *The Lake Project* images *are* beautiful, Edenic, despite the horrors represented. The colors seduce and repel, attract and horrify. They offer a transformation of aesthetic to one which recognizes the tension between the sacred and profane, the artificiality of the act of photographing and the construct of nature, and the potential for redemption found within the images of a flawed Eden. Eden has been poisoned. But within the Fall also comes rebirth; in the words of Marx (2000:221), "There is nothing inorganic." Humans – and the rearrangement of the land caused by human activities – are as much a part of the Garden as the "natural" world. The photographs in *The Lake Project* embody this potential. Maisel's images demonstrate how aesthetics can be violently rearranged, in ways that offer a transformation of our notions of beauty – and our notion of Eden and our place within it.

Works Cited

Adams, A. and N. Newhall 1960. *This is the American earth*. San Francisco: Sierra Club.
Adams, R. (with forward by J. Szarkowski) 1974. *The new west: landscapes along the Colorado front range*. Boulder: The Colorado Associated University Press, 1974.
Adams, R. 2010. *The place we live, volume one*. New Haven, CT: Yale University Press.
Berger, A. 2006. Reclaiming the American west. New York: Princeton Architectural Press.
Burnett, C. 2011. "New topographics now: simulated landscape and degraded utopia," In G. Foster-Rice and J. Rohrbackh (eds) *Reframing the new topographics*. Chicago: Center for American Places at Columbia College Chicago, University of Chicago Press 139–158.
Carson, R. 1962. *Silent spring*. New York: Houghton Mifflin Company.
Cronon, W. (ed) 1999. "The trouble with wilderness; or, getting back to the wrong nature," in W. Cronon (ed) *Uncommon ground: rethinking the human place in nature*. New York: Norton 69–90.
Digrappa, C. 1980. *Landscape Theory*. New York: Lustrum Press.
Dunaway, F. 2005. *Natural visions: the power of images in American environmental reform*. Chicago: University of Chicago Press.
Dunaway, F. 2011. Beyond wilderness: Robert Adams, new topographics, and the aesthetics of ecological citizenship," In G. Foster-Rice and J. Rohrbackh (eds) *Reframing the new topographics*. Chicago: Center for American Places at Columbia College Chicago, University of Chicago Press 13–43.
Evernden, N. 1992. *The social creation of nature*. Baltimore, MD: Johns Hopkins University Press.
Foresta, M. 1992. "Between home and heaven: contemporary American landscape photography," in M. Foresta (ed) *Between home and heaven: contemporary American landscape photography*. Washington, D.C. and Albuquerque: National Museum of American Art, Smithsonian Institution and University of New Mexico Press 38–47.
Rohrbackh, J. 2011. "Introduction," In G. Foster-Rice and J. Rohrbackh (eds) *Reframing the new topographics*. Chicago: Center for American Places at Columbia College Chicago, University of Chicago Press xiii–xxv.
Jenkins, W. 1975. *New topographics: photographs of a man-altered landscape*. Carlisle, MA: Pentacle Press.
Limerick, P. 1999. "Paradise altered," In P. Pool (ed) *The altered landscape*. Reno: Nevada Museum of Art 1–21.
Marling, K. 1992. "Not there but here," in M. Foresta (ed) *Between home and heaven: contemporary American landscape photography*. Washington, D.C. and Albuquerque: National Museum of American Art, Smithsonian Institution and University of New Mexico Press 132–139.
Marx, L. 2000. *The machine in the garden: technology and the pastoral ideal in America*. New York: Oxford University Press.
Merchant, C. 1999. "Reinventing eden: Western culture as a recovery narrative," in W. Cronon (ed) *Uncommon ground: rethinking the human place in nature*. New York: Norton 132–159.
Muir, J. 1912. *The Yosemite*. A public domain book: Kindle e-book file.

National Drought Mitigation Center 2014. "Drought in the dust bowl years," in *The dust bowl*. Lincoln, NE: The National Drought Mitigation Center. Retrieved from http://drought.unl.edu/DroughtBasics/DustBowl.aspx.

National Park Service 2014. *John Muir in Yosemite National Park, California*. Washington, DC: U.S. Department of the Interior, 2014. Retrieved from http://www.nps.gov/yose/history culture/muir.htm.

Olson, S. 1961. The spiritual aspects of wilderness. In D. Brower (ed) *Wilderness: America's living heritage*. San Francisco: Sierra Club Books 16–25.

Porter, E. 1962. *Wildness is the preservation of the world*. (Introduction by J. W. Krutch) San Francisco: Sierra Club.

Porter, E. 1979. *Intimate landscapes*. New York: Metropolitan Museum of Art.

Salvesen, B. 2010. *New Topographics*. Gottingen: Steidl.

Smith, H. 1950. *Virgin land: the American west as symbol and myth*. Cambridge, MA: Harvard University Press.

Solnit, R. 2007. *Storming the gates of paradise: landscapes for politics*. Berkeley: University of California Press.

Szarkowski, J. 2001. *Ansel Adams at 100*. Boston: Little, Brown and Company.

Thompson, J. 2013. "Unrecoverable spin," in D. Maisel (ed) *Black maps: American landscape and the apocalyptic sublime*. Göttingen, Germany: Steidl 158–162.

Thoreau, H. 1993. *Three complete books: the Maine woods, Walden, Cape Cod*. New York: Gramercy Books.

Turner, F. 1994. "The invented landscape," in A. Baldwin, J. De Luce and C. Pletsch (eds) *Beyond preservation: restoring and inventing landscapes*. Minneapolis: University of Minnesota Press 35–66.

Varnelis, K. 2013. "A dread so close to zero," in D. Maisel (ed) *Black maps: American landscape and the apocalyptic sublime*. Göttingen, Germany: Steidl 90–94.

Williams, R. 1980. *Problems in materialism and culture*. London: Verso.

Young, M. 2009. *The spiritual journal of Henry David Thoreau*. Macon: Mercer University Press, 2009.

Devin Wilson
Anatta in Buddhism and Games: Emptiness and the Magic Circle

This chapter grows out of a project to develop and apply a Buddhist approach to game studies, comparing Buddhist philosophy with the formal qualities of games, as they've been described by key figures in this nascent field of media studies. In this paper, I mean to show how the Buddhist concept of *anatta* is exhibited in games by virtue of their "magic circle", a phenomenon identified by modern game scholars to be fundamental to all games.

Anatta, which basically means "not-self", is one of Buddhism's Three Marks of Existence. The Three Marks of Existence are a set of characteristics which Buddhists believe are necessarily identifiable in all phenomena. The other two Marks are *anicca* and *dukkha*, which – roughly translated, mean "impermanence" and "unsatisfactoriness" respectively. I'll refer back to these other Marks of Existence (in their rough English translations) a little bit at later points in this paper, but my focus today is on *anatta*, which – again – means "not-self".

The word *anatta* is sometimes translated from its original Pali to "no-self", but many Buddhist scholars think that describing it instead as "not-self" can avoid many of the pitfalls that someone new to the idea may encounter. Ultimately, the truth of *anatta* reflects the fact that there is no phenomenon that can *ultimately* be taken to be an absolute "I", "me", or "mine" . . . not even *nothingness*, which distinguishes Buddhism's teaching of *anatta* from nihilism, or what may emerge from a "no-self" translation.

The historical Buddha argued that, because of the other two Marks of Existence–impermanence and unsatisfactoriness, there is no phenomenon worth clinging to as "I", "me", or "mine". Being subject to impermanence, our bodies age, decay, contract diseases, and eventually die (all these things producing unsatisfactoriness), so taking the body as an absolute self would be foolish. Our consciousness is also subject to impermanence. Upon examination of one's faculties, a Buddhist will conclude that the self that we take for granted in everyday life is just a flowing aggregation of sense media.

With this inspection through the lens of *anatta*, a Buddhist argues that the things we commonly take for "I", "me", or "mine" don't fit what we would ascribe to a self worth holding as such. A "self" suggests a degree of stability that our bodies and consciousnesses simply do not afford us, and – if the things we commonly take for self were *worth* taking for self – we would not be so dissatisfied with them. This is how impermanence and unsatisfactoriness – respectively – inform *anatta*, or "not-self".

For a Western analogue, this insight (particularly regarding consciousness) is not completely unlike David Hume's "bundle theory" of identity (Fieser, 2011). Both Hume with his bundle theory and a Buddhist with the concept of *anatta* refuse the idea of a substantial, enduring, permanent, independent, immutable, essential identity of one's self or, ultimately, any other object, a position that is in opposition to much of Western philosophy's metaphysical assumptions.

In a Buddhist conception of identity, a thing is only what it is insofar as its relationships to other things. These things, in turn, are defined only by *their* relationships to other things. This makes an independent self utterly impossible, as there is no object that is not dependent on a complex web of other objects. This understanding of *anatta* was developed with tremendous sophistication by the Buddhist philosopher Nagarjuna and the Madhyamaka school of Buddhism. The principle of *anatta* applied to all things, not just our personal selves, culminates in the Buddhist concept of *suññatā*, or "emptiness".

"Emptiness" (or sometimes "voidness") can be a troublesome translation for *suññatā*, though. It can quickly be distorted into "nothingness", which is inaccurate and devolves these ideas into a type of nihilism. Early canonical Buddhist texts are quite clear that these views are not to be taken as nihilism (Thanissaro Bhikkhu 2010) which is why "no-self" is rarely the preferred translation of *anatta*. Unfortunately, early European translations of Buddhist texts made the mistake of associating Buddhism with nihilism when, in fact, we know now that the Buddha refused to state that there absolutely is a self or is not a self, cautious to not lend credibility to the extremes of eternalism or annihilationism (Thanissaro Bhikkhu 2012).

Rather than suññatā being read as "nothingness", it could be more useful to see it as meaning something like "no-thingness". Taken this way, we can avoid nihilism and reflect the meaning of *suññatā* in how it refutes that anything is the thing it is based on a stable, independent qualification for it being that thing. Hence, it has no absolute "thingness" or essence, rendering a "no-thingness" translation far more accurate than "nothingness" would be. Any given object is not nothing; it simply possesses no absolute, independent "thingness".

Buddhist scholar David Loy writes that translations of *suññatā* "must be supplemented with the notion of 'pregnant with possibilities'" (Loy 1992: 233), a move that is in line with the word's etymological roots. It is this possibility space that makes *suññatā* not a nihilistic concept, but one that allows any phenomenon the freedom to be dynamic. In the Heart Sutra, a key Mahayana Buddhist text, the Buddha teaches that "form is emptiness" and "emptiness is form".

The past few decades have seen the academic recognition of the many parallels between Buddhist philosophy and postmodern thought. David Loy has made such a comparison between *suññatā* and Jacques Derrida's deconstructionism. Loy argues that "*[suññatā]*, like *différence*, is permanently 'under erasure', deployed for tactical reasons but denied any semantic or conceptual stability" (Loy, 1992: 234). Indeed, Nagarjuna, arguably the main author on the topic of *suññatā*, insisted that "emptiness" is itself empty as well (Nagarjuna and Garfield 1995: 316).

The upshot of *anatta* and *suññatā* is what has come to be known as Buddhism's Doctrine of Two Truths. There is the ultimate truth of *suññatā*, as well as a conventional/relational truth. Jay L. Garfield says in his commentary on Nagarjuna's foundational text, the *Mulamadhyamakakarika*, that "[conventional truth] denotes a truth dependent on tacit agreement" (Nagarjuna and Garfield, 1995:29).

Perhaps the best-known formulation of this element of play is one that is often cited in game studies literature: that of Gregory Bateson's text "A Theory of Play and Fantasy". Bateson argues that there are metacommunicative cues that indicate whether or not some activity is play or not. These cues are understood by the participants and they inform how actions are to be read. They are, in fact, a "tacit agreement", to use Garfield's description of conventional truth. Bateson writes in reference to animal play, "The playful nip denotes the bite, but it does not denote what would be denoted by the bite" (Bateson 2006:317). The nip can then be understood to be a bite under the conventions of play. Beyond that, it is arguably not a bite. The bite is empty; it has no independent, absolute bite-ness.

The nipping animals know that they are not really biting, but they unquestionably operate under provisional assumptions to the contrary while they play. This happens in human forms of play, as well. The play-reality of a game is taken to be absolutely real at the time of play. Johan Huizinga argues that, during play, "an absolute and peculiar order reigns . . . [play] creates order, *is* order" (Huizinga 1949:10). Huizinga's formulation of the play space as meaning-making extends to both ordinary games and ritualistic "magic circles", a phrase that Katie Salen and Eric Zimmerman borrowed for their theories many decades later.

Salen and Zimmerman name the boundaries of any game its "magic circle". They write that, "Within the magic circle, special meanings accrue and cluster around objects and behaviors. In effect, a new reality is created . . ." (Salen and Zimmerman 2003). With a new reality comes a new truth, or set of truths. Salen and Zimmerman continue, "once the game begins, everything changes. The [game's] materials represent something quite specific . . . All at once, the relationships between the players have taken on special meanings". Recall the Two Truths doctrine of Buddhism: there is the ultimate truth (that the game's materials are empty) and then there is the conventional or relational truth (the meaningful relationships as understood by those in the magic circle).

We see this sentiment from other authors, as well. Greg Costikyan argues that meaning in games is endogenous. In his words, this means that, "A game's structure *creates its own meanings*" (Costikyan 2002:22). Costikyan gives an example:

"*Monopoly* money has no meaning in the real world . . . Yet when you're playing *Monopoly*, *Monopoly* money has value . . . *Monopoly* money has meaning endogenous to the game of *Monopoly* – meaning that is vitally important to its players". Once more, the analogue to the Two Truths doctrine is clear: *Monopoly* money is utterly empty outside of a game of *Monopoly*, yet its meaning is clear and unambiguous during the game (which defines a set of conventions and relationships).

We see a sentiment similar to Costikyan's argument from Roger Caillois. He writes, "the game has no other than an intrinsic meaning. That is why its rules are imperative and absolute, beyond discussion. There is no reason for their being as they are, rather than otherwise" (Caillois 2001:7). The rules and their associated fictions are plainly true (or true enough), but they are also without any substantial footing. As Caillois says, "There is no reason for their being as they are", which means that *suññatā* is also true. There is no rule-ness absolutely upholding the rules. For all of their compelling qualities, they are merely conventional.

Salen and Zimmerman write that "To play a game is in many ways an act of 'faith' that invests the game with its special meaning" (Salen and Zimmerman 2003). In everyday life, to call a chair a "chair" and not remain completely silent about whether it's an object at all is a similarly pragmatic act of faith, which corresponds to conventional truth while not being directly applicable to the ultimate truth of *suññatā*, or "emptiness". Similarly, to call a carved piece of wood a "knight" is a pragmatic act of faith that chess players take, which – again – corresponds to a conventional truth while not directly corresponding to the ultimate truth of *suññatā*.

If chess is neither available nor adopted as a reference for conventionality, a chess piece has none of the meanings that chess affords it. The object is ultimately empty. This emptiness allows a child to play with a knight piece as though it were a horse figurine, with the child imagining it galloping freely across the carpet. The child can make this "knight" (as chess players would name it) go diagonally, forward and backwards in straight lines, in circles, *et cetera*. Whatever rules the child has imagined for this toy inform the actions and meanings available to it.

During a chess match, however, this same piece of wood/marble/plastic may only move in its signature L-shape, or else there is a completely unacceptable violation of the game's "absolute and peculiar order", to quote Huizinga. Both sets of meanings are obviously true to their players, but this truth is not based on some independently real substance or essence.

Furthermore, this truth is not necessarily based on the physical form of an object. We know forms that are more or less recognizable as pawns, knights, rooks, et cetera, but a proper game of chess can still be played without objects that look like these types of figures. There is no shortage of themed chess sets, and–for a completely legitimate chess match–we could even use two differently-colored sets of office supplies, with paperclips being pawns, pushpins being rooks, and so on. As long as these things can be mapped to the rules of chess and manipulated reliably on an eight by eight grid, a true chess match – however untraditional – may be played. As Jesper Juul says, "No matter how the pieces are shaped, the rules, gameplay, and strategies remain identical" (Juul 2005). When we play a game, some part of us knows (or at least knew) that we agreed to a set of ultimately empty object-meanings. We reify the selfhood of our avatar, our game tokens, our actions, and the laws which govern any game, but it is also abundantly clear that these selves are just provisional, relational, and conventional. When examined closely, we can't identify any permanent, independent essence to associate with any of these objects. They are empty.

Buddhist monk Thich Nhat Hanh says in his commentary on the Heart Sutra, "'Emptiness' means empty of a separate self . . . To be empty does not mean non-existent . . . Thanks to emptiness, everything is possible" (Thich Nhat Hanh 1988:15). This is especially apparent in games: the emptiness of a game's objects and actions is what allows for meaning and dynamism to emerge. The emptiness of a World of Warcraft character allows us to project ourselves onto it and control it in a virtual world. The emptiness of a chess match allows us to be good sports about it after the fact, to shake hands in the spirit of equanimity.

At their best, games provide rich possibility spaces for us to cheerfully explore. Buddhist nun Pema Chödrön writes that *anatta* "manifests as inquisitiveness, as adaptability, as humor, as playfulness" (Chödrön 2010.:45) When we play games, we are often at our most inquisitive, our most adaptable, our most humorous, and–almost by definition–our most playful. Buddhist practice could be said to be taking these parts of the playful attitude and maintaining them in situations that don't mark themselves so explicitly as gamelike. As Buddhist scholar Stephen Batchelor writes, "Reality is intrinsically free because it is changing, uncertain, contingent, and empty. It is a dynamic play of relationships."

Game scholars and most ordinary game players alike know that a game's reality is not ultimate reality. In the case of game objects, the ultimate truths of *anatta* ("not-self") and *suññatā* ("emptiness") are far less difficult to accept and far more obvious than is the case with more mundane objects. As such, these interrelated Buddhist concepts of are expressed extraordinarily well in all games, making games an exceptional model for understanding core elements of Buddhist philosophy.

Works Cited

Bateson, G. 2006. "A Theory of Play and Fantasy," in K. Salen and E. Zimmerman (eds) *The Game Design Reader*. Cambridge, MA: MIT Press.
Caillois, R. 2001. *Man, Play and Games*. (Trans. Meyer Barash). Urbana and Chicago: University of Illinois Press.
Chödrön, Pema (2010). *Pema Chodron Datebook*. Portland: Amber Lotus.
Costikyan, G. 2002. "I Have No Words & I Must Design," in. F. Mäyrä (ed) *Proceedings of Computer Games and Digital Cultures Conference*." Tampere: Tampere University Press.
Fieser, J. 2011. "David Hume." *Internet Encyclopedia of Philosophy*. 30 June. <http://www.iep.utm.edu/hume/>. Accessed 30 June, 2011.
Huizinga, J. 1949. *Homo Ludens*. London: Routledge.
Juul, J. 2005. *Half-Real: Video Games between Real Rules and Fictional Worlds*. Cambridge, MA: MIT Press.
Loy, D. 1992. "The Deconstruction of Buddhism." *Derrida and Negative Theology*. Eds. Harold Coward and Toby Foshay. Albany: State University of New York Press.
Nagarjuna and J. Garfield 1995. *The Fundamental Wisdom of the Middle Way: Nagarjuna's Mulamadhyamakakarika*. Oxford: Oxford University Press.
Salen, K., and E. Zimmerman. 2003. *Rules of Play: Game Design Fundamentals*. Cambridge, MA: MIT Press.
Thanissaro Bhikkhu 2010. (translator) "Vajjiya Sutta: About Vajjiya (AN 10.94)." *Access to Insight*, 4 July. <http://www.accesstoinsight.org/tipitaka/an/an10/an10.094.than.html>.
Thanissaro Bhikkhu 2012. (translator) "Ananda Sutta: To Ananda (SN 44.10)." *Access to Insight*, 12 February. <http://www.accesstoinsight.org/tipitaka/sn/sn44/sn44.010.than.html>.
Thich Nhat Hanh 1988. *The Heart of Understanding*. Berkeley: Parallax Press.

Solmaz Mohammadzadeh Kive
The National Museum and Religious Identity: The "Islamic Period" at Iran's National Museum

Since its advent in the late eighteenth century, the museum has represented and reenacted national identity. While exhibiting objects of the past to validate the present of the nation and establish its place in the world, many museums extend their scope beyond the historical and geographical boundaries of their respective nations. Especially, universal survey museums, like the Louvre, the British Museum, the Hermitage, and the Metropolitan Museum of Art, collect and exhibit objects from around the globe. While national history is typically presented in chronological order, at survey museums the diversity of collections often results in a more complex arrangement. Over the past few decades, the classificatory structure of the museum and its corresponding art historical system have received much criticism. For instance, Robert Nelson (1997) lists the divisions within contemporary art history, including Egyptian, Ancient Near Eastern, and Classical Art, Early Christian, Byzantine and Medieval Art, Renaissance, Baroque, and Eighteenth-Century Europe, and Nineteenth-Century and Twentieth-Century Europe. Beyond these traditional classes, the list includes not only racial, national, or regional classes, like Art of the United States and Canada, Native American, Pre-Columbian and Latin American Art, Asian Art, African Art, and African Diaspora, but also media-based classes, such as Photography and Film, as well as religious designations like Islamic art. As Nelson reminds us, there is nothing natural in this mixture of geographical, chronological, racial, and material taxonomies. Yet to this date, it has dominated both art history discipline and survey museums. Among many categories of the museum, the so-called "Islamic art" is one of the few religious-based designations to emerge only in the late nineteenth century at the intersection of art history and the exhibitionary realm.[1] Early-twentieth-century "Islamic art" displays included (as they still do) artworks, architectural fragments, textiles and carpets, decorative art specimens, manuscripts, articles of faith, medieval scientific artifacts, objects of everyday use,

---

1 Systematic collection of what later became "Islamic art" started in the mid-nineteenth century in museums of decorative arts such as the Museum of Manufactures (today's V&A). Initially, these objects were not categorized as "Islamic art" but placed in material-based exhibitions alongside Western objects. By the end of the century, some exhibitions under a unifying religious rubric appeared, starting with the 1893 *Exposition d'Art Musulman* in Paris. In the early twentieth century, Islamic art departments were established in major European survey museums

etc. These diverse religious and secular objects often came from different countries. Subsuming a wide range of objects with various places of origin under a single category, "Islamic art" exhibitions of Western survey museums often reduced regional or national characteristics into variations on the same theme.

As the idea of the museum spread across the globe, Muslim countries, led by Egypt and Turkey, started to create national museums. Containing among other collections, Islamic art objects, these museums both resembled Western precedents and differed from them. Inasmuch as they adopted their institutional form from the West, they used the same principles of acquisition and arrangement and employed similar exhibition techniques. However, their collections were often arranged differently. Whereas Western museums tended to overlook regional differences and historical changes to display "Islamic art" as a single, monolithic category, the museums in Muslim countries limited the scope of their collections to the country's present or past political borders. More importantly, they often categorized Islam as just one period within a larger national history. Arguably, the nationalistic undertone of the museums within Muslim countries often promote a historical perception of an "Islamic period," differing from the ahistorical notion of "Islamic art" in Western survey museums. However, the desire to construct a national history has rarely resulted in a mere subordination of the faith under nationality. Time and again, the conception of Islam as a timeless essence is set against the modern notion of the nation-state.

This chapter discusses two alternative constructions of religious and national identities at Iran's National Museum. Originally conceived under a secular regime with a strong nationalistic agenda, the National Museum in Tehran initially framed Iran as the extension of the ancient Persian Empire (553–330 B.C.E.). Accordingly, its Islamic collection was rendered as merely one period within a long historical continuum. However, following the Islamic Revolution of 1979, the desire to represent an overarching religious identity supplanted that of a secular national history and the National Museum was refurbished to present Iranians primarily as Muslims. Although significantly expanded, the collection of the Islamic Museum was not radically different from the previous phase. However, the museum reformulated its narrative of Iranian identity simply employing a different set of curatorial and spatial strategies. This chapter discusses some of these strategies to explore the two major trends of framing Islamic art objects in the museum.

---

beginning with Berlin's Kunglichmuseum (1904) and the Louvre (1906). For a history of Islamic art exhibitions in the West, see Vernoit (2000).

Iran Bastan Museum

Iran Bastan Museum, also known as "the National Museum," was inaugurated in 1937 as the first major museum in the country. Opened to the public at the peak of an intense nation-building and modernization process, it was both an outcome of the state-sponsored nationalism and an instrument to promote nationalistic sentiments. Like many other national museums in the world,[2] Iran Bastan was envisioned as a place where the nation would imagine itself as a whole, rehearse the memory of the "ancient time," and celebrate the "civilizations of [its] ancestors," as one official account put it (*Bunyad va Gustarish-i Muzih dar Iran* 1977).

Under the secular Pahlavi Regime, the Persian Empire was celebrated as the foundational epoch of the nation, which allegedly assimilated all the earlier civilizations into one vast country. Aligned with other media, the National Museum was given the task of glorifying that mythicized origin and connecting it to the present time in a single unbroken and organic narrative. At the discursive level, the museum catalog and promotional reviews explicitly emphasized a narrative of cohesion and continuity, evoking potential disjunctions only to deny them. For instance, a typical review claimed that "Ashurbanipal, Alexander of Macedonia, Arabs, and Turks, with all their devil power of massacre, plunder, and devastation, have not been able to demolish the heritage of Iranian civilization" (Samadi, 1953). Insofar as this account attempted to downplay the magnitude of these gaps and forge an uninterrupted link between the present and the past, it reflected the fragility of the constructed continuum. The strongest point of fracture was provided by the advent of Islam, through which, as Vaziri (1993) reminds us, for almost a millennium, Iran was little more than a geographical abstraction, either subsumed under a Caliphate or divided into separate units.

While to many nationalists who saw the Persian Empire as the Golden Age of the nation, Islam had marked a Dark Age that not only fragmented the ancient country but also brought its progress to a halt, the early Pahlavi regime avoided explicit hostility towards Islam. At the beginning of his reign, Reza Shah declared "the greatness of Islam and the independence of Iran" as his dual goal (quoted in Cottam, 1979). Even later, while a secular nationalism dominated the official culture of the state and pervaded the élite class, as it did not diminish Islam's popularity

---

[2] As Duncan (1994) and many later scholars have argued, the survey museum of the Western imperial powers represents the contemporary nation as the logical conclusion of an evolving history that extends beyond the country's borders. Although significantly different in their scope and often devoid of an imperial vision, many other national museums share the desire to establish the nation as the culmination of a long history. For some examples, see Knell (2014).

among the public, the narrative of national identity could not be construed in opposition to religion. In addition to these sociopolitical considerations, the temporal logic of history required an inclusive narrative, as the exclusion of over a millennium would have rendered an unbridgeable gap between the present and the ancient past.

Here, a mixture of racial theories and anti-Arab sentiments both complicated the problem and yet offered a solution. The racial theories of the time justified nationalistic sentiment by endorsing a hierarchical perception by which Iranians were part of the "supreme" Indo-European race as opposed to an "inferior" Semitic Arab race. This racist perception allowed religious nationalists to dismiss the undesired changes after Islam as "Arab rituals," separate from the "true Islam." Against this external element of "Arab rituals," these historians employed an ahistorical notion of "Iranian spirit" as the eternal essence of the nation, which had presumably survived all changes, including the influences of the "Arab invasion." This separation of Islam (the religion) from the Arabs (the invaders) was an effective strategy to advocate a pre-Islamic identity and yet appeal to the mostly-religious population. In fact, a group of intellectuals in the 1920s and 1930s, including the circle publishing in *Iranshahr*, advocated for the close relationship between the "Iranian Spirit" and Islam and defined Shi'ism as an essentially Iranian religion (Aghaie & Marashi 2014).

That same idea of an underlying "Iranian spirit" also had strong support in the West. In *A Survey of Persian Art* (1938), Author Pope, an influential American amateur art historian, claimed that "[i]n its depths, the Iranian spirit was scarcely even stirred by these [Arab] aliens whom it could well dismiss as inferiors." In this context, art and architecture were regarded as the major venues through which the "Iranian spirit" survived and flourished. According to Iran Bastan's catalog (1948), "[f]rom the political point of view, there was an absolute break between the old and new times [. . .]. However, through a closer inspection, we realize that it is only on the surface that Iranian civilization has changed." Iranian art, it claimed, "simply continued its way, just influenced by contributions from outside." As the designer and first director of the museum, André Godard elaborated (1965), the change in "the appearance" was only "the dress in which Islam clothed the [pre-Islamic] monuments." In fact, the notion of Iranian spirit aligned the nation's identity with the pre-Islamic Iran without posing Islam as a threat to it. Paradoxically construed as both historical and ahistorical, "Iranian spirit" was defined by the pre-Islamic period and yet expanded to the entire history of the nation.

Iran Bastan Museum followed a similar ambivalent agenda of inclusion and exclusion of Islam. The collection was divided into three sections: Pre-Historical, Historical, and Islamic. Housed within the same building, the former two occupied the main floor, and the latter the upper level. Many recent critics have interpreted this segregation and the resulting secondary place of the Islamic section as a bias in favor of the pre-Islamic. The building's architectural style supports this claim since the main façade (Figure 1) was modeled after Taq-e Kasra – the seat of the Sassanid Empire, immediately preceding the advent of Islam.[3] On the other hand, the intention to forge a connection between the pre-and post-Islamic periods is evident in the incorporation of both collections within a single building, where different strategies connected the two parts. Despite the lack of objects to create a full collection, the second-floor exhibition began with objects immediately after Islam. A curator of the Islamic Period, Parvin Barzin, declared (1965), "as the temporary impacts of the Arab invasion diminished, Iranian art soon resumed and flourished." According to her, the inherent link between Iran's pre-and post-Islamic arts was proved by the museum's Islamic art collection.

Figure 1: The entrance façade of Iran Bastan Museum.

To unite its diverse collections, the museum not only created visual conformity by using identical showcases and employing similar exhibition techniques, but it also disguised the disparity among its diverse collections. On the first floor, all the pre-Islamic objects were exhibited in a uniform, single space (Figure 2), while even the chronological order was occasionally subordinated to visual consistency and unity. The succession of historical periods, which started on the first floor, continued into the Islamic section, loosely following a chronological order. However, unlike the first floor, here, the exhibition space was divided into twelve galleries (Figure 3), an

---

[3] The building façade was in a hybrid style combining Modernism with what was considered the Classic Iranian style. It was in part an incident of a rather common practice of dressing the museum building in a revivalist style appropriate to its content.

arrangement that did not entirely correspond to the divisions within the catalog. Some objects from a single period occupied more than one gallery; other collections shared the room with another period. Nevertheless, the successive identical units of space worked as a visual device to imply a rhythmic progression, a quality associated with historical continuity.

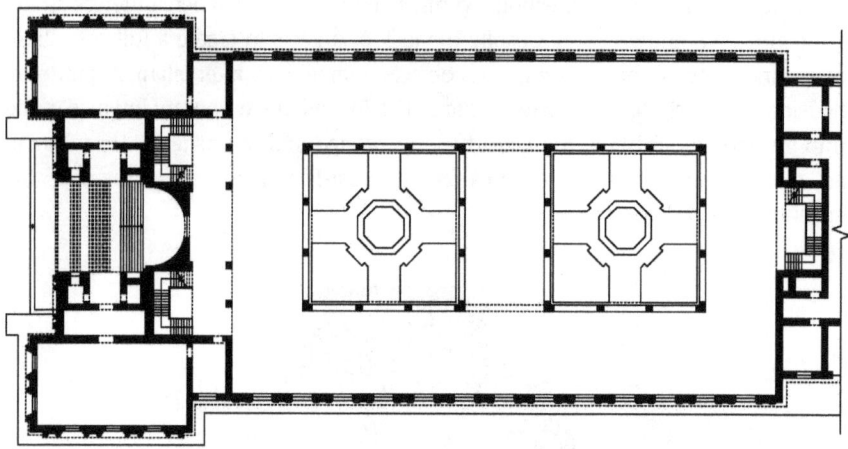

Figure 2: Iran Bastan Museum, first floor.
Created after the museum catalog.

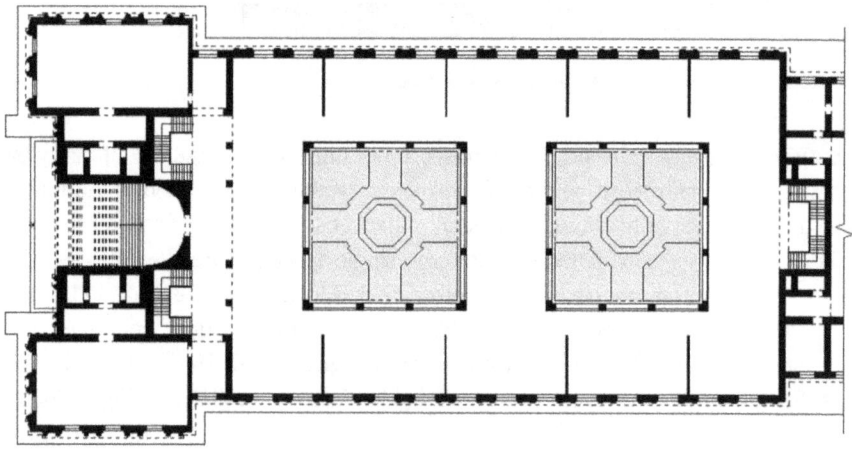

Figure 3: Iran Bastan Museum, second floor.
Created after the museum catalog.

The separation of the pre-and post-Islamic exhibitions was a necessary measure for connecting the two collections, as it disguised their significant visual difference resulting from the nature of their uneven object acquisition strategies. Whereas the prehistorical and historical sections included small sculptures, reliefs, ceramics, urns, tablets, jewelry, and some architectural fragments (Figure 4), the Islamic collection included porcelains, Koranic manuscripts, carpets, wall paintings, and architectural elements like prayer niches and stucco panels (Figure 5). Even though the catalog overtly emphasized their formal similarities, to the untrained eye, the apparent difference between the two collections would have indicated a sharp change. Denying an independent totality from the Islamic section, the divided space of the upper floor set this section as a continuation of the first floor's exhibition. In addition, two internal courtyards at the center of the museum connected the two floors, physically and metaphorically through a four-garden scheme – presumably, a fundamental characteristic of Iranian architecture throughout its history.

Figure 4: The Historic Section on the first floor of Iran Bastan Museum.
© The National Museum of Iran's Archive

Figure 5: The Islamic Section on the second floor of Iran Bastan Museum.
© The National Museum of Iran's Archive

The message of continuity and unity was once more repeated at the Treasure Hall at the end of the visiting path where, according to an official account (*Bunyad va Gustarish-i Muzih dar Iran* 1977), a selective collection of "masterpieces" brought together objects from all three sections, emphasizing the omnipresence of the Iranian spirit to all "the people who inhabited Iran" regardless of their race, region, and time. This overarching narrative subsumed the Islamic period under the larger umbrella of Iranian art and artifacts. As it framed Islam as a temporal event rather than an ahistorical truth, it is no surprise that Iran Bastan Museum's initial arrangement did not survive later ideological changes.

The Islamic Period Museum

Following the Islamic Revolution of 1979, the components of Iranian identity underwent a significant reconfiguration. While the new regime maintained the emphasis on national unity, the essence of this unity was now grounded in Islam, which was perceived as a timeless truth. History books were rewritten to marginalize the pre-Islamic Iran and render the nation as "an Islamic community." Nevertheless, nationalism was not completely dismissed, as, under the political necessities caused by events like the Iraqi invasion of 1980, the government chose to promote nationalistic sentiments. However, it was now subsumed under a religious identity. This shift in perception of the relationship between religion and nation is well-illustrated in a 1991 note from Iran's then-president, Akbar Hashemi Rafsanjani upon a visit to the Persepolis – the Persian Empire's most important surviving monument. Hashemi Rafsanjani's note started by praising "the incredible remains" that "provoke considerable national pride in every [Iranian] individual." He, then, underlined the significance of history and added: "By seeing these remains, our people will discover their own capabilities and the cultural background of their country." However, he was quick to frame these "incredible remains" within a contemporary Islamic identity. According to him, by discovering the past, Iranians "will trust that they will recover their historical role in the future to uphold upon this talent and foundation, the blazing torch of Islam to light the path of other nations" (translated in Abdi 2001). In this narrative, the Persian Empire was appropriated and glorified only as a testimony of the nation's talent and its potential for embracing Islam.

This narrative of a primarily Islamic community significantly impacted the National Museum's agenda. Soon after the Islamic Revolution, the museum's name changed from "Iran Bastan," meaning "Ancient Iran," to the "National Museum of Iran." In another gesture, the original inscription on the entrance wall, which was a poem in praise of the former regime, was replaced by Koranic verses.

However, more substantial changes were to come in less than two decades. As its former director, Mohammadreza Kargar put it (2006), the National Museum, which was "originally conceived according to the ideological vision of the 1930s, [. . . needed to be] dramatically and deeply reconverted." This dramatic change involved relocating the Islamic collection from the original building into an adjacent structure, which according to Kargar, would be refurbished "with due consideration for Islamic art and philosophy."

The building that housed the Islamic Period was designed under the previous regime as an ethnographic museum, yet the final installation was never undertaken. After the Revolution, this building was used for temporary exhibitions, lectures, and other cultural activities until 1991, when the renovation project started. Opened to the public in 1996, the new museum was named the "Islamic Period"; the former building gained back its original name – "Iran Bastan" – and the entire complex was called "the National Museum of Iran." While housing a similar body of objects (Figure 6), the new arrangement reconfigured the Islamic collection to "display Islamic art in an Islamic context, for a public familiar with the historical and cultural background of the objects," as its curator, Zohreh Roohfar, put it (1999). Different curatorial strategies aided this transformation of the museum's narrative.

Figure 6: The Islamic Period Museum.
© The National Museum of Iran's Archive

The new agenda was in part a reaction to the former nationalism. A few years before the Revolution, Ali Shariati – a highly influential theorist of Shiite ideology – had claimed that Iranians "[could] not find their roots in these civilizations. They were left unmoved by the heroes, geniuses, myths, and monuments of these ancient empires." To him, Iranians neither remembered anything from that past nor were interested in learning about it. He then concluded, "to return to our roots means not a rediscovery of pre-Islamic Iran, but a return to our Islamic, especially Shiite, roots" (quoted in Abdi, 2001). In fact, Shariati's passage highlights two interconnected strategies of redefining Iranian identity: denial of ancient Iran's relevance to the present nation and reformulation of the national identity as, first and foremost, a religious one. The renovation project reflected this same twofold strategy: first, ancient Iran was rendered remote and archaic; then, Islam was placed, both literally and metaphorically, at the center of the exhibition.

One strategy focused on shifting the perception of the Persian Empire from the embodiment of the "Iranian spirit" to a glorious, yet archaic, period. This approach is well presented by Mahdi Hodjat, one of the founders of the Iranian Cultural Heritage Organization (ICHO), after the Revolution. Hodjat criticized (1995) the naming of the original museum as "Iran Bastan," which "[s]urprisingly [. . .] was not called National Museum." Referring to the "many words in the Persian language, which mean 'past,' among which the word bästan means very old or ancient, particularly meaning prior to Islam," Hodjat concluded, "the first Iranian museum [. . .] was a constant reminder of our pre-Islamic heritage." Foreshadowing many other critics, he also condemned Iran Bastan Museum's revivalist façade, "which strongly recalled the memory of what had been overthrown by the Muslims" (Hodjat 1995). The renovation project would redefine "what had been overthrown" as a bygone past.

To counteract the former emphasis on the pre-Islamic as the nation's origin, the renovation project reformulated the relationship between the pre-and post-Islamic periods as a rupture. Established by splitting the two collections into separate buildings, this divide was then reinforced through the arrangement within the Islamic Period Museum. The Islamic collection appeared on two floors of the new building where the main level was given to the thematic exhibitions of objects like lighting devices, astronomical instruments, glassware, medical instruments, metal works, and textiles and the upper floor housed architectural fragments, archeological objects, artworks, and similar items. The historical collection on the second floor was arranged chronologically, starting with the first century of Islam, precisely where Iran Bastan Museum's exhibition ended. However, placed on the upper level, it would be visited after the thematic exhibition on the lower level. This interruption effectively challenged any perception of continuity and dispensed with the implication of a pre-Islamic origin. As it became independent from the "ancient time," the Islamic collection was defined as not only a whole in itself, but also the nation's "true beginning." The pre-Islamic objects remained on display to reclaim the country's historical status. The pre-Islamic period, however, was kept sufficiently remote so as not to suggest a potential rival to the religious identity.

While aligned with the ideological imperative of the Islamic Republic, the segregation of Islamic and pre-Islamic collections was based on a renovation plan developed under the former regime. As the then-director of the Iranian Center for Archaeological Research reported (Bagherzadeh, 1978), the collection had outgrown the original building, causing officials to consider transferring the Islamic section to the neighboring building. The original plan would both refurbish the new building, to be named "Iran and Islam," and expand the pre-Islamic collection of the original museum, taking advantage of the space that formerly housed the Islamic section. Although the post-Revolution renovation project used the previously designated building for the Islamic collection, it stopped short of renovating Iran Bastan's displays. As a result, while the Islamic Period enjoyed advanced exhibition technologies of the time, Iran Bastan looked outdated. Now framed within a binary opposition, even the contrast between the pre-Islamic revival style of Iran Bastan and the modern style of the Islamic Period (Figure 7) signaled the archaic nature of Iran Bastan's collection and, by extension, the pre-Islamic identity.

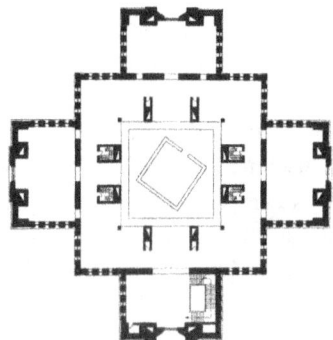

Figure 7: The Islamic Period Museum, floor plan. Reproduced after the museum catalog.

While the abovementioned features dismissed the relevance of the pre-Islamic period to the present time, another set of strategies established the central place of Islam in Iranian identity. The challenge that the original museum posed to the idea of an Islamic identity was not simply its lesser emphasis on the Islamic period compared to the pre-Islamic time, but the historical approach to Islam. When perceived as a historical period, Islam could have been subsumed under a different identity. The renovation project responded to this issue at different levels. The collection previously perceived as "the Islamic Period of Iranian history" (Iran Bastan Museum, 1948) was now called the "Islamic artifacts" (Roohfar, 1999), clearly deemphasizing the significance of both nationality and temporality. The preface to the new museum's catalog, *An Anthology from the Islamic Period Art*, framed the museum in the context of

Islam's impact on "culture and civilization of various lands." With no reference to Iran, it concluded:

> This is a museum where splendid relics of Islamic art and civilization are displayed for further meditation and acquaintance; a museum calling the Muslim community to contemplate anew its own abundant taste, art, knowledge, and science; a museum of unity and concord; the museum of friendship and affection among the Muslim community.
> (Kazerooni, 1996)

This emphasis on "Muslim community" was epitomized by a map placed at the beginning of the exhibition. As Ali Mozaffari notes (2012), in a clear nod to pan-Islamism, this map, centered on Mecca, depicted the entire Islamic world, while Iran's territory remained undistinguished. Following the same logic of literally centering Islam, the building's central hall housed a Koranic installation to serve as "the focal point of the museum," in the words of its curator (Roohfar, 1999). The galleries on both floors were arranged around this center in such a way that visitors would repeatedly return to this "focal point" (Figure 8). Throughout the exhibition, the juxtaposition of Koranic calligraphies with other objects and subtle use of Islamic motifs reiterated the message of Islam's centrality to national identity. While the thematic exhibitions of the entrance level illustrated various aspects of Muslim's "taste, art, knowledge, and science," the chronological arrangement of the upper level depicted the development of "Islamic art and civilization" throughout history. Using this well-known canon-making strategy, the museum introduced Islamic belief as the underpinning force behind the displayed arts and scientific artifacts, an essence unaffected by geographical, temporal, or political changes on the surface.

Figure 8: The Islamic Period Museum.

The Koranic Installation

While the placement of a Koranic exhibition at the center of the building was an instance of a common technique of highlighting a theme or an object, the installation itself featured some unique strategies. The Koranic exhibition took place on a square, raised platform surrounded by showcases of Koranic manuscripts and a few other objects, like a mihrab (prayer niche), a door, and a window with carved Koranic verses (Figure 9). Despite their historical and artistic values, the objects of the Koranic exhibition were treated primarily as religious items. The most dominant object of this installation was the mihrab with a prayer rug laid in front of it, a familiar arrangement that could be completed in visitors' minds with an imam leading the communal pray. According to its curator, Roohfar (1999), the installation would "notify visitors that they [were] entering an entirely spiritual area whose holy atmosphere [was] complemented by a stone prayer niche [. . .] a superb prayer rug and the heart-warming incantation of verses from the Holy Koran."

Figure 9: The Koranic installation in the Islamic Period Museum.
© The National Museum of Iran's Archive

Going beyond an objective representation and invoking religious sentiments, the Koranic Exhibition featured an unusual approach to the museum object. The mihrab was first and foremost an architectural device to indicate the direction of the Qibla. Its raised platform rotated so that it would align accurately with the Qibla. While the mihrab was placed on one end of the platform, the koranic showcases defined the entrance on the opposite side, which directed visitors to enter the area facing the mihrab, and thus the Qibla. Added to the rituals, to arrive at this point of entry, one had to perform a partial circumambulation of the Koranic installation. This reenactment of religious experience challenged the objective appearance of the museum. Unlike the common practice of the time, the installed mihrab was not simply an object on display. Rather, it continued to indicate the Qibla, maintaining its original function beyond the museum walls. Similarly, the Koranic manuscripts were treated not as historical texts, but as holy words infusing the space.

By maintaining their original everyday identities, objects of the Koranic installation refused to become museum objects, denying both art and ethnographic/archaeological designations – the two most common museum categories. In fact, a reference to everyday use was common in ethnographic displays, where objects were valued only as documents. A typical ethnography exhibition of the twentieth century placed objects in visual/material settings that would resemble their allegedly original contexts. The constructed contexts would work as the points of reference and thus allow the visitor, as the subject of knowledge, to maintain a distance from the objects of representation. Seeing the object as merely a representation of its original function, the visitor would engage with it not as a user (or performer), but only from the distance of an observer. By contrast, the Koranic installation clearly avoided any ethnographic context, denying the visitor a distance from the installation. Here, the mihrab and other objects were not representations on display, but real objects in full function, creating a holy atmosphere. Avoiding rich colors, dramatic lighting, overwhelming masses of objects, or other strategies of creating an atmospheric immersion, the installation maintained a neutral appearance. On the other hand, the Koranic installation was not an artwork either. While bearing some similarities to art in their treatment as singular objects, the artifacts in the Koranic installation differed from artworks in their refusal to represent specific stylistic features, provoke intellectual meditation, or stimulate aesthetic pleasure. Conceived as a "holy atmosphere" (Roohfar 1999), the Koranic installation invited visitors to immerse themselves within a religious experience.

Similarly, the placement of the Koranic installation called upon the visitor's lived experience. To align with the Qibla, the square platform broke with the building's geometry that defined the central hall housing the Koranic installation. The resulting pattern of a square rotated within another square resembled a well-known feature of many traditional buildings where the liturgical requirement of facing the Qibla was met by rotating prayer halls (and consequently the adjacent courtyards) against the building enclosure shaped by the urban fabric. While not limited to religious structures, this pattern of rotating squares easily recalled the Qibla orientation.[4] Although Roohfar did not explain the concept

---

[4] This pattern of squares rotated one inside the other has attracted generations of architects looking for a modern, abstract interpretation of the so-called "Islamic architecture." A recent application of this pattern can be found in the renowned architect, I. M. Pei's design for the Museum of Islamic Art in Doha.

behind this design, it is very likely that this was employed to evoke the memory of the traditional religious spaces, perhaps to intensify the "holy atmosphere" of the exhibition. Regardless of its curator's intention, the museum's educated, native visitors could easily recognize this historical reference and its religious symbolism.

Retreating from an objective approach to the exhibition and extending its narrative beyond the museum walls, the Koranic installation could successfully capture visitors with a religious predisposition. However, since it relied primarily upon religious sentiments, the installation stopped short of expressing patriotic ideas. Those who opposed the religious definition of Iranian national identity could not relate to the "holly atmosphere" of the Koranic installation. In addition, the described pattern of rotating squares, which was modeled after traditional architecture, failed to reproduce the spatial and visual experiences of its precedents. Despite its central position, this installation did not integrate with the larger space, making no connection to the enclosing building. Seating against the strong right-angle geometry of the building, the abrupt, sharp rotation of this small area was not modified by any architectural device. The resulting visual tension only intensified on the upper floor where the installation was not experienced from within but viewed only from above. This lack of integration could potentially symbolize the resistance and indifference of a foreign element, as Islam was perceived by the nationalists. This most dominant installation of the Islamic Period Museum did not play a unifying role and only added a symbolic dimension to the pre-and post-Islamic duality.

The Islamic Period Museum was closed for refurbishment from 2008 to 2016. The overgrown Iran Bastan Museum, too, was eventually rearranged. In 2006, a renovation design team lamented the national collection's division into two different buildings, which had paid "the regrettable price of imposing an artificial, though inevitable, separation" (La Torre, 2006). While eventually, this division remained in place, both museums altered their arrangements. The new Islamic Period follows a chronological order, starting on the second floor with the early post-Islamic period to continue the chronological sequence of Iran Bastan. While the central hall still maintains a Koranic installation, the former enclosed platform has been replaced by a smaller, bright surface, which holds one large Koranic manuscript (Figure 10). Unlike the former alignment towards Mecca, this central piece integrates into the building by following its geometry. The former barriers created by the manuscript showcases have moved to the corners, opening up the area and aligning with the main structure.

Figure 10: The Koranic installation in the Islamic Period Museum in 2017.

Conclusion

By 1937, when Iran Bastan Museum was inaugurated, the notion of "Islamic art" had already been established in the West. While many other Muslim countries followed the Western paradigm, Iran Bastan deliberately defied that dominant approach.[5] Explaining the Islamic section, its catalog emphasized (1948), "when the common expression, 'Islamic' art is applied to Iran, it does not mean that Iranian art was overthrown by Islam; but it refers to the art of the so-called 'Islamic period' of Iranian civilization." The overarching notions of "Iranian civilization" or "Iranian spirit" allowed the museum to counteract the pre-and post-Islamic divide imposed by the concepts of "Islamic art" and "Islamic civilization."

On the other hand, the pan-Islamic narrative of the 1979 Islamic Period Museum bears a striking similarity to the mainstream trend of exhibiting "Islamic art" in the West. Despite the apparent differences in their underlying ideologies, both practices are grounded in an essentialist understanding of "Islamic art" as the product of the "Muslim mind." Just a few years before Iran's Islamic Revolution, the 1976 festival of the "World of Islam" in London adopted the theme, "the Unity of Islam." In collaboration with other media, including public lectures, academic seminars, books, and film series, the "Arts of Islam" exhibition at Hayward Gallery was designed to "present the totality of Islamic culture and civilization" (Keeler, 1976). The festival director, Paul Keeler, listed the "essential aspects of the [Islamic] culture" as "the arts, the sciences, urban and nomadic life, poetry and music, and of course what

---

5 Although using strategies different from Iran Bastan's, the Ottoman Imperial Museum offered an earlier example of resistance against the Western discourse of periodization through. See Shaw (2000).

lies at the heart of the civilization, the Koran and its teachings." Since Islamic art was defined as essentially religious, its objects were reduced to representations of the "World of Islam." While chronological order was rejected as "undesirable and impractical," a thematic arrangement was employed to "define the essential character of Islamic art [. . .]; to identify the Islamic creative spirit" (Jones, 1976). There is no surprise that, as Lenssen points out (2008), this approach led to stereotyping displays.

Most contemporary "Islamic art" exhibitions of survey museums postulate a similar concept of the art produced by, and representative of, a uniform "Muslim world." Even though many of the objects of this art class do not serve any religious purpose, the idea of the "Muslim world" validates the term "Islamic art." A typical passage from the Metropolitan Museum of Art on "The Nature of Islamic Art" justifies the designation of "Islamic" for objects that were not "created specifically in the service of the Muslim faith" based on the assumption that Islam "is not only a religion but a way of life." Accordingly, it claims, "Islam fostered the development of a distinctive culture with its own unique artistic language that is reflected in art and architecture throughout the Muslim world" (Department of Islamic Art, 2001). For roughly a century, many exhibitions of Islamic art have used different strategies of segregation and isolation to demarcate this allegedly "unique artistic language." While the overall uniformity of galleries often reaffirms the unity of the "Islamic civilization," immersive gallery spaces and visual signs, like pointed arches, arabesque and geometric patterns, are occasionally employed to create an "Islamic ambiance." Needless to say, exhibition designs vary over time and place. However, Islamic art displays often support the idea of a common "unique artistic language."

Over the past four decades, the politics of exhibition and the ideological function of the museum have been critically examined. In response to these criticisms, many museum practices have been reconsidered. However, among many other structures, the survey museum's classificatory system (largely inherited from the second half of the nineteenth century) shows little change. Especially, in the case of "Islamic art," despite recent scholarly challenges, not only this category has been perpetuated in survey museums, but also a few museums have appeared that are solely dedicated to Islamic art of the entire "Muslim world." The current century has witnessed many renovation projects, new titles, updated interactive technologies, contextualized exhibitions, academically correct arrangements, and visually appealing designs. However, in terms of the unity of Islamic art, all but reinforce the category. Although equally charged with ideological agendas, alternatives such as the original Iran Bastan Museum could challenge the essentialist notion of "Islamic art," which has been made into a natural category through many media, perhaps most notably, the museum.

Works Cited

Abdi, K. 2001. "Nationalism, Politics, and the Development of Archaeology in Iran," *American Journal of Archaeology* 105: 51–76.
Aghaie, K. and A. Marashi 2014. *Rethinking Iranian Nationalism and Modernity*. Austin, Texas: University of Texas Press.
Bagherzadeh, F. 1978. "Introduction," In J. Pope, F. Koyama, and F. Bagherzadeh (eds). *Iran Bastan Museum*. Tokyo: Kodansha.
Barzin, P. 1965. Ba Muzeh-i Iran-i Bastan Ashna Shavid [An Introduction to Iran Bastan Museum]. *Honar va Mardom* 39,40: 39–49.
Bunyad va Gustarish-i Muzih dar Iran 1977. [Establishment and Development of the Museum in Iran]. Tehran: Vizarat-i Farhang va Hunar, Idarah-i Kull-i Muzihīha.
Cottam, R. 1979. *Nationalism in Iran*. Pittsburgh: University of Pittsburgh Press.
Department of Islamic Art 2001. "The Nature of Islamic Art," In *Heilbrunn Timeline of Art History*. New York: The Metropolitan Museum of Art. Retrieved from http://www.metmuseum.org/toah/hd/orna/hd_orna.htm; access 15/6/2016.
Duncan, C. 1884. "Art museums and the ritual of citizenship," In S. Pearce (ed.) *Interpreting Objects and Collections*. 279–286.
Godard, A. 1965. *The Art of Iran*. New York: Praeger.
Hodjat, M. 1965. *Cultural Heritage in Iran: Policies for an Islamic Country* (phd thesis). The King's Manor University of York.
Iran Bastan Museum 1948. *Guide de Musée Archéologique de Téhéran*. Tehran: Le Musée.
Jones, D. 1976. "Foreword and acknowledgements." In: G. Michell (ed.) *The arts of Islam: Hayward Gallery* 8 April-4 July.
Kargar, M. 2006. "History of the Museum," In E. Salimi (ed.) *The Renovation Program of Iran Bastan Museum*. Tehran: Gooya House of Culture & Art 7–11.
Kazerooni, S. 1996. "Preface," In Z. Roohfar (ed.) *An Anthology from the Islamic Period Art*. The Iranian National Museum.
Keeler, P. 1976. "Preface," In: D. Jones and G. Michell (eds.) *The Arts of Islam: Hayward Gallery* 8 April-4 July. London: Arts Council of Great Britain.
Knell, S. 2014, (ed.) *National Museums: New Studies from around the World*. Routledge, 2014.
La Torre, C. 2006. "The Godard Museum," In E. Salimi (ed.) *The Renovation Program of Iran Bastan Museum*. Tehran: Gooya House of Culture & Art 143–59.
Lenssen, A. 2008. "Muslims to Take Over Institute for Contemporary Art: The 1976 World of Islam Festival," in A. Lenssen, *Middle East Studies Association Bulletin* 42(1): 40–47.
Mozaffari, A. 2012. "Islamism and Iran's Islamic Period Museum," *International Journal of Heritage Studies* 19(3): 1–11.
Nelson, R. 1997. "The Map of Art History," *Art Bulletin* 79(1): 8–40.
Pope, A. 1938. "A survey of Persian Art, from Prehistoric Times to the Present (Vol. 1)," in Tehran; London; Tokyo: Persian Art; Oxford University Press; Teiji Shobo.
Roohfar, Z. 1999. Fourteen Centuries of Islamic Culture: the Iranian Islamic Period Museum. *Museum International* 51(3): 26–31.
Samadi, H. 1953. "Muzeh-i Iran-i Bastan," *Ravanshenasi va Olume Tarbiati* 26: 437–444.

Shaw, W. 2000. "Islamic Arts in the Ottoman Imperial Museum, 1889–1923," *Ars Orientalis* 30: 55–68.

Vaziri, M. 1993. *Iran as Imagined Nation: The Construction of National Identity*. New York, NY: Paragon House.

Vernoit, S. 2000. "Islamic Art and Architecture: An Overview of Scholarship and Collecting, c. 1850–c. 1950," In S. Vernoit (ed.), *Discovering Islamic Art: Scholars, Collectors and Collections, 1850–1950*. I.B.Tauris & Co Ltd Victoria, 1–61.

Magali do Nascimento Cunha
Media, Religion, and the Fabric of Culture and Communication in Contemporary Brazil

This is an exploratory study of the phenomena that represent the media and religion interface in contemporary Brazil, in search of clues to new research paths in this area. To reach this objective, cultural studies, particularly Latin American ones, are raised, with emphasis on the contribution of the Spanish-Hispanic scholar Jesús Martin-Barbero.

Martin-Barbero, in an initiative in the last two decades of the 20th century, had drawn attention to the need to shift the center of the understanding of the phenomenon of communication from media to mediations: "The axis of the debate must move from media to mediations, that is, to the connections between communication practices and social movements, to the different temporalities and the plurality of cultural matrices" (Martin-Barbero 1997:258, our translation).[1] It means to think communication from culture, ways of being and doing – the shift of the analysis of communication processes from the media to the point where it is produced, to the extent of interactions and social uses, the "cultural mediations of communication."

He points out three fundamental places of mediation: family daily life, social temporality and cultural competence. Also, taking culture as the key mediation of all social processes, he lists three relevant mediations to understand the communication-culture relationship: (1) sociability (everyday practices of social subjects to negotiate the power of any authority, and the negotiation of space with each other); (2) rituality (routines, repetition of practices, the way constructed by society to make reception and operability possible, without being a mere movement that generates no meaning); (3) technicity ("perceptual organizer" material that articulates discursive innovations in social practices, ie, represents the technique and the constitutive dimension of communication, which transforms social practices into new forms of socialization).

---

[1] NB, for each quotation from the original Portuguese I include here, I provide a free translation into English in the text but will include the original Portuguese version in a footnote: "O eixo do debate deve se deslocar dos meios para as mediações, isto é, para as articulações entre práticas de comunicação e movimentos sociais, para as diferentes temporalidades e para a pluralidade das matrizes culturais".

However, social transformations experienced in the transition from the 20th to the 21th century in the sociopolitical, economic and cultural fields, according to Martin-Barbero, called for changes in this understanding.

> (. . .) it was crucial in the 1990s to re-territorialize communication: as a movement that crosses culture and shifts culture. (. . .) Changes in the scope of technicality and identity are demanding imperiously to think on the communicational mediations of culture, a new map that takes into account the complexity of the constitutive relations of communication in culture, since the media started to be a key area of condensation and the intersection of cultural production and consumption, while they catalyze today some of the most intense networks of power".[2] (Martin-Barbero 2004:228–229, our translation)

It is not a matter of reemphasizing media over mediations and reversing the order of the first theory based on the move from media to mediations (the "cultural mediations of communication"). By proposing that the view be turned in the new century to "communicative mediations of culture," Martin-Barbero does not suggest a conflict between the two terms, instead there is harmony. Mediations continue to be thought of as something that brings meaning to social interactions, seeing media as what makes them possible, among other things. He thus aligns himself with a way of thinking about the communicational processes in evidence in contemporary times from the perspective of "mediatization," that is, the new interactional (in the social sphere) processes that "takes place quite differently in specific societies," and that develop according to the logic of the media (Braga 2006, our translation).[3]

Martin-Barbero explains:

> I reverse my first map and propose the communicative mediations of culture which are: "technicality"; the growing "institutionality" in the media as social institutions and not just devices, institutions of economic, political, cultural weight; "sociality" – how the social bond

---

[2] " . . . fez-se crucial nos anos 1990 re-territorializar a comunicação: então como movimento que atravessa e desloca a cultura. Pois o lugar da cultura na sociedade muda quando a mediação tecnológica da comunicação deixa de ser meramente instrumental para se converter em estrutural: a tecnologia remete hoje não à novidade de alguns aparelhos mas a novos modos de percepção e de linguagem, a novas sensibilidades e escritas, a mutação cultural que implica a associação do novo modo de produzir com um novo de comunicar que converte o conhecimento em uma força produtiva direta. E o lugar da cultura na sociedade muda também quando os processos de globalização e econômica e informacional revivam a questão das identidades culturais – étnicas, raciais, locais, regionais – até o ponto de convertê-las em dimensão protagonista de muitos dos mais ferozes e complexos conflitos bélicos dos últimos anos, ao mesmo tempo em que essas mesmas identidades, mais a de gênero e as de idade, estão reconfigurando a fundo a força e o sentido dos laços sociais e das possibilidades de convivência no nacional".
[3] "se realizam de modos bastante diversos, em sociedades específicas".

is changing for young people, how the relationships between parents and children, and between couples are changing. [. . .] and finally, the new "ritualities" that take place in relation to the new industrial formats made possible by "technicity." Somehow, in that moment I accept that it changes the place from which I was looking. [. . .] It was necessary to assume not the priority of the media, but that the communicative is becoming a protagonist in a much stronger way.[4] (Martin-Barbero, 2009: 151–152, our translation)

Therefore, Martin-Barbero's approach challenges researchers to focus their attention on the sociocultural phenomena in progress, considering a new way of being in the society in which the logic (or the "culture") of media crosses and permeates the social order and, together with technologies, mediates forms of being and perceiving the reality. Social practices, interactional processes and social organization itself are made with reference to the mode of existence of this mediatic culture, its logic and its operations, based on connection, on network, on fluidity, and on non-linearity.

It is based on this theoretical background that a picture of the changes and challenges in studies of media, religion and culture in Brazil in the years 2010 is outlined here. I aim to make a correlation between the mediations of "the religious" in media communication and the media-communicational mediations of religion (or – following the logic above – the processes of mediatization of religion in Brazil, a more intense challenge).

My inquiry here will emphasize Christianity, which is the majority religion in the country. It represents 86.8% of the population – almost nine out of 10 Brazilians claim to be Christians, according to the 2010 Census. Within this religious group there are essentially two segments: Roman Catholics at 64.6%, and the various Protestants groups at 22.2% (popularly known as Evangelicals – a term applied to all all non-Catholic Christians in the country). These Evangelicals (Protestants) are found in a myriad of churches, in turn synthetically grouped as the historical ones (Protestants who came to the country in the 19th century through immigration and missionary work from the United States), Pentecostals (from the early 20th century, known colloquially as divine healing churches) and

---

4 Inverto meu primeiro mapa e proponho as mediações comunicativas da cultura que são: a "tecnicidade"; a "institucionalidade" crescente nos meios como instituições sociais e não apenas aparatos, instituições de peso econômico, político, cultural; "a socialidade" – como o laço social está se transformando para os jovens, como as relações entre pais e filhos, e entre casais estão mudando. [. . .] E, finalmente, as novas "ritualidades" que acontecem em relação aos novos formatos industriais possibilitados pela "tecnicidade". De alguma maneira, nesse momento aceito que muda o lugar a partir do qual estava olhando. [. . .] Era preciso assumir não a prioridade dos meios, mas sim que o comunicativo está se transformando em protagonista de uma maneira muito mais forte.

neo-Pentecostals (new movements of the late 20th century, characterized by their preaching of the pursuit of material prosperity and their exorcism practices).

However, there is a much broader religious plurality that is found in Brazil, culturally-rooted in Aboriginal, Portuguese and African roots. It is commonplace in religious studies in Brazil to refer to a "Brazilian religious matrix," or a generic or basic Brazilian religiosity formed by elements of these three cultural roots. This "matrix" then permeates Christianity and all other relevant religions in the country, through such expressions as Kardecist Spiritualism and Umbada. Immigration and cultural exchange processes also made brought Brazilians into contact with other religious forms such as Islam and Buddhism (these other faiths comprising a total of 5%). This portrait of Brazil's religious geography would not be complete without highlighting the 8% of Brazilians who claim to have no religion (a growing number according to the Census – and something Brazil shares with the major countries of the developed world).

This religious matrix, as a significant cultural reality, is present in everyday life and – in what matters in this chapter – in religious expressions in the media. It materializes as an element of religious mediation in media communication, as it will be seen, and is transformed by media-communicational mediations in the religious sphere.

From this perspective in research on communication and religion, we strive to overcome the functionalist scholarship that predominated from the 70s to 90s. This approach is still privileged in some studies, for instance those that analyze the "use" of the media by churches. These studies have a role in understanding the processes of religious communication but have been theoretically exhausted and do not account for the meaning, value and place of communication in the practice of religious groups, nor the changes in the nature of religious communication that the media produced in the churches.

The methodology for this study consists of a review of research already undertaken by the author of this work, in the light of theories of social mediatization, from the *Barberian* perspective of mediations. It also includes the identification of emerging themes through continual monitoring of religious media programming and religious themes in major media through projects of the Research Group on Communication and Religion of the Brazilian Society on Interdisciplinary Studies on Communication (INTERCOM).

Identifying the Mediations of the "Religious" in Religious Communication

In the context of Brazilian Christianity, the predominant forms of social communication in churches has been mainly print literature, radio and then TV. Cinema has been very little valued as a vehicle of religious communication.

The strength of the written word in Christian tradition, as in religious book publishing, is seen in the high level of production that still occurs in the country. The study "Portrait of the Book in Brazil" (Pro-Book Institute/Ibope Inteligência, 2011) found that 57% of respondents regularly read a religious book. The Brazilian Book Chamber records that the revenue from sales of religious works exceeds $ 500 million per year. According to a last survey by the Brazilian Economic Research Institute Foundation (Fipe), 72.4 million copies were sold in 2013, and at least 30% of those titles refer to religion.

At the same time, Brazil's strong oral culture, as well as the ease of acquiring broadcasting concessions from the government or buying spaces in the schedule has made radio a privileged vehicle for religious communication. According to the Brazilian Association of Radio and TV Broadcasters (Abert), there are around 300 religious radio stations in Brazil, registered as such, representing 8% of radio stations in the country. This number, in fact, falls well short of reality as radio leasing is common, especially among evangelical churches.

Initially, the emphasis in radio was in the transmission of services and masses and in programs made of meditations and religious preaching and prayers, including exorcisms, predominantly among Pentecostals. Among Catholics, meditations and prayers had ample space in radio programs but they also provided social services and education. In the first decade of the 2000s, with the growth of the religious phonographic industry, musical programming grew to prominence and entertainment programs appeared in the form of talk shows, interviews, debates and games.

Television, with less intense presence due to its high costs of acquisition, costs of airtime and production, followed the same trajectory of radio and, in the 2000s, also saw an increase in entertainment programs with presentations of religious singers, talk shows, round tables, games and dramatizations in the format of the *telenovelas*.

The 1990s saw the consolidation of church-linked small media empires, especially among evangelical – and then Pentecostal – groups. One of them, the Universal Church of the Kingdom of God (IURD), is now prominent as one of the "11 families" who own all media in Brazil. IURD owns several media, with varied content (not only religious) and occupies the second place only to the colossus

Rede Globo in Brazil in TV audience through the Rede Record Network (TV and Radio). Following IURD in prominence but still significant are the International Church of the Grace of God, the Reborn in Christ Church, and the Roman Catholic Church. There are others seeking to share this market. There is a political lobby of growing influence among religious groups since broadcasting concessions are public and there is competition to win federal government approvals. It is largely because of this interest in broadcasting, and the necessity of influencing government that the Evangelical Caucus in the National Parliament was initially formed and now has growing influence (Figueiredo Filho, 2005). In the Bolsonaro era, this caucus's influence has spread well beyond interests in broadcasting approvals alone.

Another significant area emerging in the 2000s is the increasing presence of religion on the web. This is seen through the numerous institutional websites and a multitude of internet pages and social media accounts, from different groups. These of course give visibility to institutions that sponsor them, but in the web alternative, independent, and dissident voices can also be found (Cunha 2014).

Besides all these practices that fit under the rubric of spreading of the Christian faith through traditional religious preaching, there is emerging the religious presence in the media as a strategy of visibility, image, or brand. Institutional advertising and the creation of a religious market through the offer/sale of products are increasing in presence and importance. This is also a market, where competition in the religious field rewards those who can grow larger audiences, networks, and circulations.

Hence, there is a weakening of what had been the presumed purpose of religious communication: the preaching of religious conversion and of the appeal to repentance of sins. This had been typical of the 70–80s under the influence of the US televangelists (Assmann 1986) in which "the religious" (what is relative or proper to religion) mediated the salvation of the soul and the recruitment of members to the churches.

Today, religious media groups are more interested in audience capture than they are in increasing the number of faithful/adherents. This market logic favors the preaching of personal success with Prosperity Theology, which emphasizes the realization of God's blessings in the life of the believer through the accumulation of material wealth (Cunha 2007). In this sense, the "religious" mediates the processes of inclusion in the socioeconomic system of neo-liberal globalization and its markets. The narratives (testimonies) of success of small businessmen who were formerly unemployed presented in radio and TV programming of the IURD and the Reborn in Christ Church promote these economic ideas.

Identifying the Mediations of the "Religious" in "Non-Religious" Communication

There is also mediation of "the religious" present in the media communication processes of "non-religious" media: in journalism, literature, music, entertainment, advertising. This is a field of research still under development, as it frees itself from the functionalist framework to think about how religion manifests itself in supposedly non-religious contexts. This involves understanding such things as imaginary significations and sociocultural representations both in the processes of production and in the processes of reception.

In the production of news, literature, songs, *telenovelas*, films and advertising campaigns, there remains the hegemony of Catholic religiosity (Cunha 2016). For example, at Christian feasts such as Christmas and Easter, news coverage privileges the Roman Catholic approach. When it comes to specific feasts of the Catholic calendar, a remarkable amount of space is still given in journalism. The same is true in advertising: if there is to be a religious framing, then it is the Roman Catholic faith expressed including in the images of leaders such as priests, nuns and the Pope, or in the authority of the canonical saints that predominates (Folis 2012). In literature, in popular songs and films, it is possible to see expressions of Candomble and Umbanda and of the very popular Kardecist Spiritism.

The religiosity that is, in fact, marginalized in these sectors of communication is that of the evangelicals. Media content producers seem to see this religious expression suspiciously or even pejoratively. This is reflected in journalism and in comedy shows, where evangelicals are connected prominently to scandals or are treated as objects of curiosity. Evangelicals have been largely absent from films, popular music, and advertising.

This is changing. There is a growing representation of evangelicals in TV entertainment productions such as music programming, interviews, debates and as soap opera characters. It is a reflection of the popularity of the evangelical growth (numerically and geographically) over the past two decades expressed not only in the number of supporters but in the presence in political parties, public acts, the music market and the commodity marketplace. It is a new movement that must be monitored which introduces a standard of the evangelical faith that forms good people, encourages charity but is conservative in many sociocultural aspects, especially concerning sexuality (Cunha 2015).

The predominance of Catholicism in the non-religious media is not only related to the issue of numerical superiority but is the result of the fact that Catholicism, within itself, has lived with syncretisms and has considered as Catholic all the people reached by its preaching and its sacraments. In this sense, Catholicism became a cultural form in Brazil (Seidl 2014).

In these communicational expressions, there are also the traits of a popular mystical religion, such as individualism (as the devotion to the saints), utilitarianism (doing what needs to be done to deserve God's favor) and egalitarianism (the idea of that all have sinned and are equal before God, given the unequal world that poor people faced), characteristics of the Brazilian religious matrix (braga Filho 2003).

A significant illustration of this aspect was the Catholic World Youth Day and Pope Francis' visit to Brazil in 2013. It was remarkable that the coverage of the event by the country's largest media group, Rede Globo, was classified by analysts as "evangelism" (Cunha 2013). The station that ran the pool of networks responsible for capturing and distributing images of live flash events throughout the program had full-length speeches by Pope Francis. Anchors left their newscasts to perform in sites visited by the Pope, while the broadcaster's drama director, famous actors and actresses played a prominent role in creating and performing the *Via Sacra* staging on the sands of Copacabana Beach. All of this was fueled by strongly positive speeches from every moment shown, with touches of explicit emotionalism by journalists.

Journalist Paulo Victor Melo observed, "News broadcasts have practically become extensions of the Vatican press office . . . a series of information devoid of critical sense that leaves journalism and the public interest and opens up an intimate relationship between media and religion in Brazil. " (Cunha 2013).

Identifying the Communicational Mediations of Religion

Four important factors then emerge to explain the contemporary process of mediatization of religions – particularly of Christianity – in Brazil: (1) The emergence of media churches; (2) Access to the sacred by actors in the media marketplace; (3) The potentiality of spectacular religion; and (4) The consolidation of digital religion. I'll review each of these.

It is worth reiterating that the term "mediatization" is used here as a synonym for what Martín-Barbero calls "communicational mediations of culture." José Luiz Braga (2006) takes this understanding to argue that mediatization occurs under two conditions: one that consists of specific social processes triggered by the logic of the media; another that represents the mediatization process of society itself. According to Braga, mediatization is an ongoing process of interaction. It is not established but is being implemented, and is becoming a reference point in society.

The Emergence of Media Churches

One of the elements that signal the mediatization of Christianity in Brazil is the emergence of churches that have media in their very constitution, central project and as the essence of their practices. Religion has always been mediated, but increasingly depends to a greater or lesser extent on the media. This is not a purely a technical issue, on the contrary,

> From the moment the religious field restructures its practice and its discourse, different meanings are generated. Therefore, we are facing a new religion that carries symbolic and marks of the logic of the media and its process of meaning production.
> (Borelli 2010:17, our translation[5])

In this sense, media churches are characterized by locating media as their primary communication channel and as their own religious project. In the very functioning of these churches, it is possible to identify elements of this characteristic. For example, the worship spaces, the actual church premises, do not exist without media equipment including sophisticated sound systems, text and image projection devices, big screens, and integrated systems for the transmission of websites, radios, TV channels. Time and space gain different meanings than in ordinary religious groups.

The mediatization of these churches also involves the control of multiple media (print publications, conventional and web radio and TV channels, phonographic and video productions, web portals and social media). This has resulted from, and made necessary, the direct political activism I mentioned earlier, engaged in in order to protect these interests and initiatives.

The dynamics of operation under media logics is significant beyond the mere use of technological devices. It involves and engenders discourses and religious action based on fluidity, immediacy, image privilege, spectacularization of practices, fragmentation, emptying of spontaneity, distancing/virtuality, and an address to audiences (Kellner 2001). This describes well the neo-pentecostal churches: Universal Church of the Kingdom of God, International Church

---

5 A partir do momento em que o campo religioso reestrutura a sua prática e o seu discurso são gerados distintos sentidos. Portanto, estamos diante de uma nova religião que carrega simbólicas e marcas das lógicas da mídia e de seu processo de produção de sentidos.

of the Grace of God, Reborn in Christ Church, The Heal Our Earth Church, and the World Power of God Church, all important players in Brazilian mediatized religion.

Accessing the Sacred through the Media Marketplace

In the logic of neo-liberal market culture, media and marketing communication play a major role in the interactions that produce marketplace citizens – those who participate in the market through the consumption of goods and services. Christians then become a specific market segment with products and services specifically designed to meet their religious needs, whether they are for the consumption of material goods or for leisure and entertainment. In the logic of mediatized religion, consumption is not only an action that responds to the logic of the market, but it also constitutes an element that produces religious values and meanings (Campos 1997).

The Religious market was already strong through the print media and radio until the 1990s, but its expansion happened mainly due to the consumption of music. This niche drove the success of "religious radio", especially on the FM band, in the 1980s, with significant audiences in metropolitan areas and the explosion of the Christian music industry. The considerable increase in the number of products (goods and services) marketed to Christians built on this base. It is now possible to find a variety of products available, such as clothing, cosmetics, food, and travel, with brands comprised of religious slogans, Bible verses or simply the name of Jesus. Catholic and evangelical fairs (major trade events) that exhibit products specifically aimed at these consumers are becoming increasingly successful.

At the same time, major (secular) media adopt these approaches and produce programs, or portions of them, to compete for Christian audiences. They have offered space for contemporary Christian music ("gospel") and its artists, sponsorship of music festivals and mega street events, and broadcasting of religiously themed entertainment programs (by creating religious characters for soap operas and even editions that have 100% of religion in their thematic).

Rede Record Network (owned by the Universal Church of Kindgom of God or IURD), whose primary programming identity is not religious, built a strategy of conquering the religious public during this same period, with focus on audience. The strategy involved the transmission of religiously-themed *telenovela* soap productions (based onBiblical narratives) and has yielded satisfactory results in the competition for audience ratings.

The emphasis on consumption and the new treatment for Christians as a market segment give the evangelical media a new character and a new role. The classic aspects of religious programming (prayer sessions, studies, debates and sermons) are no longer the way to recruit. Instead there is now an emphasis on soft themes (Christian fashion, overcoming of depression, attention to children, happiness in marriage) aimed at gathering media audiences and markets for the products offered (Cunha 2007). Advertising appeals often tie in the purchase of the products and services offered to the possibility of getting closer to God or receiving a blessing.

By these means, religious media programs and literature become mediators of a consumer community where ecclesiastical attachment is no longer what matters. Instead it is a religious experience and the consumption of goods and culture that make it possible to approach God and get "healthy" entertainment. This is the Christian appeal of mediatized religion.

Jesus Martin-Barbero anticipated such a new context when reflected on the theme of the "electronic church":

> [. . .] in my view electronic churches are churches that have been converted especially to radio and TV, making TV and radio a fundamental mediation of religious experience. That is, the medium is not simply a help in amplifying the voice but it is an important element, a fundamental element of religious contact, religious celebration, religious experience.
>
> As I see it, the electronic church is returning magic to religions that had become intellectual, that had cooled, that had become disenchanted. [. . .] It is not simply a matter of expanding worship, it is about adding, continuing, intensifying one's religious experience.
> (Martin-Barbero 1995, 75–76, our translation)

The practices of local religious congregations are also transformed by these marketplace and media-consumption logics. They have begun to assimilate the principle that they also have products to offer along with their religious services and can compete for believers which they increasingly see as "audience." Along these lines, countless offerings of specialist professional marketing consultancies in the religious field are available to churches to contribute to the creation of strategies to achieve these results. One sign of the strength of these cultural currents has been the adoption of marketing language in church discourses: they create "strategic planning" with targets for membership recruitment and property acquisition; identify themselves (as companies do) through "a mission," "a vision" and "values".

The Realization of Spectacular Religion

Consumption and entertainment are components of media culture. In the contemporary Brazilian religious landscape, consumption and entertainment find in religious media an important mediation. Through religious FM radio stations Christians have access to religious music productions, participate in the programming by requesting their favorite songs and get free gifts that bind them to the religious scene (tickets to live performances; artists' promotional items; personal contacts with artists). This is how the repertoire sung in musical moments of worship accompanies the religious music "hit parades": new songs are permanently inserted, and exhaustively repeated, while others are soon discarded or sporadically sung as flashbacks.

Listeners also receive non-musical content – interviews, debates and messages ¬– that work with language that privileges the repertoire used in churches, so that the programming has no identity with this or that specific group and seeks to work with common themes across broad evangelical circles. They touch issues highlighted in the evangelical setting, such as female pastoral practice, ecumenism, political participation, homosexuality and church-state relations. Many of these issues are requested directly by listeners or pointed through church surveys among the audience.

This non-musical programming also works to reinforce the content that feeds the prosperity-centered discourse of neo-pentecostal churches: the symbolic war against evil spirits, and the intimate perspective of cultivating faith. Respondents and debaters are generally recognized leaders in the religious or church-related setting, as well as personalities from the regional or national sociopolitical-economic-cultural setting (Patriota 2008). Advertising space includes sponsor commercials and the dissemination of church and group programming. Consumption and entertainment are essential components, as in any media. Therefore, the religious field seeks to follow the format of the other radio fields, adapting to the musical repertoire keen to the popular taste, ensuring the continuing support of audiences and sponsors.

As it is the case with secular radio, religious radio is primed to launch new fashions and trends and put the public "on top" of what is most current in the religious scene. At the same time, they present themselves as vehicles in the service of God, as instruments of a divine mission, which promotes acceptance among church adherents (Fajardo 2011).

Radio has a strong reach rooted in oral culture, as I noted above, but the power of image gives programs on TV, albeit with lower audience numbers, strengths of their own. This is further intensified by the internet. The religious has adopted the practices of the recording industry and has invested heavily in the production and distribution of gospel music videos that support the promotion developed through radio. The visualization of the music (the way singers perform, supporting choreography, and other production values) serves as an inspiration and model for musical groups that perform live during worship in the different churches as well. Worship becomes, then, a spectacular performance.

Other programs include great variety. Examples include debates on topics such as drug use, professionalization of religious musicians, political participation, interviews with gospel singers, promotion of religious spectacle and Biblical messages and reflection. These are presented as informative programming along side such entertainment as games shows, mimicking the format of secular programs.

As with radio, TV shows do not privilege a particular denomination as their target audience. They seek to develop a language that downplays identification with a specific group and aims at the broad evangelical segment, as I've said (Cunha 2007). Examples are games that involve groups of different denominations in competition with one another, as well as debates where people from various churches are invited to present their ideas.

In addition, these television programs have in common their adoption of formats and production values intended to insert these religious groups into the broader media logic. Plots, the presentation of the talent and the settings, costumes and language all demonstrate that this mediatized religion assimilates what is mediatic and modern. They want to make certain that they have moved past the classic premise that "religious believers are funny outdated faces" who live in the past and who look in media as though they do. The aim seems to be to make it obvious what has been true of religious music content for some thime: having faith does not mean distancing oneself from fashion, modern technology and contemporary entertainment. This new cultural form has announced the disappearance of the conservative evangelical cliché isolated on the outskirts of big cities. Instead it visualizes the image of modern people wearing fashionable clothes, shopping, having fun and consuming music (Burity 2008).

The Consolidation of Digital Religion

The popularization of the internet has emerged in this context. The dimension of participation and the transformation of receivers into transmitter through practices of interaction made possible the radical change of the church-media relationship through the digital media. It is a challenge to be answered to list all Christian groups websites located by search engines: they are thousands and vary from the institutional in all Christian denominations, to the handmade assembled by groups of churches. The sector also includes the most sophisticated and most accessed belonging to music groups or media groups (Sbardelotto 2012).

In social media, a plethora of articulations and spaces presents itself. Churches and Christian groups have realized that these media are able not only to present religious preaching and give them visibility, but can also articulate, promote sociality and build community. This has given a new character to the church's relationship with the media. Moreover, with the convergence of media (TV, radio, computer, phone on a mobile device, smartphones), a program is no longer only designed to broadcast but can add the dimension of stimulated interaction. More space has been opened for meetings, the exchange of ideas, debates, information, dissemination. The dimension of communication as interaction is enhanced. The sociality promoted by digital media facilitates Christian exchange and evangelization.

On the other hand, churches now no longer have the control of the sacred and of doctrine they once had (Hoover 2014). Openness to participation and contribution by anyone who professes a faith – whether or not they are formally linked to a church – to freely express ideas, reflections and opinions has taken control of the content out of the hands of religious leaders. It is enough to have a blog or a free account on the most popular social media, and space for free expression is guaranteed.

Therefore, theological doctrines and traditions have come to be relativized along with the authority of the classical leaders: the ecclesiastical authorities. Confessional statements are debated, not simply accepted, and criticisms are made explicit. This is a strong feature of digital media spaces: people feel liberated and encouraged to express what they would never express in a face-to-face encounter. This process also gives birth to new religious authorities that emerge from the media – celebrities (media pastors and priests, preachers, gospel singers), bloggers – who become a reference for the way of thinking, acting and seeing the world of many Christians.

The loss of control of religious discourses and symbols by ecclesiastical authorities has also opened the door for playful experiences in digital media that express classic elements of faith in entertainment and humorous forms. This is well received by some audiences while it is a nuisance for others, which has introduced new controversies in digital networks.

Another element that stands out in this process of "Christian occupation of digital media" is the space now able to be taken in religious discourse by the unconnected (from the ecclesiastical point of view): the so-called unchurched or churchless (Campos 2012). These are people who profess the Christian faith but who, for a variety of reasons, have decided on institutional disengagement but at the same time wish to continue sharing faith in community and publicly expressing reflections, ideas, experiences and opinions. To the extent that this was already happening through the long-standing phenomenon of alternative communities, through digital media the possibilities for meeting and interacting are increased through the formation of hundreds of virtual communities.

Perspectives

The portrait outlined here indicates new and rich possibilities for research on the religion and media beyond the classical understanding of the phenomenon of churches in the media as message producers and carriers. It is a changing reality, a dynamic whose movements must be monitored, taking in all its nuances. Among these, or course is the strong and growing presence of religion in politics in Brazil, something that is beyond the scope of this treatment, and something that has taken on new force and significance since the election of Bolsonaro.

Research efforts and their accounts give shape to the mediatization of Christianity in Brazil. Through them it is revealed to be the process of the production of meanings through which Christians have sought to understand, communicate and transform themselves through an extensive array of media practices, especially now using digital technologies. As a result, religious mediations in culture and the communicational mediations of religion are phenomena that have achieved a high profile in Brazilian sociocultural processes and function with increasing intensity. To understand them requires openness to new approaches, new theory and new research.

Works Cited

Assmann, H. 1986. *A igreja eletrônica e seu impacto na América Latina*. Petrópolis: Vozes.
Bittencourt Filho, J. 2003. *Matriz Religiosa Brasileira: Religiosidade e Mudança Social*.
    Petrópolis: Vozes, Rio De Janeiro: Koinonia.
Borelli, V. 2010. "Dispositivos midiáticos e as novas 'formas' do fenômeno religioso". In Mídia e religião: entre o mundo da fé e do fiel, edited by Viviane Borelli, 15–30. Rio de Janeiro: E-Papers.
Braga, J. L. 2006. *A sociedade enfrenta sua mídia: dispositivos sociais de crítica midiática*. São Paulo: Paulus.
Burity, J. A. 2008. "Religião, política e cultura". *Tempo Social*, v. 20, n. 2: 83–113.
Campos, L. S. 2012. "Rebanho virtual", fator que contribui para o individualismo religioso evangélico?". Interview by Thamiris Magalhães. *IHU On Line*, 400. http://www.ihuonline.unisinos.br/artigo/4592-leonildo-silveira-campos-4

Campos, L. S. 1997. *Teatro, templo e mercado. Organização e Marketing marketing de um empreendimento neopentecostal*. Petrópolis/São Paulo/São Bernardo do Campo: Vozes/Simpósio/Umesp.

Cunha, M. 2014. "Interseções e interações entre mídia, religião e mercado: um objeto dinâmico e instigante". *Horizonte*, v. 12, n. 34, Apr./Jun., 284-289.

Cunha, M. 2013. "A Jornada Mundial da Juventude e a visita do Papa Francisco ao Brasil: notas reflexivas sobre mídia, religião e política". *Cadernos de Teologia Pública: Papa Francisco no Brasil, alguns olhares*, ano VII, n. 79, 74-84. http://www.ihu.unisinos.br/images/stories/cadernos/teopublica/079_cadernosteologiapublica.pdf.

Cunha, M. 2015. "Chaves teórico-interpretativas do processo de aproximação das Organizações Globo com o segmento evangélico no Brasil: audiência, mercado, política e poder". *Comunicação & Inovação*, Mai-Aug: 59-75. http://seer.uscs.edu.br/index.php/revista_comunicacao_inovacao/article/view/3038

Cunha, M. 2016. "Religião no noticiário: marcas de um imaginário exclusivista no jornalismo brasileiro". *E-Compós*, v. 19, n. 1, Jan/Apr, 1-21. http://www.e-compos.org.br/e-compos/article/download/1204/883

Cunha, M. 2007. *A Explosão Gospel. Um olhar das ciências humanos sobre o cenário evangélico no Brasil*. Rio de Janeiro: Mauad.

Fajardo, A. 2011. "A Atuação dos Evangélicos no Rádio Brasileiro: Origem e Expansão". Master Thesis, Universidade Metodista de São Paulo.

Figueiredo Filho, V. 2005. *Entre o palanque e o púlpito: mídia, religião e política*. São Paulo: Annablume.

Follis, R. 2012. "Interseções entre publicidade e cultura: uma análise da presença do religioso em comerciais televisivos". Master Thesis, Universidade Metodista de São Paulo.

Hoover, S. 2014. "Mídia e religião: premissas e implicações para os campos acadêmico e midiático". *Comunicação & Sociedade*, v. 35, n. 2: 41-68. https://www.metodista.br/revistas/revistas-ims/index.php/CSO/article/view/4906

Kellner, D. 2001. *A cultura da mídia. Estudos culturais: identidade e política entre o moderno e o pós-moderno*. Bauru: EDUSC.

Martin-Barbero, J. 2009. "Uma aventura epistemológica". *Matrizes*, v. 2, n. 2: 143-162.

Martin-Barbero, J. 2004. *Ofício de Cartógrafo: travessias latino-americanas da comunicação na cultura*. São Paulo: Loyola.

Martin-Barbero, J. 1997. *Dos meios às mediações – Comunicação, cultura e hegemonia*. Rio de Janeiro: Editora UFRJ.

Martin-Barbero, J. 1995. "Secularizacion, desencanto y reencantamiento massmediatico". *Dialogos de la comunicación*, n. 41, mar., 71-81.

Patriota, K. 2008. "Mídia e Entretenimento: Em Busca da Religiosa Audiência". Revista de Estudos da Religião, Sept 2008: 69-88. https://www.pucsp.br/rever/rv3_2008/t_patriota.pdf

Sbardelotto, M. 2012. *E o Verbo se fez bit: A comunicação e a experiência religiosas na internet*. Aparecida: Editora Santuário.

Seidl, E. 2014. "Apresentação do dossiê 'Catolicismo e Formação Cultural'". *Pro-Posições*, v. 25, n. 1, Jan./Apr., 25-30. http://dx.doi.org/10.1590/S0103-73072014000100002.

Steven Hu
Digitizing Jesus: Expanding Publics and Cultivating Civility with the Jesus Film Smartphone App

Since its debut in 1979, the *Jesus* film, a motion picture of the life of Jesus produced by the evangelical parachurch organization Cru (formerly known as Campus Crusade for Christ)[1] has been screened in every country in the world and translated into some 1,750 languages (Jesus Film Project 2019a). Conceived as an evangelistic film, its purpose is "bring Christ-centered video to the ends of the earth" and "to introduce Jesus to the world" since "movies cross barriers of communication both culturally and geographically," they "offer the most dynamic way to hear and see the greatest story ever lived" in the viewer's own "heart language" (Jesus Film Project 2019b). Based on a verse-by-verse rendering of the Good News Bible's version of the Gospel of Luke, the film's portrayal of the gospel narrative of Jesus's birth, life, death, and resurrection demonstrates how scripture may be transposed into various media formats.

In making the film more readily accessible to a wider and global audience, *Jesus* is now available as a smartphone app where "everything on the app is free to watch, download, and share with anyone you meet, wherever you meet them" (Jesus Film Project 2019b). The driving goal of the app, which is downloadable via the Apple App Store and Google Play, is to place scriptural and evangelism resources in the pockets of Christians as "the tool that can equip anyone, anywhere to introduce people they love to Jesus" (Ibid) making every user a missionary. In addition to short films on topics such as Christian prayer, worship, and finding peace in difficult times, the app contains 40 "Conversation Starters" clips designed to be used in proselytization engagements. The *pièce de résistance* of the app is the original *Jesus* film. The app allows users to view the 128-minute film in 61 short segments and also allows them to share and discuss the film via email and social networking sites. Indeed, the story of Jesus has gone digital.

The digitization of *Jesus* represents a religious organization's ability to adopt new technologies in mediating the use of scripture for the individual thereby creating a novel experience for the user. Scholars examining the intersection of

---
[1] Since its founding in 1951, the evangelical parachurch organization has been known as Campus Crusade for Christ. Its name was changed to Cru in 2011 to avoid the negative connotation associated with the word "crusade."

religion and media have noted the use of new media technologies by religious communities, especially the internet, has affected the innovation and transformation of religious practices and experiences (O'Leary 1996; Brasher 2001; Dawson and Cowan 2004). However, studies holding the simple assertion that the adoption of digital technologies as a religious innovation miss the need to examine how new technologies enable the creation of new discursive spaces that cultivate self-making in such spaces. This chapter suggests the mediation of scripture/religion via new media technologies allows *Jesus* to extend its reach to a wider audience thereby increasing its public. My analysis focuses on the development and format of the *Jesus* film smartphone app and how the app is designed and deployed as a proselytization tool that prompts individual users to seek out others in order to show them content in their "heart language" for the purpose of dialogic engagement. I examine the digital distribution channels of the *Jesus* film app to demonstrate how it expands its public by producing an increasing "space of discursive circulation" (Warner 2002) for the *Jesus* film while aiming to narrow the distance between the user and the strangers they seek to proselytize.

For the user, the *Jesus* film app also engenders a new subjective experience since the utilization of the app cultivates an ethical disposition in the individual user toward the stranger. Since the app is designed as a tool for Christian evangelism, users are primed to use it in public settings where they encounter strangers, specifically who they perceive as "internationals." Users are trained to approach and engage strangers by first introducing the app on their smartphones, viewing the contents of the app together with the stranger, and then dialoging with them regarding what they watched. During the course of these encounters, users intentionally seek out personal details from strangers by asking "Where are you from?" and "What language to do you speak?" in order to customize the content shown to them. By taking a phenomenological approach toward understanding the concept of intentionality (Husserl 1973; McIntyre and Smith 1989), I show the deployment of the *Jesus* film app requires the user to consciously conceptualize the stranger as an object of her own reflection prior to the encounter. Since the other is conceived as the object of proselytization, users are primarily concerned with bringing the contents of her reflection into a real relationship with herself. This mode of knowing the other generates a sense of intimacy between strangers and illuminates the practice of care in which users engage with strangers. I follow Marian Barnes's (2012:5) assertion that care should be thought of as practices that are perceivable and observable. Care is indeed "a set of values, or 'moral principles' . . . that offers a way of thinking about what is necessary for human well-being, flourishing and indeed survival." Therefore, care for others is discernable when we attend to social relationships generated in the use of the *Jesus* film app as a tool for Christian evangelism.

This chapter demonstrates that the specific kind of care deployed in the usage of app is the practice of civility. I define civility broadly as the consideration of and respect for others – especially strangers – what Richard Boyd calls "formal civility" that includes polite manners, courtesies, and the formalities of face-to-face interactions in everyday life (Boyd 2006: 864). Formal civility involves practices of etiquette, respectful speech, and other social norms as these are both formal and conventional ways of interacting with others. In examining how the *Jesus* film app is deployed, I show that practices of formal civility engendered by the app cultivate conditions conducive for "civic equality" and generates a sense where participants know they are "part of one moral collectivity or public" (Ibid: 865). Civility is treating others as equals, and when practiced, results in the "deference to the social and democratic identity of an individual" (Papacharissi 2004: 267). Thus, civility allows individuals to communicate their "wishes or injunctions to fellow citizens – whatever those wishes may be – so long as we agree to subscribe to common conditions on the means we may legitimately use in the pursuit of those self-chosen ends" (Boyd 2006: 864). I demonstrate that in seeking to evangelize others, *Jesus* film app users approach strangers with genuine solicitude and engage them dialogically regarding both personal matters and content of the app. They do so while also recognizing others as *different*. The communicative acts engendered in these encounters points to the formation of a public when the app is utilized. I also show that care for others through the practice of civility is predicated on the app's ability to generate a public or a realm in which users and strangers recognize one another as equals *and* different in order to discursively interact in such space.

I begin with a brief sketch of the history of *Jesus* which situates the smartphone app within the proselytization goals which Cru originally had envisioned for the film. I move next to an analysis of the smartphone app digital strategy and the technical platform on which the app is designed, focusing on the specific ways the app allows itself and its content to be distributed across multiple software platforms by different Christian organizations which has the effect of increasing the *Jesus* film app's reach and audience. Finally, in the last section this paper examines in its attempt to extend itself to a wider public, the app allows the user to cultivate a concern for the Other. In using the app, the user is encouraged to consider someone "who needs the message of the Gospel." I demonstrate how it is in this relational encounter between the user and the Other, that the app is able to increase its reach and cast a wider net of audience.

A Brief History of the *Jesus* Film

The idea for an evangelistic motion picture of Jesus's life was first conceived in the 1940s by Bill Bright, founder of Campus Crusade for Christ (founded in 1951), and evangelist Billy Graham (Dart 2001). Bright believed the medium of film could be harnessed as an effective tool for spreading the Christian gospel to a wider audience. After unsuccessfully approaching Cecil B. DeMille to direct and produce a film about Jesus in 1947, Bright shelved the idea for the next 30 years due to lack of interest and funding (Eshleman 2000). The film project was revived when filmmaker and producer John Heyman sought Bright's assistance in marketing his "New Media Bible" to mainline and evangelical churches. As a major player in Hollywood, Heyman produced several movies in the 1970s and 1980s, including *A Doll's House*, *D.A.R.Y.L.*, and *A Passage to India*. Heyman went on to help finance major films such as *Chinatown*, *The Rocky Horror Picture Show*, *Grease*, *Saturday Night Fever*, *Home Alone*, and *Edward Scissorhands*. His International Artists Agency represented the likes of Elizabeth Taylor and Richard Burton (Dagan 2017). In 1974, Heyman founded his own production company, the Genesis Project, to render the Bible verse-by-verse into film (Dart 2001; Stone 2009). The film was to be offered along with other media – filmstrips, audio cassettes, study guides – for $2,000 to churches and synagogues as a way to promote biblical literacy (Blau 1976). Heyman's aim was authenticity and fidelity to the biblical text and he consulted a number of biblical scholars across denominational lines for the project. By the time he approached Bright, Hyman had completed a film version of the book of Genesis consisting of eight 15-minute films and two additional films of the first two chapters of the Gospel of Luke (Blau 1976; Eshleman 2002). Hyman previewed these films to Bright in 1976 with hopes of securing funding for the Genesis Project. Sensing an opportunity to add film to Campus Crusade for Christ's evangelism tool chest, Bright agreed to collaborate with Heyman in producing a feature film on the life of Jesus that would be suitable for showing in theaters nationwide (Dart 2001; Eshleman 2002; Lindvall and Quicke 2011).

The final version of *Jesus* is a verse-by-verse rendition of the Gospel of Luke shot on location in Israel and contains a narrated six-minute "altar call" segment at the conclusion of the film that introduces viewers to the historicity of the virgin birth, Jesus's life, death and resurrection. The viewer is then asked to become "a follower of Jesus" and pray a pledge of his belief and faith in Jesus. After the prayer, the narrator exhorts the viewed to read the Bible, pray to God on a regularly basis, meet with other Christians, and tell others about Jesus.

Since the primary goal of *Jesus* is evangelism, the film must reach a wide and global audience Bright and his team at Campus Crusade for Christ had five criteria in making the film:

(1) The film must be as archeologically, historically and theologically accurate as humanly possible; (2) the presentation must be unbiased, acceptable to all as a true depiction of Jesus's life; (3) the film story must appeal to all ages; (4) the script must be easily translatable into virtually any language on earth; and (5) the film must be of high quality and effective with both urban and rural audiences. (Nichols 2009; Stone 2009)

Funding for most of the $6 million to produce the film came from Campus Crusade for Christ donors. Heyman also asked several major studios including Columbia Pictures, MCA, Universal Pictures to finance and distribute *Jesus* with hopes that revenues would offset the cost of making the film (Eshleman 2002). The film opened on October 19, 1979 in 250 theaters and eventually played in 2,000 theaters in the U.S. through a distribution arrangement with Warner Brothers but saw little commercial success (Eshleman 2000; 2002). The film was also reformatted to be shown on HBO, ShowTime, and the Movie Channel. Campus Crusade for Christ later secured international distribution rights and began dubbing the film's soundtrack into different languages for viewing outside the U.S. (Dart 2001; Stone 2009).

By the end of 1980, *Jesus* was translated into 31 languages and within five years, the film had been rendered into over 100 languages (Dart 2001; Jesus Film Project 2019c). The first foreign telecast took place in India where a Hindi version of the film was seen by 21 million viewers (Eshleman 2002). Despite being a distinct artefact of American evangelicalism (Walsh 2003; Peperkemp 2005; Merz 2010), the producers of *Jesus* continue to translate it into new languages. According to the film's website, *Jesus* currently exists in 1,750 language versions and has been viewed more than eight billion times globally (see Fountain, Kindon, and Murray 2004; Merz 2010; Shreve 2015; Jesus Film Project 2019a). More than 60 million *Jesus* products including film, video, and audio media have been distributed (Jesus Film Project 2019a). To better facilitate the translation of distribution of the film, Campus Crusade for Christ formally established Jesus Film Project in 1985.

Because it was explicitly conceived as an evangelistic film, *Jesus* has been adapted to various media from its original film format to facilitate distribution and transmission. The film was first distributed in 35mm then in 16mm four-reel format for film teams (Bright 1999). This smaller format made it easier for wider distribution, especially screenings in rural areas around the world. India and the Philippines were the first locales where Campus Crusade for Christ organized film teams in 1980 (Dart 2001; Stone 2009; Jesus Film Project 2019c). These teams consisted of local Christians and Jesus Film Project staff carrying cumbersome film reels and projector equipment. Teams would trek for days before reaching a small village to show *Jesus* (Eshleman 2002). By 1999, Jesus Film Project employed over full-time 2,100 film teams worldwide (Bright 1999).

As new media technology developed, the format of the film evolved as well. Soon the film was distributed via audio and videotapes, and VCDs. In 1997, *Jesus* was made available to download via the internet and an DVD format was released a year later (Eshleman 2002). In an ongoing effort to expand its viewership and reach a global audience, producers developed new distribution channels and methods. In locales where security was an issue (such as communist Eastern Europe and the Soviet Union), Jesus Film Project adopted the strategy of allowing lay people on short-term mission trips to distribute *Jesus* media products such as audio and video tapes, and DVDs (Schmidt 1991; Bright 1999). In the U.S., churches were trained by Campus Crusade for Christ and Jesus Film Project to canvass their neighborhoods and distribute *Jesus* videotapes. Church members would return with two weeks to follow up on those who indicated "they have received Christ" (Bright 1999). Direct mailing campaigns were employed to extend the reach of the film in the U.S. By 2005, 20 million copies of the film on DVDs and videotapes have been sent to addresses in Alabama, Hawaii, North and South Carolina, Ohio, and Texas (Foer 2004; Dewan 2005). Jesus Film Project worked in conjunction with other Christian organizations and institutions such as American Bible Society, Samaritan Purse, World Relief, and the Roman Catholic Church in distributing *Jesus* film and video materials (Eshleman 2002; Turner 2008; Jesus Film Project 2011). Non-evangelical Christians also used *Jesus* in their proselytization efforts. In Poland, for example, founder of the Light-Life movement and Roman Catholic priest Franciszek Blachnicki saw the film as a powerful medium for evangelization especially during the tumultuous years of the Solidarity movement and collaborated with Campus Crusade for Christ to screen *Jesus* in parishes and universities where the communist state had no control (Peperkamp 2005). Since 1997, Campus Crusade for Christ and Jesus Film Project has partnered with the Southern Baptist International Mission Board, the largest Protestant missionary organization, in making *Jesus* more widely available (Turner 2008; Lindvall and Quicke 2011). These organizations served as additional distribution channels expanding the global reach of *Jesus*. Similar methods and strategies for increasing viewership of the film will be re-deployed in the development of the *Jesus* film smartphone app.

Jesus Goes Digital: The Jesus Film Smartphone App

Since *Jesus* was conceived as an evangelistic film to take Christianity "to the ends of the earth" (Eshleman 2000), its translatability to other languages and adaptability to different viewing contexts have largely determined how the film is distributed.

In its ongoing "aggressive" effort to expand its global viewership (Noll 2009), Jesus Film Project developed a smartphone app as the digital extension of the film. Launched on October 2, 2012 on both Apple App Store and Google Play, the app contains the canonical two-hour re-mastered and high-definition *Jesus* film fully restored with a new musical score along with other content such as the hour-long *Magdalena, Released from Shame* (2007). *Magdalena* is a retelling of the *Jesus* film from the perspectives of various women in the Bible narrated by Mary Magdalena and contains new material interspliced with selected scenes from the *Jesus* film (Wood 2007). *Following Jesus*, also released in 2007 for an Indian audience, also incorporates clips from the original *Jesus* deals with illness and divine healing and. Jesus Film Project released three additional film in 2011: *Rivka*, a 12-episode series about the everyday lives of women during Jesus's ministry in first-century Palestine; a five-part series called *Walking with Jesus*, "produced by Africans for Africans," helps viewers understand the basics of Christian belief in "common African life scenarios" using "narrated storytelling techniques created for members of an oral culture" and clips from the *Jesus* film (Jesus Film Project 2012); and the animated short film *My Last Day*, which uses audio from *Jesus*, depicting the regret, repentance, and redemption of the thief on the cross. *My Last Day* was conceived to reach a younger audience since its animé style "visually translates" the *Jesus* film (Jesus Film Project 2011).

The smartphone app allows users browse an existing digital video library of over 330 clips of full-length films and shorts. The app also provides users a political map of the world. Users can choose a preexisting pin placed on a country and this will pull up a list of languages available in that country. When the user selects the desired language, the app will display all content available in the language. The app also contains a search function that lets viewers search for any video clips by country, language, keyword, or title. Other features of the app's user interface allow viewers to share and download any video content. Included with each video clip are discussion questions. Viewers can use these questions to discuss themes presented in the clip. Lastly, the user interface also includes a button when clicked opens the website, knowgod.com. The website contains the *Four Spiritual Laws*, the tract conceived by Bill Bright in the 1960s as the mainstay of Cru's evangelistic method (Turner 2008). Like the tract, the website presents a "distillation of theological truth" concerning God, sin, and salvation and prompts its reader for a decision to convert to Christianity (Turner 2008).

According to the Jesus Film Project, the smartphone app was developed as a part of the overall strategy of "reaching everyone everywhere in their heart language by helping people to engage with Jesus Christ" Telp[hrough the original *Jesus* film (Brubaker 2013). As the "digital expression" of the film (Jesus Film Media 2014), the app was conceived, designed, and developed out of Jesus Film

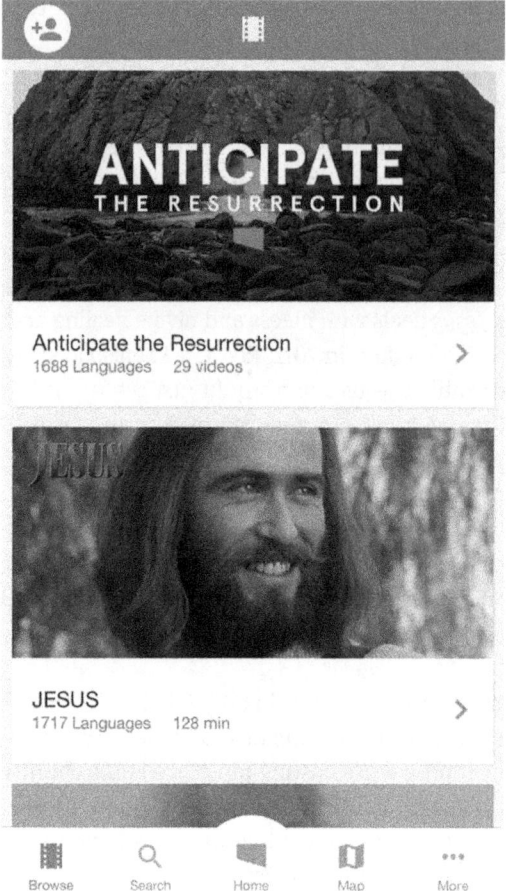

Figure 1: Screenshot fom the Jesus Film App © 1995–2021 Jesus Film Project ®. All rights reserved.

Project's attempt to utilize the increasing popularity and ubiquity of smartphones and tablet devices. According to the development team, the app was designed and deployed according to four goals (Brubaker 2013):

(1) "Unprecedented access: Everyone, everywhere can connect with Jesus through film." The app is the vehicle through which the Jesus Film Project can disseminate its video content, making it available to anyone. This includes end users and organizations who wants to partner with the Jesus Film Project.

(2) "Others focused: 90% of all views of Jesus Film project content would happen on other's branded sites and apps." Along with the app, an API (application programming interface) was also developed. Jesus Film Project has made all

Figure 2: Screenshot fom the Jesus Film App © 1995–2021 Jesus Film Project ®. All rights reserved.

of its content available to other organizations so that virtually most viewing of its media content would take place on third-party websites or apps. The API houses all Jesus Film Project content, metadata (keywords, bible scriptural references, film descriptions, images) and is freely available to third-party entities. Third-party organizations can access content and metadata via the API for their own purposes without storing the content on their own servers. The API therefore allows external organizations to utilize and distribute content, thereby extending the reach of Jesus Film media.

(3) "Permanence: All of our links will work, always." This is to ensure that the API, the software engine that makes it possible for third-parties to use Jesus

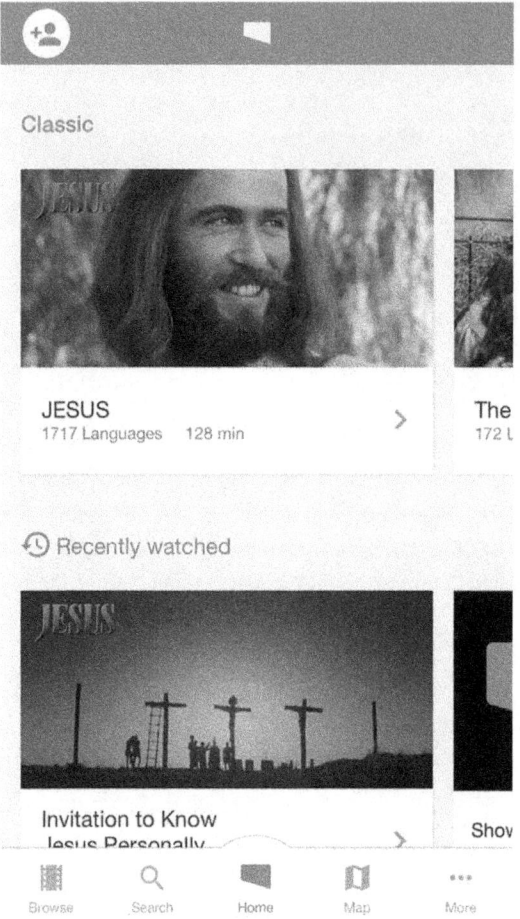

Figure 3: Screenshot fom the Jesus Film App © 1995–2021 Jesus Film Project ®. All rights reserved.

Film Project content, remains stable. This will allow a continuous link between the Jesus Film Project content third-party platforms.

(4) "Business intelligence: We will be good stewards by making decisions on how to strategically invest and be accountable to partners." Built into the API is an analytic system that gives the app development team access to metrics such as the number of downloads, app installations, number of views, etc. Analytics help the app development team to refine their digital strategy. Such statistics also serves to provide hard numbers for donors. (Jesus Film Project relies solely on donors for funding.)

Since its launch in October 2012, the Jesus Film app has been installed over 1.7 million times on both iOS and Android devices. According to its statistics, over 149 million instances of *Jesus* related video content were viewed on the app in 2018 (Jesus Film Project 2019a). The top five countries with the most installations of the app are: U.S., India, Ghana, Nigeria, and Tanzania (Jesus Film Project 2018).

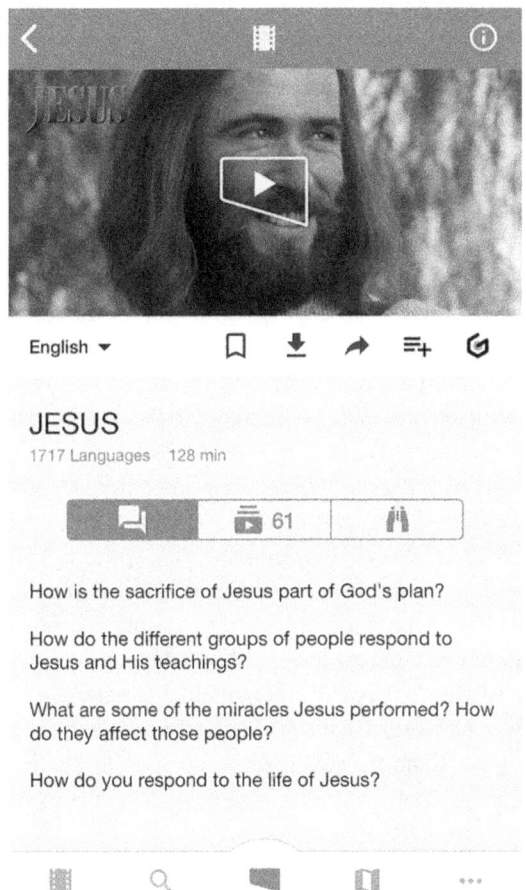

Figure 4: Screenshot fom the Jesus Film App © 1995–2021 Jesus Film Project ®. All rights reserved.

Expanding Publics with the *Jesus* Film App and API

These four goals demonstrate the primary purpose of the Jesus film app is to circulate and increase the viewership of the film and related content. This circulation involves two entities: a discourse and an audience. The discourse circulated among the viewers of the Jesus film app generates shared ideas, sentiments, and moods which all constitute a public. At its simplest definition, a public is constituted by reflexively circulating discourse as an "ongoing space of encounter" that is not static (Warner 2002: 62). The public is also inherently poly-vocal and is constructed by the involvement of various interlocutors (Warner 2002: 63). In the same way, as third-party organizations utilize the Jesus film app API and distributes the film, the discourse and ideas of the Jesus film is further circulated, and its public enlarged.

The kind of mediation enabled by the Jesus film app allows for the possibility of networked public(s). By this I refer to Mizuko Ito's (2008) description of how circulation of discourse becomes increasingly complex through networks that are "bottom-up, top-down, as well as side-to-side" (Ibid: 2–3). In the case of the Jesus film app, networked publics are constituted and configured by geographical locales. When the app is installed on smartphones and utilized in various locations around the globe, users thereby participate in various different publics in their engagement with and discussion of the media content. The tablet user in Boulder, Colorado and a Nigerian user belong to separate publics alongside other, smaller publics, each constituted and conditioned by local, cultural, language, and geographical conditions. Though Jesus film app users may be separated by these local factors, different publics are potentially linked to one another due to new media technology mediating the film, that is, through online forums, sharing functions within the app, etc. While users from two different locations and languages watch Jesus related content in their own situation, they can still participate in discussion regarding the film's content on an online forum. Thus the Jesus film app facilitates the formation of a "networked religion" (Campbell 2012) allowing for opportunities where "individual create webs of connection between different social contexts to create a personalized network of relations" (Ibid: 69).

Networked publics can also take the form of "(re)makers and (re)-distributors, engaging in shared culture and knowledge through discourse and social exchange as well as through acts of media reception" (Ito 2008: 2–3). The processes of remaking and redistributing can be seen in how third-party organizations and developers other than Jesus Film Project utilize the app's API. Working in conjunction with Kolo Group, Jesus Film app developers made all of its African language film content available without cost to Kolo. Kolo then developed its own app called "Kolo Africa" which contains the Bible in video and audio format in almost 500 African languages. The purpose of the Kolo Africa app is to leverage "Applied digital strategy, cloud computing and mobile technologies for accelerated missional impact in heart languages of the world" (Kolo 2014). In Nigeria, the app has been deployed by local users and missionaries in Christian evangelism and church planting (Brubaker 2013). Screenings of segments of *Jesus* through the Kolo app has also taken place in these locales. Missionaries also use this media for bible studies which allows the formation of discussion groups around a discourse consisting of a passage from the Bible.

The Kolo Africa app therefore acts as a distributor of Jesus and related content in the African context. For years, the Kolo Group and its partner organizations had been active in Nigeria. Kolo assisted missionaries in starting churches by providing them with audio bibles and screening Jesus. The film was so popular that local Nigerians asked the missionaries for more screenings to be shown in their villages. Due to lack of film projectors and equipment, these requests were turned down by the Jesus Film Project. The primary reason why the Jesus Film Project made its content available to Kolo Group is due to a lack of presence of Jesus in Nigeria. The Kolo Group developed the Kolo Africa app to circumvent this problem to provide a "church-planting toolkit in the pocket of every Nigerian Christian" (Brubaker 2013). In deploying its app, Kolo Group became a distributor but on its own terms. In making its content and material available through its API on the Kolo Africa app, the Jesus film extended its public where it had no presence. In a way, Kolo Group "re-made" Jesus by embedding it in its app, and adapted it for use in its own software eco-system.

Cultivating Care and Civility for Strangers with the Jesus Film App

In recent years, scholars have taken interest in how media, with their forms of circulation and usage, shapes practices of religious mediation, knowledge, discipline, and the making of religious subjects (cf. Meyer and Moors 2006; Hirschkind 2009; Meyer 2009; Johnson 2018). I close this chapter by examining how the *Jesus* film app cultivates an ethical disposition of care for others through practices of civility in the user. When users seek and engage strangers with the app for the purpose of evangelism, they do so with the politeness and courtesy characterized by "formal civility" (Boyd 2006: 864). *Jesus* film app users practice the conventions of face-to-face everyday interactions – respectful speech – that treat others as equals. In a typical encounter, *Jesus* film app users approach strangers with a real desire of knowing the other through dialogical queries regarding their personal history, family life, and place of origin.

When the app was first launched in October 2012, its development team hosted training sessions for users who were missionaries working with Cru. Because it is capable of accessing over 1,500 language versions of the *Jesus* film, the app was promoted as a tool to engage non-English speakers with the Christian gospel. Users were trained and instructed to use the app to show the *Jesus* film and related content in the viewer's native language. The users I interviewed indicated they deployed the app in settings where they intentionally sought out strangers whom they perceive as "internationals" for engagement.

For one *Jesus* film app user, having the app available on her iPhone made her "more attuned to internationals whose native tongue is different" because it provides her something "readily accessible to talk about religion, to share Jesus with others, and to have something relatable that we can watch and discuss afterwards." This user describes how she used the app when she encountered an Iranian man working at the International Cottages in Balboa Park, San Diego.[2] Upon entering the Iranian cottage house, the man greeted her by saying that he would be willing to discuss anything regarding Iran and Iranian culture except for issues related to politics or religion. She agreed to the invitation and injunction. The conversation took a personal turn when the user told the man that she worked for a Christian organization which led the man to ask her about her religious background. After telling the user about his childhood in Iran, the man proceeded showed her Farsi music videos. Upon seeing these videos, the user reciprocated by asking if the man would like to watch a movie in his own language, Farsi. The man agreed and watched several minutes of the *Jesus* film on the user's smartphone. The user noted that

> the man was really surprised and stunned that we had a film in his language. We then gave him more information on which films (on the app and *Jesus* film website) to watch. This demonstrated we care and what set us apart in our faith. We follow his lead to see how far we can take the conversation. We then left him with my friend's business card and planned to build a point of connection. . . .. The app wasn't the catalyst that got us to those spiritual conversations. The app, for me, allows for a point of relevance.

In this particular encounter, the user engaged in formal civility through polite speech in a public setting. As civility is "a series of techniques of citizenship

---

[2] Located in Balboa Park, San Diego, these cottages were first constructed in 1935 representing various cultures and countries around the world "to create a spirit of understanding, tolerance and goodwill among the various national and ethnic groups represented in the community." See https://www.sdhpr.org/aboutus.html.

generated from the daily practices and experiences of public life and manifested through judgments about bodies, language, and actions" (Thiranagama et al. 2018), this user behaved civilly despite intentionally seeking out a stranger whom she perceived as different. In her engagement with the Iranian man, the *Jesus* film app user respected the man's initial request not to discuss religion and politics. Her public engagement with the Iranian man displayed restraint and respect in the face of cultural and religious difference.

In intentionally seeking people who are different from them, users of the *Jesus* film app engage others with genuine solicitude. One user noted the app "aroused curiosity and opened up an opportunity" to talk about family with a Slovenian taxi driver he met in Chicago since he showed *Jesus* in the driver's "heart language." The same user recounts a similar reaction from a Ghanaian waiter at a restaurant in Little Rock, Arkansas. After viewing *Jesus* in his own native language, the smiled since "he's thousands of miles from his home." Viewing the film together generated a point of connection between the user and the waiter which further allowed them to dialog on everyday and personal issues. The app did not lead the user into a discussion regarding Christianity or an attempt to evangelize the viewer, but it did provide him an entry point to relate to a stranger.

Because the Jesus film app is designed for evangelism, users are primed to use the app in settings where they purposely seek out others for such engagement. In the cases discussed above, these "others" – people who hail from different parts of the world whose "heart language" is not English – already exist in the user's mind as an object of his own reflection and creation. The Jesus film app user is conscious of these things as something he or she brings into their minds. In representing others as possible objects of evangelization, the user is creating intention toward them that results in a certain state of affairs in their minds (McIntyre and Smith 1989: 148). Such "representational character of mind or consciousness – its being 'of' or 'about' something" as a mental phenomenon is defined as intentionality (McIntyre and Smith 1989: 147). In engaging with the stranger through the app, the user aims to bring this person into a knowing relationship with him through a mutual exchange of queries, dialog, and even debate. In this manner, care in the form of civility – the conscientious and respectful interaction with the stranger, to bring others into a knowing relationship – is facilitated and enabled by the Jesus film app.

I suggest that the ethical disposition of care for others that is manifested through formal civility in these encounters supports the formation of and participation in a public centered on the Jesus film. Users are primed by the Jesus film app to attend to others in order to bring strangers into relationship with themselves. As Michael Warner (2002) points out, a public is where "strangers come into relationship by its means" and "unites strangers through participation alone" (Warner 2002: 56). As a relation among strangers, a public is a space where strangers engage in public discourse and construct a sense of commonality. While publics are indeed constituted through rational-critical engagement via discourse, dialog, and debate, their formation are also facilitated and catalyzed by enacting practices of care and civility. It is in and through this encounter and civil engagement with others, mediated through the Jesus film app, that strangers are invited into the ever-expanding, networked public of the Jesus film.

Conclusion

The digitization of *Jesus* represents a new way in which the message of the Christian gospel is constituted, distributed, and consumed through the deployment of a smartphone app. By rendering the original film into a digital version viewable on smartphones, the app facilitates the expansion of the film's viewing public across geographical boundaries and linguistic barriers, allowing users to potentially become more interconnected. This interconnectedness is made possible by the technical mediation of the *Jesus* film which facilitates the formation of a public that is constituted by a reflexive circulation of discourse centered around the content of the film. As with all publics that cannot exist apart from the discourse that addresses them, this space of discursive circulation is self-organized and networked. The *Jesus* film app also has the potential to link local publics to a wider, global, networked Christian community.

The mediation of the Gospel of Luke as presented in the *Jesus* film app has the effect of fragmenting the original 115-minute *JESUS* Film into 61 segments thus enabling a new viewing experience for its audience in that the film no longer needs to be consumed in one sitting. Not only does the app offers the potential for new viewing experiences for a postmodern audience, the app also engenders new subjective experiences for the user by allowing the her to cultivate an ethical disposition of care as practiced through civility for strangers. Users orient themselves toward others out of a concern to engage them in Christian evangelism. Ironically, these strangers are thus brought into the public of the *Jesus* film through discussion of personal, intimate matters. Such discussions of intimate matters, however, are enacted to increase the ever-expanding, networked public of the *Jesus* film discourse.

Works Cited

Barnes M. 2012. *Care in Everyday Life*. Chicago: The University of Chicago Press.
Blau E. 1976. "A Movie Translation of Entire Bible Begun to Transmit Faith to Today's Nonreaders." *The New York Times* January 26, 1976. https://www.nytimes.com/1976/01/26/archives/new-jersey-pages-a-movie-translation-of-entire-bible-begun-to.html. Accessed December 5.
Boyd R. 2006. "The Value of Civility?" *Urban Studies* 5/6: 863–878.
Brasher B. 2001. *Give Me That Online Religion*. San Francisco: Jossey-Bass.
Bright B. 1999. *Come Help Change the World*. Orlando, FL: New Life Publications.
Brubaker M. 2013. Director of Digital Outreach and Strategies, Jesus Film Project. Interview. December 19.
Campbell H. 2012. "Understanding the Relationship between Religion Online and Offline in a Networked Society." *Journal of American Academy of Religion* 80/1: 64–93.
Dagan C. 2017. "John Heyman, Distinguished Financier and Producer, Dies at 84." *Variety* June 9, https://variety.com/2017/film/news/john-heyman-dead-dies-producer-1202460783. Accessed February 9, 2019.
Dart J. 2001, "The making of *Jesus*." *Christian Century* 118/18: 26–31.
Dawson L, 2004. Cowan D, editors. *Religion Online*. New York: Routledge.
Dewan S. 2005. "Putting Jesus in Every Mailbox." *The New York Times* August 16, https://www.nytimes.com/2005/08/16/us/putting-jesus-in-every-mailbox.html. Accessed April 16, 2019.
Eshleman P. 2000. *I Just Saw Jesus*. San Clemente, CA: The Jesus Film Project.
Eshleman P. 2002, "The *Jesus* Film: A Contribution of World Evangelism." *International Bulletin of Missionary Research* April 68–72.
Foer F. 2004. "Baptism by Celluloid." *The New York Times* February 8, https://www.nytimes.com/2004/02/08/movies/baptism-by-celluloid.html. Accessed February 10, 2019.
Fountain P, Kindon S, Murrary W. "Christianity, Calamity, and Culture: The Involvement of Christian Churches in the 1998 Aitape Tsunami Disaster Relief. *The Contemporary Pacific* 2004;16/2: 321–355.
Hirschkind C. 2009. *The Ethical Soundscape: Cassette Sermons and Islamic Counterpublics*. New York: Columbia University Press.
Husserl E. 1973. *Logical Investigations*, 2nd edition, trans. Findlay, JN. London: Routledge.
Ito M. 2008. "Introduction." In: Varnelis K, editor. *Networked Publics*. Cambridge, Massachusetts: MIT Press, 1–14
Jesus Film Media. 2014. "About Jesus Film Media." http://Jesusfilmmedia.org/about-us. Accessed on 4 January 2014.
Jesus Film Project. 2011. "Shining His Light: The JESUS Film Project 2011 Annual Review." https://www.jesusfilm.org/content/dam/jesusfilm/devteam/pdf/annual/2011-Annual-Review.pdf. Accessed January 15, 2019.
Jesus Film Project. 2012. "Life-Changing Moments: The JESUS Film Project 2012 Annual Review." https://www.jesusfilm.org/content/dam/jesusfilm/devteam/pdf/annual/2012-Annual-Review.pdf. Accessed January 15, 2019.
Jesus Film Project. 2018. "Changing Lives: The JESUS Film Project 2018 Annual Review." https://www.jesusfilm.org/content/dam/jesusfilm/devteam/pdf/annual/2018-JFP-Annual-Review.pdf. Accessed January 15, 2019.

Jesus Film Project. 2019a. "Official Jesus Film Project Ministry Statistics – March 1, 2019." https://www.jesusfilm.org/about/learn-more/statistics.html. Accessed March 15, 2019.

Jesus Film Project. 2019b. "Why film? Why we chose the medium of video to introduce the world to Jesus." https://www.jesusfilm.org/about/why-film.html. Accessed January 15, 2019.

Jesus Film Project. 2019c. "The history of Jesus Film Project." https://www.jesusfilm.org/about/history.html. Accessed January 18, 2019.

Johnson J. 2018. *Biblical Porn: Affect, Labor, and Pastor Mark Driscoll's Evangelical Empire.* Durham: Duke University Press.

Kolo Group. 2014. https://www.kologroup.org/. Access January 5, 2014.

Lindvall T. and Quicke, A. 2011. Celluloid Sermons: The Emergence of the Christian Film Industry, 1930–1986. New York: NYU Press.

McIntyre R and Smith D.W. 1989. "Theory of Intentionality." In: Mohanty JN, McKenna WR, editors. *Husserl's Phenomenology.* Washington, D.C.: Center for Advanced Research in Phenomenology and University Press of America, 147–79.

Merz J. 2010. "Translation and the Visual Predicament of the "JESUS" Film in West Africa." *Missiology: An International Review* April, 38/2: 111–126.

Meyer B, (ed.) 2009. *Aesthetic Formations: Media, Religion, and the Senses.* New York: Palgrave Macmillan.

Meyer B. Moors A. (eds.) 2006. *Religion, Media, and the Public Sphere.* Bloomington: Indiana.

Nichols S. 2009. "Jesus on the Big Screen." *American Theological Inquiry* 2/1: 41–60.

Noll M. 2009. The New Shape of World Christianity: How American Experience Reflects Global Faith. Downer's Grove, IL: InterVarsity Press.

O'Leary S. 1996. "Cyberspace as Sacred Space." *Journal of American Academy of Religion* 64/4: 781–808.

Papacharissi Z. 2004. "Democracy online." *New Media & Society* 6/2: 259–283.

Peperkamp, E. 2005. "Being a Christian the Catholic Way: Protestant and Catholic Versions of the *Jesus* Film and the Evangelization of Poland." *Postscripts: The Journal of Sacred Texts & Contemporary Worlds* August/November 1.2/1.3: 352–374.

Schmidt W. 1991. "U.S. Evangelicals Winning Soviet Converts." *The New York Times* October 7. https://www.nytimes.com/1991/10/07/world/us-evangelicals-winning-soviet-converts.html. Accessed December 7, 2018.

Shreve A. 2015. "Religious Films in Zimbabwean Contexts: Film Reception Concerning Representations of Jesus." *International Journal of Public Theology* 9: 193–211.

Stone B. 2009. "Modern Protestant Approaches to Film (1960-present)." In: Lyden L, editor. *The Routledge Companion to Religion and Film.* New York: Routledge Press, 72–88.

Thiranagama S., Kelly T. and Forment C. 2018. "Introduction: Whose Civility?" *Anthropological Theory* 18/2–3: 153–174.

Turner, J. 2008. *Bill Bright & Campus Crusade for Christ: The Renewal of Evangelicalism in Postwar America.* Chapel Hill, North Carolina: University of North Caroline Press.

Warner M. 2002. "Publics and Counterpublics." *Public Culture* 14/1: 49–90.

Walsh R. 2003. *Reading the Gospels in the Dark: Portrayals of Jesus in Film.* New York: Trinity Press International.

Wood R. 2007. "The Jesus Film Project: Conquering New Frontiers in Partnership an Evangelism." *Mission Frontiers* September/October 26–27.

Seung Soo Kim
Digital Media and Imperial Formations: The 2012 Lady Gaga Controversy in South Korea

Lady Gaga is Coming!

As soon as the first concert of Lady Gaga's worldwide tour 'Born This Way Ball' was scheduled to be held in Seoul on April 27th, 2012, tickets were immediately sold out. The Korean Association of Church Communication quickly declared their opposition to the Lady Gaga concert with a statement titled 'The Problem of the Lady Gaga Concert in South Korea' on March 19th. Three days later, the Korean Media Rating Board officially announced that the concert, which was initially open to anyone over the age of 12, would be harmful to teenagers. Civilian Network against the Lady Gaga Concert on April 21st and Facebook Group against the Lady Gaga Concert from April 23rd to 27th, mobilized a protest in front of the Hyundai headquarters threatening that they would call for a boycott against Hyundai credit card products unless Hyundai the sponsor of the concert canceled the concert.

The protestors, comprising mostly conservative Evangelicals, insisted that Lady Gaga's song and performance glamorized homosexuality and suicide and thus her concert would have a dangerous impact on the overall morality and spirituality of South Korean youth. The severe protest of Evangelicals against the Lady Gaga concert, however, reignited a prevalent hatred of Protestantism in Korean society that was derived mostly from its offensive evangelism and the moral corruption of prominent Protestant pastors. Liberal media opined that their aversion to Lady Gaga and homosexuality is absurd and irrational. Conservative media, on the contrary, expressed their concern over the moral consequence of Lady Gaga's concert although they did not explicitly support the protest of the Evangelicals. The Korean controversy on the Lady Gaga concert was introduced several international news media, including some US and French online news media. Despite the huge controversy, however, the event was successfully held at Seoul Olympic Stadium on 27th April 2012.

The 2012 Lady Gaga Controversy and New Digital Media

Is Lady Gaga a philanthropic celebrity standing for human rights of social minorities or is she instead a pathetic anti-Christ worshipper caught by Satan? Or, is she just a brilliant late-modern cultural product acquiring attention and controversy by provocatively appropriating sacred symbols of Christianity? The question of which category Lady Gaga would fall into cannot be irrelevant to that of how Korean society has engaged with homosexuality, Evangelical belief, and freedom of expression to name a few. In fact, Evangelicals' aversion to homosexuals, which became vividly prominent during the controversy, generated disputes over how Korean society should respond to their fundamentalist belief which seems irrational and anachronistic.

At the beginning of the controversy, Korean mainstream media mostly covered Lady Gaga's tremendous impact on the economics and cultural politics of the U.S. and the globe. However, emergent fierce protests of conservative Evangelicals refracted the overall media coverage on it. Especially prominent liberal online news media, such as 'Pressian,' 'OhmyNews,' and 'Cine 21,' played a significant role in shaping and providing a social space where issues such as freedom of expression and the public presence of conservative Evangelicals in Korean society could be problematized and disputed. Liberal online news media were not the only generator of the controversy, of course. The extremely high rate of Internet connection and mobile broadband access in South Korea was a material condition for the development of the controversy online and offline, where lots of social media users could actively circulate, share and comment on the news articles and columns critical of the Evangelicals against Lady Gaga and Korean Protestantism.[1]

For those familiar with the celebratory discourse of 'new media resistance' which promises free information distribution, democratization, and even political revolution, such protest against the conservative sexual moral order of Korean society might be seen as an exemplary case for a resistance to

---

[1] The internet penetration rate of South Korea in 2010 was 81.1% And the 2014 rate was stated at 84.8%(www.internetworldstats.com, last accessed March 10th, 2019). South Korea also had the cheapest and fastest broadband in the World around the time of 2012 (http://www.nytimes.com/2011/02/22/technologytechnology/22iht-broadband22.html?_r=1&, last accessed March 10th, 2019). In addition, in 2005 already, 96.8% of Korean mobile phones had internet access (Ahonen, T. & O'Reilly, J., 2007, p.242). According to OECD statistics, the wireless mobile broadband penetration rate of South Korea in 2012 was stated at 102.13% at the second quarter and 103.4% at the fourth quarter (http://www.oecd.org/sti/broadband/oecdbroadbandportal.htm, from the statistics of Historical time series, fixed and wireless broadband penetration, lastly accessed on March 10th, 2019).

the dominant social order, particularly enabled by the affordance of digital media. Such a view on new media technology, however, might be leading us to only a part of the whole picture of this controversy for the following reasons:

First, the impacts of new media are conditioned by social and cultural contexts (Chen et al., 2002). The meaning of resistance should be explored with the questions of to what social order(s) new digital media is used to resist and what other order(s) its resistance serves in reverse in what concrete historical context of the given society. And the questions call for scrutiny on the concrete context and history of the social world where new media use influences and is influenced by particular cultural projects and imaginaries of the new media users.

Regarding such focus on the concrete context and history of the social world where new media is used and practiced, I am indebted to Nick Couldry's works theorizing media as a practice to construct the social world rather (Couldry 2004; 2012) and research projects of the Center for Media, Religion, and Culture in Boulder illuminating how digital media afford in-between space where 'the religious' can be newly imagined and practiced for religiously-oriented new media users who have their own projects and imaginaries different from those of institutionalized religion (e.g. Hoover & Echchaibi Forthcoming; Hoover & Kim Forthcoming). Reconstructing this controversy into the complicated interplay of human and non-human agents including Lady Gaga, the Evangelicals against her, new digital media, representations of Korean Protestantism in modern Korean history, and what I capture as the imperial 'social imaginary (Taylor 2004)' of the linear and universal world history, this chapter aims to complicate the discourse of 'new media resistance' which has often been uncritically imposed on and associated with digital media use for social change in the non-Western world.

Second, especially in the contemporary modern world easily leading us to cultural relativism, a single fixed social order hardly dominates a society. Various social orders likely compete and negotiate with each other within particular geopolitical and cultural boundaries. A dominant social order is always on its making, transforming, and unmaking while struggling with the other ones that are constantly being formed in society (Hall 1981; 1982). If a certain collective use of new digital media contributes to a resistance to *a particular social order*, then it can contribute to the hegemonic formation of *one of the other ones*. In this chapter, I argue that, while new digital media afforded the formation of a resistance to the censoring power of Korean Protestantism and the heterosexual moral order held by it, they also generated a social space where the social imaginary of the singular and universal History, which the case study finds imperial and teleological, was significantly manifested, circulated and legitimized.

Third, the concepts of resistance, democratization, modernization and liberalization, readily associated with new media, could be addressed in a particular social imaginary that constructs, orders, and naturalizes what I describe as an *imperial* one. This case study finds that there is a subtle resonance between the received understanding of such terms and the secular liberal social imaginary of the linear and universal History. It also illuminates that Korean liberal online media significantly contributed to the mediation and circulation of the social imaginary, representing the Evangelicals as the 'pre-modern' Other who threatened and endangered the complete modernization of Korean society in the course of the 2012 Lady Gaga controversy.

Social Imaginary

The significance of mediating and circulating imaginaries for the construction of modern social world, has been noted by thinkers such as Benedict Anderson (1983), Arjun Appadurai (1990; 1996), and Charles Taylor (1995; 2004) just to name a few. Theoretical concepts such as "imagined communities" (Anderson, 1983), "community of sentiment" (Appadurai, 1990), and "modern social imaginaries" (Taylor, 2004) highlight the *social* aspect of such imaginaries which bind individuals into a collective world in which they come to imagine, feel and experience the real together. For these thinkers, the imaginary is not the opposite of the real but *the condition of perceiving and experiencing it* (Dawney 2011). There is no embodied experience of the real without imagination. It can generate collective action and practice in reality and further transform it (Castoriadis, 1987).

Charles Taylor (1995; 2004; 2007) uses the concept of social imaginary to narrate the rise of Western modernity as the transition from the pre-modern imaginary where social agents' position is hierarchically allocated with transcendental meaning to the egalitarian modern one characterized by reciprocal interest pursuit and respect among equal individuals detached from any sacred order and/or transcendent being. Social imaginary is involved in how people recognize their whole circumstances by offering a broader grasp of order, time, and history in which people understand their existence and practice. Taylor illuminates its *normative* aspect as well as its cognitive one. By social imaginary, he refers to "the ways people imagine their social existence, how they fit together with others, how things go on between them and their fellows, *the expectations that are normally met*, and *the deeper normative notions and images that underlie these expectations* (Taylor 2004, p. 23)." As it accompanies "a widely shared sense of legitimacy (Ibid., p. 23)," social imaginary shapes people's immediate sensorial experience of the (un)just and thus a collectively shared moral judgment. It is a sense of *moral order* which "provides an imperative prescription" for the reality (Ibid., p. 7). Digital space in the 2012 Lady Gaga controversy opened up an opportunity to capture the formation and circulation of what I would call an *imperial* social imaginary where Korean society is imagined to lag far behind in the linear, universal, and singular timeline of world history because of the allegedly pre-modern presence of Evangelicals against the Lady Gaga concert.

Social imaginaries are expressed and carried through a variety of encounters with "images, stories, legends, and modes of address (Gaonkar 2002, p. 10)" – in fact, all of the things that the term media can stand for. And in the contemporary digital era, these images, texts, and audio-visuals carrying social imaginaries are constantly and multi-directionally mediated and circulated (Couldry 2008; Silverstone 2002). As Valaskivi and Sumiala (2014) concisely put, "society is held together (Latour 2005) by the social imaginaries (Taylor 2004) created and maintained through circulation (p. 231)."

Imperial Formations and Imaginaries on History

The question of how imperial projects have changed their ways of exercising power and maintaining hegemony, has brought to postcolonial scholarship viral discussions on empire without colonialism (Duara 2007; Stoler & McGranahan 2007), its making of a common sense understanding of reality (Coronil 2007; Dirks 1992; Said 1978), and imperial formations as an affective and intimate project (Stoler 2001; 2002). Unlike the terms of 'imperialism' and 'empire' that appear to be already fixed, materialized, and accomplished in their project, the concept of 'imperial formations' helps us focus more on the ongoing process of constructing, deconstructing, and reconstructing imperial power relations and realities. Stoler and McGranahan (2007) states,

> Empire may be "things," but imperial formations are not. Imperial formations are polities of dislocation, processes of dispersion, appropriation, and displacement. They are dependent both on moving categories and populations. Not least, they are dependent on material and discursive postponements and deferrals: "the civilizing missions," imperial guardianship, and manifest destiny are all promissory notes of transformations. (p. 8)

Imperial project is not confined to territorial boundaries. It involves cultural and social formations which construct a common sense of reality for people to receive what it *is* and *has to be*. Thinking of what Louis Althusser and Etienne Balibar (1971) call 'the concrete complex whole of social formation,' Stoler and McGranahan (2007) highlights that 'imperial formations' encompass not only economic, political, and ideological practices, which Althusser and Balibar illuminate as composing the social formation, but also cultural practices of producing epistemological claims and moving conceptual categories. Imperial projects involve moving not only populations but also categories of anything related to its project utilizing academics, international laws, policies, culture industry, education, transnational media, and last but not least celebrity culture to which the 2012 Lady Gaga controversy cannot be irrelevant.

It is noteworthy that "imperial projects are predicated on and produce epistemological claims that are powerful political ones (Ibid., p. 11)." And one of the most powerful epistemological claims in imperial projects is made regarding *history* (Chakrabarty 2000; Coronil 2007). In *Provincializing Europe* (p. 8), Chakrabarty demonstrates how non-European histories are marginalized and relegated to "an imaginary waiting room of history" which is predicated on the social imaginary of the singular and universal History in whose linear timeline we are "all headed to the same destination" though 'Europe' precedes other non-European countries (2000:8). Such imaginary of History with a capital H is "what made modernity or capitalism look not simply global but rather as something that became global *over time* (emphasis by the author), by originating in one place (Europe) and then spreading outside it (Ibid., p. 7). "In the 'first in Europe, then elsewhere' structure of global historical time," non-European histories are often imagined to be anachronic, outmoded, pre-modern, and inferior (Ibid., p. 8). This case study captures the 2012 Lady Gaga controversy as a fascinating scene where what I call imperial and teleological imaginary of the linear and universal History is mediated and circulated especially when Korean mainline liberal online media represent Evangelicals against Lady Gaga's concert in particular and Korean Protestantism in general as the uncivilized, pre-modern and dangerous Other to impede the complete modernization and civilization of Korean society.

Lady Gaga: An Evangelist of American-Style Liberal Imaginary?

Lady Gaga has particular issues that she wants to communicate with her fans all over the world through her music and fame. They include homosexuality, suicide, self-esteem, diversity, human rights and so on. She often ignites controversy on such issues and herself especially by provocatively appropriating religiously-sacred symbols in her artistic world (Turner 2011). To boldly contend, in her artistic world, religion, especially Christianity, tends to be dealt with as nothing but an empty form to convey her liberal message on issues such as homosexuality, self-esteem, and human freedom, to name a few. In her interview with *The Guardian'* on May 14th, 2011, she compares her tours to *religious experiences*, appropriating Christian rhetoric and imaginary.

> It [The show] is a religious experience. But it's more like a pop cultural church. . . . It's more self-worship, I think, not of me. I'm teaching people to worship themselves.
>
> I'm writing more about pop culture as religion, my identity as my religion: 'I will fight and bleed to the death for my identity.' I am my own sanctuary and I can be reborn as many times as I choose throughout my life.[2]

As a sincere Protestant believer submits one's volition to God's grace, Lady Gaga confesses that she "never intended for the Monster Ball to be a religious experience" and continues that "it just became one." She finds her show became a religious experience where her fans were encouraged to worship themselves, not God nor Lady Gaga. She considers her identity as her religion to "fight and bleed to the death." In this way, Christian symbols and imaginaries such as 'worship', 'being reborn', and 'martyrdom' are actively adopted, but only as an empty form to be filled by her secularist liberal values. The actual content to fill in them is not the Christian God any longer but the individualistic self who is praised as worthy of worship. She wants her fans to believe in and be dedicated to themselves as if one practices a religion. As vividly shown in the lyrics of her song Judas, she appropriates Christianity as a form that is style, rather than receiving it as the content to be preserved and handed down. In her artistic world, religion is often used as an empty form to convey a secular liberal social imaginary, in which the self who gets full autonomy no longer waits for the sanction of transcendental being on one's existence, practice, and meaning and thus the position of God is substituted for the self (Peters 1989; Kramnick 1990). And this provocative and intentional binding between the form of Christian symbols and the content of secular liberal imaginary makes religious people feel uncanny and raises controversy.

Such appropriation of religion as an empty form for the worship and prosperity of the self is not the unique story of Lady Gaga. Not surprisingly, it is also the story of the United States: its global expansion and legitimization as the imperial power. In *Migrations of the Holy* (2011), William Cavanaugh explores the two discourses of American exceptionalism which help the U.S. imagine itself as the Messianic nation: One is that America is exceptional because it is the chosen New Israel in the contemporary world history progressing under God's guidance.

---

[2] https://www.theguardian.com/musicmusic/2011/may/14/lady-gaga-interview, (accessed on March 18th, 2019)

The other is that America is exceptional because it is the first and most universal nation that accomplished the freedom of human will that is imagined to be fundamental to democracy and free markets.

If these two discourses are interwoven with each other, it is readily argued that the United States is "the vehicle that God has chosen to spread the gospel" and such evangelization is enabled only by the dissemination of *American-style liberalism*, that is believed to be "the empty form for evangelization (Ibid., p. 99)." The relationship between the form of American-style liberalism and the content of evangelization, however, is easily inverted. In the exercise of American exceptionalism, the ideology of American-style democracy and free market, which should be the vehicle/form for the content of evangelization, turns into the actual content that is spread and evangelized. America takes the position of the God that America is supposed to evangelize. And such inversion between God and America interestingly resembles what Lady Gaga evangelized during her 'Born This Way Ball' tour: *the self-worship*.

Media Representations of Korean Evangelicals against the Lady Gaga Concert

In the early phase of the 2012 Lady Gaga controversy, media coverage mostly focused on the tremendous impact of Lady Gaga on the economics and cultural politics of the countries in which her concert had been held. However, the media began to drastically shift its focus as the concert was rated to be harmful to teenagers by the Korean Media Rating Board on March 22nd and Hyundai Card decided to allow only those over 18 to attend the concert which was initially open to anyone over the age of 12 on March 30th, 2012. Mainline liberal online news media such as 'Pressian,' 'OhmyNews,' and 'Cine 21,' began to move their focus from Lady Gaga to the protest of Evangelicals against her concert. They raised questions and discussions on issues including censorship, freedom of expression, the hate speech, public presence of Korean Protestantism, and modernization of Korean society to name a few, producing columns and news articles even until June 2012.

A few columns published in the liberal online news media, represent the Evangelicals protesting against the Lady Gaga concert as the irrational and pre-modern Other whose presence is anachronic in Korean society. Han's 'Pressian' column titled *Is Christians' Slogan "Non-Believers in Hell" Freedom of Expression?*, for instance, highlights that Korean Protestantism has been in dominance society as a censoring power to threaten the freedom of expression in Korean society.[3] Han constructs the imaginary linear timeline of world civilization in which various cases of religious censorship and tolerance could be historicized, by listing from "the time of the ancient Rome" to "the Inquisition" and "witch trial" in the Medieval age, to the censorship of Islam in the modern age, to the intolerance of Christianity in the late-modern Western world. At the end of the linear and universal history of religious censorship, the columnist puts a historical memory – a form of social imaginary shared among Koreans – where Korean Protestantism fanatically opposed the public screening of *The Last Temptation of Christ and The Da Vinci Code*, for the reason of blasphemy in the recent past. It continues that Korean Protestantism "still did not learn a tolerance on the freedom yet." Then, the aggressive evangelism of Korean Protestantism is "dangerous as much as Islamic terrorism," the column asserts.

Although this might be a mere rhetorical emphasis, such association of the evangelism of Korean Protestantism with "Islam" and "terror" likely leads its readers to the recent global imaginaries and imageries of violent terrorist attacks on and after 9/11. Considering that Islam has been imagined and represented as one of the most fearful enemies of the West, liberalism, democracy, and modern civilization since the late-1970s (Said 1978, 1979,1981) and particularly in the post-9/11 era (el-Aswad 2013; Perigoe & Eid 2014), it likely prepares the readers for the sentiment of fear with moral judgment on Korean Protestantism especially in relation to the broader social imaginary of Korean society heading toward its further modernization, democratization, and liberalization. In addition, given that freedom of expression is considered in general as one of the core values of liberal democracy that is imagined to be universalized from the West to non-Western world, the column delineating Korean Protestantism as the unenlightened Other who "did not learn the tolerance on the freedom yet," successfully constructs Korean Protestantism as the obstacle to and the enemy of Korean society on its way to liberalization, democratization, and modernization.

Meanwhile, Kang's column from 'OhmyNews,' titled *The Secret of the Huge Success of the Lady Gaga Concert*, spends a quarter of the column comparing the aversion of Protestant churches to homosexuality with Hitler's persecution of homosexuals.[4] After mentioning an anonymous Protestant believer who said to him that, according to the old testament, the one who committed obscenity

---

[3] http://news.naver.com/main/read.nhn?mode=LSD&mid=sec&sid1=102&oid=002&aid=0001984126 (accessed on March 19th, 2019)

[4] http://news.naver.com/main/read.nhn?mode=LSD&mid=sec&sid1=103&oid=047&aid=0001999677 lastly accessed on March 19th, 2019.

should be stoned to death, Kang asks back why he does not pick up and throw a stone following the old testament. It reads:

> [The Protestant believer] said that according to the old testament, the one who committed obscenity should be stoned to death. If he believes that that's the duty of a believer, why does not he lift a stone and exercise the will of God? Although he did not use a stone, there was a man who practiced his faith in a similar way, who is Hitler. He . . . arrested tens of thousands of homosexuals and sent then to the gas chamber. Hitler was a Christian, cursing atheists.

His column leans more toward the construction of Korean Protestantism as the insane and irrational Other. Linking the hate speech of an anonymous Protestant believer with the mass persecution of homosexuals by Adolf Hitler, who was Christian, the column helps its readers identify Korean Protestantism with Hitler who is often imagined and narrated as the most insane dictator against, and the most powerful enemy of, humanity and reason in the history of civilization. In the comparison between the Protestant believer and Hitler, Korean Protestantism is overlaid with the traits of brutality, insanity, and dangerousness. It is imagined not merely as an obstacle to the further democratization and liberalization of Korean society, but as the potentially violent, dangerous Other whose latent brutality and insanity would be dangerous and disastrous for Korean society after all.

Korean Protestantism is imagined to be the ridiculous and inferior Other as well while being depicted by the words of "insanity," "comedy", and "premodern." The concepts of "insanity" and "comedy" to describe the Evangelicals' aversion to homosexuality accompany a sort of moral sentiment on how ridiculous and anachronic it is. Leesong's 'Cine 21' column titled *Who Calls South Korea Modern* reads:

> Who calls South Korea modern? *Bernardino*'s ghost being called out of the Middle Ages wanders everywhere. If the ridiculous season of the Middle Ages where comedy and insanity intersected with each other does not cease, modernity and democracy are just distant. If there is only one that can lay the wandering Ghost to rest in a coffin, it is reason with its eyes wide open.

Noting that the legacy of Western Medieval Christianity, demonized homosexuals and the Jewish in the name of God, remains in Korean society where "conservative Protestantism insanely abhors homosexuality," Leesong argues that modernity and democracy are distant from Korean society. And interestingly their distance is imagined as far as the historical one between the Middle Ages and the contemporary modern era.

It is noteworthy how the column draws on and perpetuates the *transition* narrative on History in whose allegedly singular, linear and universal timeline Korean society is imagined to remain at the pre-modern stage of the Middle Age.

In the universal historical timeline that such transition narrative assumes, we are "all headed for the same destination" of modernity and democracy where Europeans "arrive earlier than others (Chakrabarty p. 8)". In this way, the column makes modernity and democracy "look not simply global but rather as something that became global *over time* (emphasis by the author), by originating in one place (Europe) and then spreading outside it (Ibid., p. 7)". In the narrative of historical transition that is predicated on the "'first in Europe, then elsewhere' structure of global historical time (Ibid., p. 8)", not only Korean Protestantism is imagined to be the inferior and pre-modern Other impeding the complete modernization of Korean society, but also what could be called the imperial social imaginary of the linear and universal History is thickened, naturalized and perpetuated.

The questions of how stereotyped images and differences of marginalized groups, marked by race, gender, class and/or ethnicity to name a few, are perpetuated by the media and how such representations of marginalized groups contribute to the reproduction of the existing social order, have been central to the scholarship of media and cultural studies (e.g. Hall 1992, Hall et al, 1978; Nakayama 1988; Said 1978, 1979, 1981; Shaheen 2001; el-Aswad 2013; Perigoe & Eid 2014). Given the 2012 Lady Gaga controversy that shows the interplay between the media and religion, the series of Said's works (1978; 1979; 1981) problematizing the representations of Arabs, Muslims, and the Islamic world, are very relevant and noteworthy. In *Covering Islam* (1981), for instance, Said explores how the Western media produces untruth about Islam by portraying Arabs, Muslims and the Islamic world as the outmoded, violent and dangerous Other in the name of objectivity, freedom, human rights, liberalism, and modernity. Muslims are portrayed, constructed and categorized as the Other to threaten and endanger Western democracy, liberalism, and modernity, all of which are imagined and believed to be the most convincing path to the progress of universal human history. And what makes the 2012 Lady Gaga controversy fascinating is a few scenes where such imagery of the aggressive, uncivilized and dangerous Other who threatens liberal democracy and modernity, comes to be projected toward Korean Protestantism.

This relatively new imaginary on Korean Protestantism, which was being circulated and thickened in the controversy, is noteworthy especially considering that Korean Protestantism has been in general imagined and expected to be the media to and embodiment of Western modernity and civilization in Korean society since the late 19th century (Jang 1999; Lee 2000). The establishment of the modern nation-state was imagined and discussed revolving around Protestant discourse on civilization in early modern Korea (Kim 2002). A sense that Protestantism is essential to the civilization, modernization, and independence of Korea, was commonly shared not only by Protestant believers but also by intellectuals, political elites, and ordinary people at that time (Cho 2006; Jang 1999; Kim 2011; Lee 2000). The Protestant discourse on civilization and modernity helped Korean Protestantism proclaim itself as the sole genuine 'modern' religion that is distinguished from shamanism and traditional folk religions such as Buddhism and Confucianism. And under the enormous influence of the Protestant discourse on modernity, shamanism and superstition became a target to eradicate to transform Korea into a genuine modern nation-state not only in the Japanese colonial regime but also in the Park Jung-Hee's dictatorial regime of the 1960s and 1970s (Jeong 2012; Lee 2005). In this way, early modern Protestant discourses surrounding civilization, modern nation-state, and modern religion have considerably affected and structured social imaginaries on the relationship between modern nation-state and religion, between civilization and Protestantism, and between modernity and tradition/shamanism in Korean society. And the 2012 Lady Gaga controversy generated a few fascinating scenes where such close affinity between modernity and Protestantism in the Korean social imaginary could be significantly twisted and even destructed.

Such scene to make the imagined affinity between modernity and Protestantism doubtful, was captured at an Evangelical prayer meeting where around 30 believers prayed for the cancellation of the Lady Gaga concert at Sinchon Beautiful Church in Seoul in April 22nd. The photographs of praying believers, taken by the Associated Press, were massively circulated not only by Korean online news media, major portal sites, and social networks services such Facebook and Twitter but also by international online news media such as Reuters, BuzzFeed, and Liberation.[5] And interestingly most of the pictures taken in the prayer meeting concentrate on presenting particular moments of the Evangelicals closing their eyes, raising their hands, and loudly yelling out in a seemingly fanatical atmosphere (see Figures 1–4).

The photographs primarily focus on the Evangelicals who appear to be completely caught by 'collective effervescence (Durkheim 1961)' or a supernatural world that a secular person would not be able to comprehend. The Evangelicals look incomprehensible, out of control, and even more or less dangerous. For those critical of the Evangelicals against the Lady Gaga concert, the photographs could be seen as a self-evident proof that demonstrates the irrationality of the Evangelicals' pray for the cancellation of the concert and thus any further explanation and investigation seem unnecessary. For them, it would be unlikely

---

[5] For instance, http://next.liberation.fr/musique/2012/04/23/que-les-foudres-de-l-enfer-s-abattent-sur-lady-gaga_813724, https://www.buzzfeed.com/mjs538/south-korean-christians-praying-against-lady-gaga?utm_term=.khjp3Evap#.stGq1apEq, http://in.reuters.com/article/ladygaga-korea-idINDEE83Q07Q20120427 (all accessed on March 19th, 2019)

Digital Media and Imperial Formations — 171

Figure 1: Korean Evangelicals depicted in ecstatic prayer.

Figure 2: Korean Evangelicals depicted in ecstatic prayer.

noted that a photograph inevitably captures only a particular moment of a continuing event which could be narrativized with many other serial moments in time. Nor would it be likely noted that the photographic images posted in the news articles, were *selectively* chosen among many others which could capture different moments when the Evangelicals do not look that irrational. In this regard, such photographs produce effects of truth transforming particular *historical*

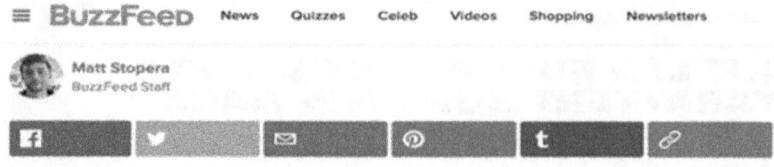

Figure 3: Korean Evangelicals depicted in ecstatic prayer.

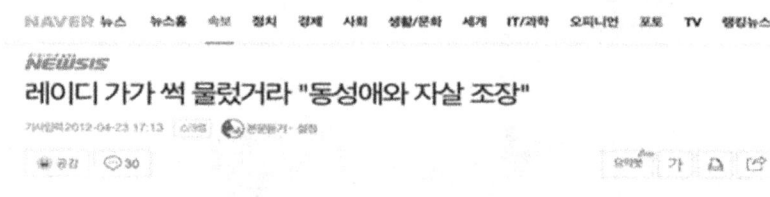

Figure 4: Korean Evangelicals depicted in ecstatic prayer.

moments of the prayer meeting into *the moment of ahistorical truth* that is claimed to reveal the intrinsic nature of the Evangelicals and Korean Protestantism.

To sum up, the columns that identify the protest of Evangelicals against the Lady Gaga concert with 'Islamic terrorism' and 'Hitler' who persecuted homosexuals, attempt to represent Korean Protestantism as the uncivilized, irrational and dangerous Other. And the discursive construction of Korean Protestantism as the uncivilized Other is likely essentialized, thickened, and perpetuated by the photographic representations, selectively chosen among others, that focus on the Evangelicals closing their eyes, raising their hand and yelling out in the seemingly fanatical atmosphere of the prayer meeting. Noteworthily, such representation of Korean Protestantism as the pre-modern Other is predicated on the imperial social imaginary of the singular and universal History in whose linear timeline we are "all headed to the same destination" of modernity which Europe arrived earlier than others (Chakrabarty , 2000, p.8). The 2012 Lady Gaga controversy generates a few fascinating scenes of *imperial formations* (Stoler & McGranahan, 2007) that are predicated on and produce powerful epistemological claims regarding history (Chakrabarty 2000; Coronil 2007). In what could be called the imperial and teleological social imaginary of the universal History where Korean society is imagined to lag way behind because of the presence of Korean Protestantism which allegedly impedes its complete modernization and civilization.

Korean and/or Imperial Citizen?

One of the most interesting scenes in the controversy is captured when several Koreans comment on the US online news articles that cover the protests of the Evangelicals against the Lady Gaga concert. Some express a deep aversion of the Evangelicals, which is a form of self-hatred, given that the commenters identify themselves as Korean or specifically Korean Christian while denouncing and othering the Evangelicals as 'doggy Christian' that is a pejorative term for Christianity in Korean society.[6] One commenter criticizes Korean society in favor of liberal values discussing a few liberal issues relevant to the Lady Gaga controversy, such as censorship and the lack of freedom of expression in Korean society.[7] Another commenter even points out Korean society's "hypocrisy" of "blaming Lady Gaga" arguing that it still shows "the highest income gap between men and women in the industrialized world and the highest per capita prostitution in the OECD."

It is noteworthy how the commenters feel ashamed of the Evangelicals or their mother country South Korea in the comment sections of the U.S. online news

Jae Beom Lim

That kind of people so called doggychristian. even I'm korean, I'm fuckin hate them.

Like · Reply · 👍 1 · Apr 23, 2012 1:51pm

Figure 5[6]

Jay Jongkyung Lee · Seoul, South Korea

that kind of people so called doggychristian. I'm the one of kor christian but I'm fuckin hate them.

Like · Reply · 👍 4 · Apr 23, 2012 1:24pm

Figure 6[7]

TK Sung · Seoul, Korea

Add "mechanical" to "arbitrary and capricious", you have Korean Media Ratings Board and the Ministry of Women and Family. They'd ban any song that includes the word "alcohol" or "tobacco". But "Soju" is ok while "beer" is not. Freedom of expression is still a foreign concept here, and censorship dating back to days of the military dictators had been resurrected under Lee Myeong-bak whose had been snooping on private citizens who are against his regime.

April 12, 2012 at 7:00 a.m. · RECOMMENDED 👍 2

Figure 7[8]

media. Separating themselves from the Evangelicals (e.g. "I am fucking hate them") and even Koreans (e.g. "Look at yourselves"), the commenters feel ashamed of and embarrassed by them in front of the imagined commenters and readers of the U.S. news media. A fascinating scene is revealed where the commenters appear to categorize the Evangelicals and Korean society as the inferior Other while identifying themselves more with those in the U. S. who are imagined to not only support liberal

---

6 http://www.buzzfeed.com/mjs538/south-korean-christians-praying-against-lady-gaga (accessed on August 30th, 2016)

7 http://www.buzzfeed.com/mjs538/south-korean-christians-praying-against-lady-gaga (accessed on August 30th, 2016)

8 http://rendezvous.blogs.nytimes.com/2012/04/11/little-monsters-in-south-korea-are-not-amused, (accessed on March 20th, 2019)

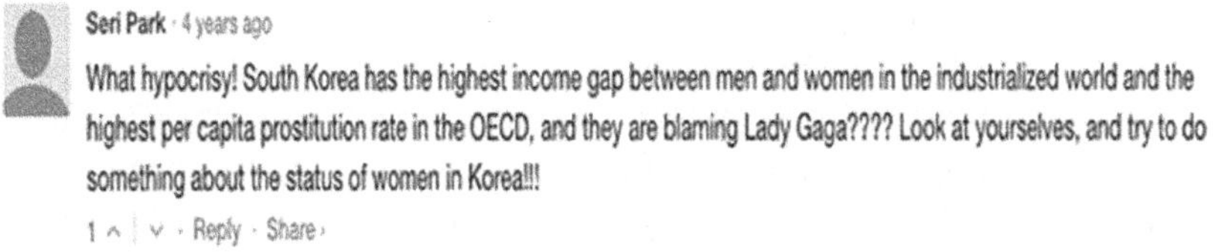

Seri Park · 4 years ago
What hypocrisy! South Korea has the highest income gap between men and women in the industrialized world and the highest per capita prostitution rate in the OECD, and they are blaming Lady Gaga???? Look at yourselves, and try to do something about the status of women in Korea!!!
1 ∧ | ∨ · Reply · Share ›

Figure 8[9]

values but also likely achieve them earlier. There emerge what could be called imperial citizens who feel an affinity more toward the imagined citizens of the U.S. in the favor of liberal values while being embarrassed or even disgusted by their own ethnic group being Korean.

Conclusion

The 2012 Lady Gaga controversy revealed the latent conflict between Korean Protestantism, which have increasingly taken a fundamentalist approach to the overall crisis of their religious meaning, authenticity and authority are grounded in a transcendental being, and pub in conflict with a secular modern society in which no ground of legitimacy for its politics and governance is rooted in such transcendental being beyond loosely shared agreements of people (Taylor, 2004). While liberal online news media in Korean society successfully represented the Evangelicals protesting against Lady Gaga's concert as the insane, anachronistic and uncivilized Other, Korean Protestantism failed to produce counter-representations of itself especially in digital space where the representations of the Evangelicals as the uncivilized Other were being significantly produced and circulated. After all, the controversy generated as well a few interesting scenes of what could be called *imperial formations* (Stoler and McGranahan 2007) that produced, and were predicated on the imperial social imaginary of the singular and universal timeline of historical transition in and through which Korean society was imagined to fall behind because of Korean Protestantism. In the imperial imaginary, Korean Protestantism was imagined to be the irrational, inferior, and dangerous Other who had endangered and threatened the complete modernization and civilization of Korean society.

---

9 http://www.washingtontimes.com/news/2012/apr/22/taking-names-lady-gaga-arrives-in-south-korea/?page=all (accessed March 20th, 2019)

New media environment involved not only Korean and international liberal online news media but also ordinary Korean digital media users in the imperial formations. With their active searching for and commenting on the US online news articles covering the controversy, the Koreans felt an affinity and identified themselves more with the commenters and readers of the U.S. online news media while othering the Evangelicals and Korean society. In favor of liberal values whose substantial achievement is often imagined to be one of the crucial indicators of civilization and modernization , some Korean commenters go beyond merely denouncing the Evangelicals as an obstacle to them. They even feel ashamed of Korean society mainly highlighting its failure to achieve the liberal values including freedom of expression and gender equality.

In this regard, digital media-related practices such as *searching, commenting on,* and *sharing* online news articles, contributed to the constructing, mediating, and circulating of what could be called *imperial* social imaginaries in the controversy (See Couldry 2012 regarding digital media -related practices of searching, commenting on, and sharing). In the hyper-connected digital spaces of Korean society, the practices of searching for, commenting on, and sharing of the online news articles that represent the Evangelicals and Korean Protestantism as the pre-modern Other, cannot be irrelevant to the mediating, circulating and thickening of the social imaginary that makes the presence of the Evangelicals felt as anachronistic, uncivilized, inferior, and even dangerous. With the analysis of how Korean and International online news media represented the Evangelicals and Korean Protestantism, this case study argues that such imaginary of Korean Protestantism being irrational and pre-modern is predicated on the teleological and imperial social imaginary of the singular, linear and universal History.

What is revealed regarding the digital spaces that mediate the 2012 Lady Gaga controversy, demonstrates the need for a careful analysis of the cultural politics of the social space where digital media is actually used. Digital media use in non-Western societies has been narrativized, to a great extent, in terms of how it contributes to democratization, liberalization and political revolution. And in such 'new media resistance' narrative the simplified idea of resistance is conventionally associated with digital media use of non-Western societies, while not showing a proper and careful interest in exactly to which social order(s) among others digital media use resists and, in reverse, to which social order(s)' hegemonic formation it contributes. The scrutiny of the cultural politics surrounding the 2012 Lady Gaga controversy illuminates that the digital media use by liberal journalism and some Korean commenters contributed not only to a liberal resistance to the traditional heterosexual moral order prevalent in Korean Protestantism but also to the mediating, circulating, and thickening of the imperial social imaginary of the universal History in whose linear timeline of transition Korean society is imagined to remain at the pre-modern stage which Europe already passed through.

What this case study demonstrates, however, is not merely an urgent need for the careful analysis of the cultural politics of the social world in which digital media is used and new media-related practices are exercised. It also raises a question of if and how terms such as democratization, modernization, and liberalization, easily associated with digital media use, are closely interwoven with the imperial and teleological social imaginary of the linear and universal History in whose singular timeline 'Europe' always and already precedes other non-European countries (Chakrabarty 2000; Stoler & McGranahan 2007; Taylor 2004). In other words, there is a subtle resonance between the received understanding of these terms and the social imaginary of the linear and universal History, whose mediation and circulation, during the 2012 Lady Gaga controversy, Korean and international liberal online media significantly contributed to.

Reminding of the significance of the imaginary to the (re)production of particular social reality and that of media technology and media-related practice to the mediation and circulation of such imaginaries, this case study illuminates a necessity to examine what social imaginaries are formed and thickened when journalists and/or intellectuals employ particular concepts and categories to explain the relationship between new digital media and social change. In this way, this case study shows how imperial formations can be predicated on the producing, mediating, and circulating of particular social imaginaries about religious subject and history especially by means of new digital media in the South Korean context.

Bibliography

Althusser L, Baliba E. *Reading capital*. New York: Pantheon Books, 1971.
Anderson B. *Imagined communities*. London: Verso, 1983.
Appadurai A. Topographies of self. In: Lutz CA, Abu-LughodLE, editors. *Language and the politics of emotion*. Cambridge: Cambridge University Press, 1990:92–112.
Appadurai A. *Modernity at large*. Minneapolis, Minnesota: University of Minnesota Press, 1996.
Castoriadis C. *The imaginary institution of society*. Cambridge, MA: MIT Press, 1987.
Cavanaugh WT.*Migrations of the holy*. Grand Rapids, MI: William B. Eerdmans Pub, 2011.
Chakrabarty D.*Provincializing Europe*. Princeton, NJ: Princeton University Press, 2000.
Chen W, Boase J, Wellman B. The global villagers. In: Wellman B, Haythornthwaite C, editors. The Internet in everyday life. Oxford: Blackwell, 2002: 74–113.
Cho ST. Kŭndae pulgyohak kwa han'guk kŭndae pulgyo [Modern Buddhist scholarship and modern Korean Buddhism]. Minjok munhwa yŏn'gu 2006; 45: 77–109.

Coronil F. After empire. In: Stoler AL, McGranahan C, Perdue P, editors. Imperial formations. Santa Fe: SAR Press, 2007: 241–271.
Couldry N. Theorising media as practice, Social Semiotics 2004; 14(2):115–132.
Couldry N. Mediatization or mediation? Alternative understandings of the emergent space of digital storytelling. New Media & Society 2008; 10(3): 373–391.
Couldry N. Media, society, world. Cambridge: Polity, 2012.
Daura P. The imperialism of free nations: Japan, Manchukuo, and the history of the present. . In: Stoler AL, McGranahan C, Perdue P, editors. Imperial formations. Santa Fe: SAR Press, 2007: 211–239.
Dawney L. Social imaginaries and therapeutic self-work. The Sociological Review 2011; 59(3): 535–552.
Dirks NB. Colonialism and culture. Ann Arbor: University of Michigan Press, 1992.
Durkheim, E. The elementary forms of the religious life. New York: Collier Books, 1961.
El-Aswad ES. Images of Muslims in Western scholarship and media after 9/11. Domes: digest of Middle East studies 2013; 22: 39–56.
Gaonkar D. Toward new imaginaries. Public Culture 2002; 14(1): 1–19.
Gatens M., Lloyd G. Collective imaginings. London: Routledge, 1999.
Hall S. Notes on deconstructing "the popular." In: Samuel R. editor. People's History and Socialist Theory. London: Routledge and Kegan Paul, 1981: 227–241.
Hall S. The rediscovery of "ideology." In: Gurevitch M, Bennett T., Curran, J, Woollacott J., editors. Culture, society and the media. London: Methuen, 1982: 56–90.
Hall S. The questions of cultural identity. In: Hall S., Held D., McGrew A., editors. Modernity and its futures. Cambridge: Polity Press, 1992: 274–316.
Hall S., Critcher C., Jefferson T., Clarke J., Roberts B. Policing the crisis. London: MacMillan, 1978.
Hoover S, Echchaibi N, editors. The third spaces of digital religion. The Pennsylvania State University Press, Forthcoming.
Hoover S, Kim SS. A Protestant vision of digital media. In: Hoover S, Echchaibi N, editors. The third spaces of digital religion. The Pennsylvania State University Press, Forthcoming.
Jang SM. Kŭntaemunmyŏng-ilanŭn ilŭmŭi kaesinkyo [Protestantism identified with modern civilization]. Yŏksapip'yŏng 1999; 46: 255–268.
Jeong YJ. Pakchŏnghŭi chŏngpuki munhwachaechŏngch'aekkwa minsoksinang [Policy of cultural assets and folk beliefs in the period of Park Jung-Hee]. Yŏksaminsokhakhoe 2012; 39: 175–213.
Kim HJ. (2002) Sikminchi sitaewa munmyŏng-munhwaŭi inyŏm [The ideology of civilization and culture in the colonial age]. Minchokmunhaksayŏnku 2002; 19(20): 91–117.
Kim SH. Hankuk kŭntaesaŭi chŏnkaewa pulkyo [Buddhism and the modern history of Korea]. Pulkyohakpo 2011; 60: 263–289.
Kramnick I. Republicanism and bourgeois radicalism. Ithaca, NY: Cornell University Press, 1990.
Latour B. Reassembling the social an introduction to actor-network-theory. Oxford: Oxford University Press, 2005.
Lee JK. kŭntae hankuk kitokkyowa pulkyoŭi sanghoinsik [Mutual recognition of Protestantism and Buddhism in modern Korea]. Hankuk kitokkyo yŏksayŏnkuso sosik 2000; 2: 145–164.
Lee YB. Musoke taehan kŭntae hankuksahoeŭi puchŏngchŏk sikake taehan koch'al [An examination on the negative viewpoint on the Korean shamanism in modern Korea]. Hankukmusokhak 2005; 9:151–179.

Nakayama T. "Model minority" and the media. Journal of Communication Inquiry 1988; 12(1): 65–73.
Perigoe R, Eid M. Mission invisible. Vancouver: UBC Press, 2014.
Peters JD. John Locke, the individual, and the origin of communication. Quarterly Journal of Speech 1989; 75: 387–399.
Said E. Orientalism. New York: Vintage, 1978.
Said E. The question of Palestine. New York: Vintage, 1979.
Said E. Covering Islam. New York: Vintage, 1981.
Shaheen JG. Introduction. In: Shaheen JG, Greider W, editors. Reel bad Arabs. Northhampton, MA: Olive Branch Press, 2001: 1–37.
Silverstone R. Complicity and collusion in the mediation of everyday life. New Literary History 2002; 33(5): 745–764.
Stoler AL. Tense and tender ties. The Journal of American History 2001; 88(3): 829–865.
Stoler AL. Carnal knowledge and imperial power. Berkeley: University of California Press, 2002.
Stoler AL, McGranahan C. Introduction. In: Stoler AL, McGranahan C, Perdue P, editors. Imperial formations. Santa Fe: SAR Press, 2007: 3–47.
Taylor C. Two theories of modernity. The Hastings Center Report 1995; 25(2): 24–33.
Taylor C. Modern social imaginaries. Durham, NC: Duke University Press, 2004.
Taylor C. (2007). A Secular Age. Cambridge, MA: Harvard University Press.
Turner F. Lada Gaga and the civil religion. Soc 2011; 48:495–7.
Valaskivi K, Sumiala J. Circulating social imaginaries. European Journal of Cultural Studies 2014; 17(3): 229–243.

Stewart M. Hoover and J. Kwabena Asamoah-Gyadu
Media Curation and Re-emergent Religion in Ghana's Roadside Public Sphere

Much has been written about the religious culture of Ghana. Well-placed both historically and geographically, it has provided a valuable field of research on contemporary African religion, on African religious history, and more recently on new and emergent forms of mediated religion. Ghana shares much with its West African neighbours. Its colonial history is one of the oldest, though, with early Portuguese explorations and exploitations finding their way to its coast very early in the so-called "age of exploration." As a result, today it boasts the oldest extant European building in sub-Saharan Africa (Elmina Castle) and is rapidly becoming a destination for educational tourism focused on Africa's colonial and slave histories.

Its religious history is also notable. Like much of West Africa, the imported and imposed religions of the colonial era confronted and contested a deep and vibrant religious culture. What we today call "African Traditional Religion" (ATR) was and is in fact a complex and layered network of practices, histories, practitioners, symbols, and resources. Treated as a monolith by Catholic and later Protestant missionaries, ATR was coded and treated as very deeply an "other" to the preferred religious histories, doctrines, and sensibilities of the European faiths. African traditions were derogated and sometimes even suppressed by violent and nonviolent means. Contemporary historians of African religion identify a deeply ironic dimension of these traditions. In comparison with other traditions encountered in the global South by the early explorers, traditional Ghanaian religiosity was and is deeply monotheistic in the sense that there is a single spirit at the center of things, with various religious practices, spirits, rituals, and saints acting as a circulation of pathways to that central meaning (Opoku 1978). Its range of locations, rituals, meanings and practitioners are all seen to circulate within a broad effort to define and locate one's life and experience in relation to that reality.

That there could be said to be one "God" at the center of religious practice made for an easier syncretism between the traditional and the colonial religions, at least in conceptual and linguistic terms. Two of the colonial religious traditions, Islam and Christianity, found a foothold in Ghana as in the rest of West Africa, though through different paths and by different means. Islam, which is more present in the north of the country, was carried to Ghana largely through the Saharan trade routes. Christianity came by sea and by land, traveling down the Coast from the West, according to received histories (Debrunner 1967). What elements of ATR they could not coopt or incorporate, both Christian and Muslim religious authorities have attempted to compartmentalize and control through processes of "othering," differentiation, and derogation. Ghanaian Christianity has inherited from traditional religion a healthy and vibrant belief in the materiality and reality of "the spiritual," and this belief has been in part instantiated and expressed through an active discourse which divides the world between those spiritualisms that are acceptable and those which are not (some of this materiality came from Catholicism; the offer of the Mass in Latin meant people did not understand much of what was being said so piety was expressed through possession and use of religious icons). The spirits of African Traditional Religion have been defined as decidedly not acceptable, while at the same time their power and importance has been emphasized. What has resulted is a generalized public acceptance of the power and importance of the religious practices of the traditional seers and healers of ATR but at the same time a fear or suspicion of them.

The dominant religious culture of Ghana for most of the 20th Century, then, saw a large and central public place for the descendants of the missional churches. The Protestant denominations, Catholicism, and Islam each found ways of drawing a bright line between themselves and the "other" of ATR. The global rise of the Neo-Pentecostal movement has found footing in Ghana (as in many other places) and has introduced some new dynamics into the religious public sphere in the country. One dimension of this has been a new emphasis among these churches on the challenges and dangers of a spiritual geography that also includes ATR. To a greater extent than the earlier missional bodies, Pentecostals have identified ATR practices, practitioners, and material artefacts as a direct threat or danger to society and to individual souls.

The rise of Pentecostalism in Ghana has become the latest wave of its religious evolution, settling yet another layer on the nation's religious geography. These churches have grown rapidly in the past two decades, and their presence in the religious public sphere has changed the nature and sensibility of religion in Ghana (Asamoah-Gyadu 2005a, 2013). While it might be assumed that these groups are the result of a horizontal, global spread of Pentecostalism, it can be argued that they also have deep roots in the African context. They have a foot in the Christian missional history of the region, of course. But they are also rooted in modes of materiality and practice that carry the signature of the context and its traditional religions. The singular characteristic of these movements is the notion of "possession" (Lehman 2001). Adherents are convinced that it is not enough to simply believe, to seize a religion. One must also be seized by their faith, a conceptual and behavior materiality that imagines the world very much in African terms. To these traditions, the objects and geographies that surround lived experience are "alive" and Pentecostal possession invests faith with that sense of aliveness.

In fact, it has been argued that the Pentecostal resurgence in Africa (and perhaps elsewhere) evidences a moment when Christianity has become African, at the same time that the developed West has become more "Post-Christian" (Sanneh 2003: 10). There are other characteristics of the Pentecostal surge in West Africa, as well, ones that give it a larger and more far-reaching significance. Most importantly, perhaps, these churches and movements arise in a context of modern mass-mediation, something that most of them have seized with great energy. Pentecostalism is not either resistant to markets or to the notion that religion might be understood in market terms. The religious market of contemporary Ghana is both an economic and a cultural market. Both these valences of market are, of course, deeply connected with and derive from a sense of religiosity as something deeply material in its conception, practice, and circulation. Their mediation, and their presence in, and embrace of, the market concept places these movements at the center of Ghanaian public culture with a particular – and particularly meaningful – set of claims. Among these claims is the implicit idea that, as prominent constituents of the Ghanaian public sphere, these religions are the logical embodiments of aspiration to participation in modern neoliberal markets and neoliberal globalization. By their mediation and their prominence, they are coded as "modern," and as "sophisticated," and as "influential." Their prominence has further given them important purchase in the Ghanaian political sphere, with prominent politicians now needing to be seen to take them seriously.

In these ways, the emergent Pentecostal presence in the Ghanaian public sphere resembles the rise of Pentecostalism in Asia and in Latin America. Its publicness and its mediation in these settings are important, even defining characteristics. This is not to say that there is much that is not unique about the West African context of Pentecostalism and of emergent Christianity. Much has been written about the Ghanaian case (for example, Gifford 2004; Goldstone 2012; Meyer 2002, 2005)

But it is the presence of religion, and of what in Latin America is called "mediatic religion" in the public sphere that is of most interest here. Ghana's history of religious mediation stretches back several decades, but experienced new momentum with changes in broadcast regulation in the 1990s. Before that time, religion on television was controlled by the state broadcaster, the Ghana Broadcasting Corporation, or GBC. After that time, a modest proliferation of television channels, the introduction of satellite and cable television and the increasing commercialization of television, opened the way for broadcasts by independent churches and ministries (de Witt 2008, 2011).

This new media-derived presence of religion in Ghanaian public life accompanied an increasing orientation to markets, advertising, and public relations in the public sphere. Religion became more prominent and individual religious movements and groups became more differentiated and relativized,[1] leading these ministries to increase their efforts, and to an increasingly vibrant public and visual culture of religion. As in other contexts, much of this public sphere is present on television and radio, but in Ghana it is also present at the roadside and streetside.

Mediatic Religion in Ghana

What has emerged as Ghana's religious media culture has some specific outlines and characteristics. It is largely Christian, owing to its history. In the years when television in Ghana was controlled by the state broadcaster, the Ghana Broadcasting Corporation, the established main churches had preferential access to air time. The end of the state monopoly over television coincided with the rise of the new independent charismatic and neo-Pentecostal churches. High-profile appearances on television by evangelical and Pentecostal leaders, many of them from outside Ghana, introduced the notion of the power of television as a tool for evangelical and Pentecostal practice, as did widespread discussion of the rise of "Televangelism" in contexts like the United States. Emergent Pentecostal leaders in Ghana thus came to assume that television could be one of the important contexts for their ministries. Television was also an open context for the particular modes of practice of these ministries, with their emphasis on visual, spectacular, and material expressions of faith and witness. The television "marketplace" has thus become a context of visual and material exchange, discourse, and competition between rival ministries, churches, and efforts.

The earlier public broadcasting era and today's wider marketplace of televisual religion are both then dominated by Christianity, with other religions and movements struggling to find access to time and attention, as are the traditional mainline Protestant and Catholic churches. While they once were nearly the sole provider of religion on television, today they must compete from a position of much less power and influence. The new, competitive, and largely commercial media marketplace of Ghana favors those who can afford to buy air time or

---

[1] These twin tendencies to religious differentiation and relativization can be argued to be nearly universal forces in struggles over contemporary religious authority. For a more complete discussion, see Hoover, 2016, Introduction.

who can achieve support through advertising. This almost by definition means that the new, growing, Pentecostal "megachurches" are the ones that will dominate the airwaves. And they do. At the time of a study by de Witte (2012), there were thirty different television programs on the air weekly in Ghana, filling 22 hours of airtime. In addition to these, prominent foreign broadcasts such as Pat Robertson's *700 Club* and the *Eternal Word Television Network* (an American Catholic broadcast) are aired.

This means that Christian religious television in Ghana occupies the same central place in broadcasting that Christianity does in radio and in the mediated public sphere more generally. Christianity, particularly the new Pentecostal Christianity, is rapidly becoming the public Religion of Ghana, and other traditions lose out. Among these are, of course, the non-Pentecostal churches, including the formerly-missional Catholic and mainline bodies, older Protestant groups, and of course the "new religions" of Buddhism, Hinduism, Sikkhism, and Sufism. There is some presence in television and the public sphere of Islam, of course, but there are many fewer Muslim programs and most of those that do air are very traditional in genre and format.[2] They are very unlike the more modern, globally-linked, sophisticated Pentecostal programs. Also very much missing, of course, is African Traditional Religion, which until recently has almost entirely lacked a presence in mediatic culture (on-air or along the roadside) in Ghana (de Witte 2013).

This mediatic Pentecostalism shares much in common with its emergence in the mediated public spheres elsewhere in the world, most notably in Asia and Latin America. Its broadcasts are colorful, lively, technically-sophisticated and to an extent daring and experimental while at the same time borrowing heavily from formats and genres in commercial television and earlier waves of global televangelism. Importantly, we would argue, they are significant as well for their "materiality," their very material way of imagining and representing faith and the fruits of faith. It is one of the compelling developments of contemporary religious cultures that the very materiality and visuality of Pentecostal practice, its spectacle and its conventions of presentation and framing, make for particularly good "media," and are comfortably articulated into mediatic cultures (again, broadcast as well as roadside, as well as – increasingly – online) that are themselves material and convinced that their field of activity is naturally a "market."

---

[2] An important emerging exception are programs of the Ahmadiyya movement that have adopted a more charismatic style of preaching featuring a single presenter speaking in English and gesturing like a modern Pentecostal pastor.

Thus, mediatic religious culture in Ghana is one that has been largely Christian and is increasingly Pentecostal and Charismatic, and is a dynamic context for the increase and spread of Pentecostal Christianity (Meyer, 2002). The dimensions of this culture we have discussed: 1) its Christianity and historic grounding in Christianity; 2) its structural and genre materiality and orientation to the visual and to spectacle; and 3) its construction of public religion as in important ways a "market" with all that can mean for practice; define a kind of new baseline for the religious public culture of Ghana, though of course, other movements, impulses, discourses, institutions, and practices endure and persist. It is just that now, increasingly, these others must see themselves in relation to this public material culture of display. In this "market," there will then be winners and losers, those who can accommodate to these new demands, and those who are unable to.

Not surprisingly, one of the significant barriers to entry in such markets is financial. The traditional mainline churches, in particular, find it hard to compete. Catholic Bishops and Muslim Imams and fraternal councils must likewise carefully consider the implications of entering the fray at the center of mediatic religious cultures such as Ghana's. There is also the factor of preferred content. The historic Catholic and Protestant churches, when they have purchased airtime, have preferred to present programs reflective of denominational interests and identities rather than a popularized message with a wide appeal to broad publics.

As even newer forms of media emerge in Ghana in coming years, it seems likely that some of these logics of the public religious marketplace will endure. The new digital and social media, as they have emerged in other contexts and as they have emerged among certain class and income locations in Ghana, have only served to enhance these tendencies toward increasingly material, visual, sensational, and market-oriented practice.

Extents of the Mediatic Religious Public Sphere

We would like to point in a slightly different direction, however: toward some contexts and consequences where other mediatic market practices and mechanisms come into play. Ghana remains a powerfully visual culture, and a culture where materiality and visuality have always played important roles in cultural, social, religious, and economic processes. Travellers to Ghana never fail to be surprised by its roadside visuality. No stretch of lane, street, or highway of any significance is without signs. These are on one level mere advertising. But on quite another level they constitute part of the outline or fabric of Ghana's public sphere, something it shares in common with other West African Countries (Ukah 2008; See also Asamoah-Gyadu 2005b). For generations, these signs have been produced by a cadre of artisans/craftsmen, independent entrepreneurs who work on commission producing them (Meyer 2008). Called "roadside artists," or "street artists," or "sign artists," their shops are ubiquitous across the country. Typically standing near an intersection or at the edge of town but near enough the business district to be noticed, they set up small stands to display examples of their work (Figure 1). These displays usually focus more on contemporary religious (megachurch pastors Mensa Otabil and Duncan Williams are widely depicted) cultural or sports figures, while the majority of their work is in the creation of commercial signs.

Figure 1: A roadside studio.

Their commercial signs are what most travelers notice. Highly visual and representational, naïve in comparison to global standards of commercial culture, they remain a commonplace fabric of Ghanaian visual public culture (Figure 2). Typical of the traditional and naïve form is the Cold Store sign, an example of which is in Figure 3, where its artist, Steven Ankutse, stands with it. This sign also demonstrates an element that is very common among such commercial signs, the business's name as a Biblical reference, allusion, or phrase. These signs thus constitute a kind of visual artefact within a larger field of practice (Morgan 2005) through which cultural gestures of the commercial, the religious, the common, and the material converge. A powerful articulation of private interest or sentiment and public gesture through shared and remembered motifs and registers of value, meaning, and representation can be said to intersect in such visual gestures, making them almost narratives of this articulation. The religious gesture in signs such as these might on one level be seen as trivial

Figure 2: Commercial images at the roadside.

Figure 3: A common type of sign.

or as profane commercialization of what should be revered about religious faith. On quite another level, though, one can see in the ubiquity and tacit ordinariness of these gestures a powerful instantiation of or marker of "the religious" in Ghanaian life.

This Ghanaian sensibility of the public visual is more obvious in another trajectory of commercial visual practice: funerary traditions (Witte 2001). Funerals are of great symbolic and embodied experience in Ghana. A complex structure of conventions and commitments define practice around funerals, which are public events made even more public and material through their visuality. While the public spectacle of the funeral itself is highly material and visual, we would point to three gestures associated with Ghanaian funerals that are more precisely focused on our project here. These are more ancillary to the funeral festivities themselves but are significant to our discussion here because they are designed to persist outside the context of the actual funeral ritual, enriching in particular the publicness of the practices and processes of commemoration and mourning. First, there is a long and rich history and tradition of representational and other memorial statuary in Ghana (Figure 4 shows sign artist Gilbert Forson at work on one). Such statues are by no means universal, in part due to the expense involved, but the tradition is nonetheless significant for its visuality and materiality.

Figure 4: At work on a sculpture.

Second, Ghana is world-famous for its traditions of representational casket art. Ghanaian caskets are exhibited in museums around the world. We present two interesting examples here, both from the catalogue of a roadside casket artist. Figure 5 is a casket in the shape of a bible, Figure 6 a casket made for a cocoa farmer in the shape of a cocoa fruit.

Figure 5: A casket-maker's catalogue.

Figure 6: A casket-maker's catalogue.

The third funerary tradition, and the one more significant here, is the tradition of the funeral notice. Many families, in preparation for an upcoming funeral, will engage a roadside artist to create a poster-obituary that is then printed and posted in the community. An example is at Figure 8. As informant Steven Ankutse told us, ". . . funeral posters are a big part of what I do." And, as the example there demonstrates, these artists have begun to expand their genre repertoire with the development of the digital age. While they once concentrated on what an informant called "manual posters," those that are hand-painted, today a younger cadre of these artists are comfortable with digital materials. Figure 9 shows informant Ankutse with such a product. Accommodating the creative potential of digital media has allowed these artists to experiment with more modern and sophisticated-looking products, including in funeral announcements such as in Figure 7.

Figure 7: A funeral announcement.

Interestingly, the mass-produced funeral posters aside, the majority of even the digital work of these artists remains in single posters, produced by specialist shops that print them on adhesive-backed, plasticized materials that can be easily posted on the metal or wooden boards that have traditionally been the canvasses of these artists (Ankutse interview 2012). The creative product and creative logic of these producers, then, is less focused on the mechanical mass production of the images than on the potential for digital materials to make possible entirely new possibilities and gestures in representation (Ankutse interview, 2012).

We would describe the field of practice of these artists as one that exists in the larger context of Ghana's emerging public visual culture, but that at the same time invigorates and helps constitute it. Even the most ambitious major commercial signboard will be surrounded with the work of these smaller, more local, artists. We would further describe this field of practice as one that responds to the conditions of the larger, more dominant visual sphere (the one that links powerful media sources such as television and radio with the commercial – and religious – advertising articulated to it). It is conscious of that culture and of its conventions and demands (Woets 2016:305). But it is also one that responds to its own fields of action and agency, responding to its own – more local and specific – networks of social and economic relations. And – most importantly to our discussions here – it also articulates religion into its work product.

These artists regularly take commissions from churches, religious organizations, and even mosques. This work often involves the production of posters or signs that advertise revivals and other spectacular events. When they do so, they produce with a keen consciousness of the conventions of such advertising in the larger, more national and international contexts (Ankutse interview, 2012). But the important point is that these artists are at the center of a field of production of such materials that results in the representations of roadside visual culture seen everywhere in Ghana.

New Forms in the Religious Public Sphere

We want to argue that roadside sign artists represent a kind of curatorial engine of this religious public sphere, and that they are providing yet another iteration in the ongoing struggle between religious authority and emergent religion and religious cultures in Ghana.

There has been a broad and growing scholarly discourse focused on the interactions of religion and media in modernity. New media (those emergent since the dawn of the "mass media" era late in the 19th Century) have demonstrated a growing capacity to reform and remake the ways religions are understood and practiced. These implications cross religious and cultural boundaries and structures and definitions of specific religious traditions (for a review, see Hoover, 2016, Chapter 1). While much of this literature has focused on the so-called "developed world," growing literatures also consider these developments and their implications beyond the North Atlantic West (see, for example, Meyer 2008; Asamoha-Ghyadu 2013; Hoover (ed.) 2016; Clark (ed.) 2012).

Among the most important questions that arise in relation to the interaction of media and religion are those surrounding the implications for religious authority. In a review of this turf, Hoover (2016) has argued that the significant challenges to authority lie in a number of specific areas. 1) Media cultures make it impossible for religious authorities to control the boundaries and limits of their realms of action. They can no longer have a "private conversation." 2) In the context of mediated marketplaces, religious lose control over their own symbols. 3) Religions today become "differentiated" in the media-cultural marketplace, needing to "brand" themselves in order to exist in public. 4) These differentiated religious authorities also find themselves "relativized" in a cultural marketplace where they must compete with other confessions and traditions. The "major" or "historic" traditions lose their claim to particular authority.

The outlines of this challenge to authority are obvious in the Ghanaian cultural marketplace as we have described it. The growth in "mediatic" churches and the emergence of new media markets in Ghana have afforded a growing media marketplace within which all religious traditions must now co-exist and organize themselves. Ghanaian media and religious markets have evolved together, and the consequence of this has been a shift the bases on which religious cultures express themselves in Ghanaian society. The once-dominant traditions of denominational Protestantism, Catholicism and Islam have had to come to grips with powerful emergent mediatic Pentecostal churches. This has been a fact for more than a decade. But there is more to this evolution. We would argue that the voluble spaces and practices of the media marketplace in Ghana have created conditions for broader, more layered, and more subtle transformations of presence and authority in Ghana's religious cultures.

The commercial visual culture of the Ghanaian road- and street-side has emerged as a major context for these transformations. Important religious institutions and figures – along with a variety of commercial advertisers – have long engaged in advertising and promotion in that context. But we point to the invigoration of a layer of this context long overlooked or undervalued: the vibrant and voluble productivity of roadside visual culture curated by Ghana's community of sign artists.

And, we point to a particularly significant transformation that they have brought about. The challenge to authority they pose can be seen most clearly in relation to a relatively recent development: the increasing presence in their work of practitioners of African Traditional Religion (ATR). As we noted above, the confrontation with ATR was one of the definitive characteristics of the formerly-dominant religious institutions of Africa. A large part of the evolution of Christianity and Islam in West Africa (regardless of their provenance in recent missional activities or older formations) has been a story of their defining themselves *vis a vis* Africa's prior traditions. This has meant that, for much of the colonial and post-colonial history of Africa, a variety of public institutions, both colonial and indigenous civil societies, have tended to suppress the representation of ATR.

In Ghana, this situation seems to be changing. On the streetsides of Ghana's cities, as well as the roadsides of its major and minor auto routes, such signs have begun to appear. The particular aesthetic traditions and practices of the sign artist guild are obvious. Some new conventions are emerging. The collective significance of this curation is the emergence of ATR as a more tacit, taken-for-granted dimension of the Ghanaian cultural marketplace, something that has important implications for religious authority in Ghana.

A representative group of these signs reveals emergent conventions and practices that show interactions between the "sensational forms" (Meyer, 2014) of mediatic religion in Ghana, national and international forms in the secular media marketplace, and these emergent forms.

According to informant Stephen Ankutse, the major aesthetic division in the signs is between those that are hand-painted and those that are digitally-produced and printed.[3] There are trade-offs between the two forms. The newer digital forms allow for a different kind of visual imagination, making it possible to incorporate a variety of images from commercial culture, in the process borrowing credibility and charisma from that context. The older hand-painted forms allow their own kind of aesthetic experimentation and fluidity, and carry a characteristic familiarity. The hand-painted signs can also be more vivid in their colours. The hand-painted signs are also more durable, and thus preferable in rural settings or locations where they are more likely to be weathered by the sun.

---

[3] Perhaps surprisingly, the fact that they can be printed does not mean they are mass-produced. Most are "one-off" creations, produced on large printers on adhesive stock and intended to be singular. In this way, they are consistent with the traditional hand-painted form, in that there was no expectation of mass production.

Figure 8 is a hand-painted sign along a rural roadside near Axim, on the Western end of Ghana's coast with the gulf of Benin. Its simplicity and banality obscures its significance as a form that resists traditional conventions in the representation of ATR. The practitioner chooses a contemporary framing for her work, calling herself a "native doctor," thus connecting her practice with "health," and with natural sources and materials. The visual symbols depict representative instruments of ATR, combining them with the very modern listing of her phone numbers, something typical of commercial advertising. It is a kind intersection between form, tradition, market, commodities, and resistant religious culture.

Figure 8: A traditional practitioner's roadside sign.

Figure 9 illustrates how this simple and banal form can introduce other layers and trajectories of meaning and history. In this case, the significant inclusion of the ubiquitous Yoruba water goddess Mami Wata. Most often depicted as a kind

Figure 9: A traditional practitioner's roadside sign.

of mermaid, she is a powerful figure, nearly universal in West African, Afro-Caribbean, and Afro-Brazilian contexts. Here, she spits power directly into the mouth of the practitioner, connecting him with deep historical, spiritual, and identity meanings. As with the prior sign, traditional ATR spiritual objects are also depicted, along with the very modern gesture of his telephone number. These two figures establish the foundation of the media articulation that is achieved in the quotidian context of roadside advertising. Tradition, spirit, and enchantment are articulated together with a very Protestant concern with the utility of modern publicity and modern communication. The handmade form, simple as it seems to be, incorporates traditional power with the pressing technologies of modernity.

Figure 10 is in a less rural location, along a roadside near Accra, the capital. It also slips into a slightly different register. The practitioner is depicted with a different sacred creature, this time a crocodile, which he has tamed and positioned with a very non-traditional object, a football. This sign also gets specific (in very modern-advertising style) about what he can address – a list that is very much in line with the "health and wealth" appeals of the Neo-Pentecostal churches. This might suggest an emergent sub-theme in these appeals, occasioned by the prominence of the claims and rhetorics of those churches.

Figure 10: Sign featuring traditional healing and contemporary symbols.

The capacity of these signs toward an elasticity and positioning regarding other traditions is also seen in Figure 11, which unlike the others here, was displayed as part of a public exhibit of cultural artifacts. In this case, the ATR practitioner is clearly gesturing toward Islam. Again, he is described as a "native doctor," and lists some of the maladies he can treat, including "spiritual matters," a curiously "modern" formulation. As with other signs we review here, the form seems

Figure 11: A sign including Islamic features.

to beckon both to tradition and to modernity, using these spaces as ways of gesturing toward commonplaces in modern, globalized languages and idioms.

The term "spiritual" and connection to specific powers carries forward in Figure 12, a digitally-produced sign, which was seen on the main road near the Asante capital of Kumasi. The technology allows a photograph of the practitioner himself to appear, along with a second image of him with sacred objects, and text connecting him with a broader group of practitioners in the Kumasi region. This sign demonstrates the positives and negatives of the digital form. Realist depiction is possible, but the actual aesthetic power of the image is somehow reduced in comparison to the hand-painted signs we include here. Their dynamism is illustrated in Figure 13, which incorporates a wider range of phantasmal images, bodies, and forms.

Figure 12: A sign incorporating photography.

The phantasmagoria depicted in Figure 13 incorporates tradition, the modern, appeals to modern public mediation and its cultural authority, technology, tradition, the past, the present. These are signaled both by the images themselves and by their framing within technological traditions and appeals to secular popular culture as well as emergent gestures in Pentecostal culture. These references to popular culture in the work of sign artists (also noted by Meyer, 2008) are obvious in Figure 14. Here, the digital affords an elasticity of visual gesture, of course, but includes in the artist's "palette" the possibility of adopting or appropriating material directly from popular culture, thus incorporating both the specific image and some of the sensibilities of that context. In this case, Mami Wata becomes not a figure of power (see Figure 9 but also compare to Figure 15) but a more passive figure, and in this case accompanied by sexualized feminine images more typical of (and borrowed from) filmic popular culture. And, at the same time, this work exists in trajectories deeply embedded in the visuality of Ghanaian cultural and religious history.

Figure 13: A collection of images on one sign.

The larger significance of Figure 15 is one we've hinted at: that these visual practices at one and the same time confirm this complex of visual practices at the Ghanian roadside and suggest that it has a particular and significant effect today. That effect is the emergence into these spaces of articulations of African Traditional Religion. ATR thus finds itself able to be represented in public culture in new ways and in new, more public locations. This affordance is both a function of technology, and of practices of visualization that use technologies in new ways. Further, it suggests that the authority to visualize and normalize representation is now dispersed and diffuse, and now in the hands of curators whose provenance is commercial, not religious (though many of them may themselves be people of faith).

Figure 14: Incorporating Mami Wata.

Figure 15: Another use of Mami Wata.

They represent a significant contemporary illustration of a phenomenon that dates back to the emergence of printing and its relation to the European Reformation. As Elizabeth Eisenstein pointed out in her definitive work on printing, the significance of printing was not only in the distribution of books or of literacy, but in the emergence of a locus of authority in the political economy of publishing (Hoover 2016). Publishers, who through their foundation in the commercial marketplace and their ability to monetize and thus achieve independence from settled state and church authority, thus became "the media," as we know and use that term today. And the independence of "the media" to operate independently of the authority and sponsorship of church or state is a significant explanation for their implication for those other sectors of authority. Thus roadside sign artists in Ghana stand in a long and distinguished lineage of such economies of publication. And, in this case, they can be seen to be curating a context where a suppressed religious form, African Traditional Religion, can find a location of public articulation, in defiance of settled authorities in Ghanaian Christianity and Islam.

Conclusion: Roadside Curation as a Location of Emergent Religious Authority

We want to argue that the roadside is thus a complex geography of curation that locates itself within the religious public sphere and at the same time expands that sphere. These sign artists are at one and the same time commercial practitioners and the curators and thus the authorities defining the limits, capacities, and affordances of that sphere. It is not just that tradition cannot control these spaces – or even delimit the spaces of public religion–neither can it control the standards and conventions of framing there. But this is not a simple matter of social actors in media spaces confronting settled authority. It is a much more complex story than that, one that we've identified as a set of trajectories that intersect in the curational space of the roadside.

The first of these is in the history, traditions, aesthetics and sensations of Ghanaian visuality. Ghana is not alone among cultures where "the visual" obtains specific and particular meaning or function. But, each culture can in a way be a "universal singular" and in this case we can see in Ghanaian practices a specific place for visual representation. Visual evidence is thought about in specific ways, most importantly in relation to visual practices being able to connect concrete, lived experience with sensations of meaning and transcendence beyond. More importantly, perhaps, visual expression has a long and deep history in Ghana, particularly in informal, popular, even banal contexts. Thus there is a public experience with, and acceptance of, visual expression as more or less ubiquitous in spaces of lived everyday experience.

This is seen and felt most presently in the context of the roadside and streetside. The ubiquity of visual culture is in its very everydayness, and in its accessibility in a broad and suffused circulation that is seen and experienced by all. The practices of creation for this large heterogenous and anonymous context of reception enforce an aesthetics that is necessarily realist and commonplace, While it might be easy to dismiss this context and these expressions for their banality, it is in that commonness that their significance lies, particularly when specific visual gestures, such as those we've discussed here, are present. Articulations by ATR practitioners achieve a normalcy and presumed acceptability in a context where everything is normal, accessible, and acceptable.

That the visual context of the roadside can be imaginable as a geography that can be marked by religion is rooted both in practices of visual production and in ways that Ghanaian religion has come to be marked by visual and mediatic framings. Ghanaian neo-Pentecostalism's easy adoption of these gestures also serves to establish the plausibility of the banal, commonplace, media framings typical of commercial practices. The whole question (often asked in other contexts) of whether religion retains its legitimacy when it enters the commercial marketplace is elided in a context where important religious forms openly embrace the gestures of that marketplace. The boundary between "sacred" and "secular" can no longer be inscribed in traditional terms of "legitimate" vs "profane" or "commodified" religious practice. What were once purely secular or profane gestures are now openly embraced and adopted by mediatic Pentecostal churches. This may have served to broaden the range of legitimate mediated affordances of religion, including in sign art at the roadside.

We've wished to argue that this nuanced, layered, and ambiguous context illustrates in a specific and located form the larger implications of changes in media practices for the prospects and aspirations of religions and specifically of religious authority. In this case, this is best demonstrated in relation to the changing prospects of African Traditional Religion. These practices, long discouraged, even suppressed, by established religious authority in Christianity and Islam have long had a complex and ambiguous place in Ghanaian social practice. While they necessarily existed at the margins of Ghanaian culture in the colonial and post-colonial periods, they have persisted and maintained a kind of social currency. More recently, they have begun to surface into public consciousness. Our explorations here show how this resurgence has been enabled by changing popular media practice in the particular context of sign art. These artists – who we've argued can be described as the "curators" of this mediatic context – have become an instrument through which ATR might become more and more present, both materially and visually, in the commonplace contexts of Ghana.

Technology is in a way at the center of these developments, but in a nuanced and ambiguous way. The curation of the roadside has a long and deep history in practices of visual representation and visuality. The sign artists and indeed the whole political economy of the roadside and streetside offer an established set of practices, aesthetics and representations. They have for decades crafted a materiality of representation that was public, plastic, voluble, and protean, made the more significant by its tacitness and taken-for-granted-ness. That these practices were "mere" commercial practices undoubtedly served their banalization. The introduction of digital technology played a role in the elaboration of these artists' conceptual and practical "palettes," and opened their practice to interaction, remediation, and circulation in conversation with broader streams of popular and commercial culture. This expanded palette may well have also encouraged new markets and new clients, and in an era when traditional practitioners saw opportunities to connect themselves with emerging public taste cultures which increasingly push the boundaries of what is "acceptable" public representation of "the religious."

The evolving material practice we've described thus sits at the intersection of a range of forces significant of hypermediatic cultures of the emergent neoliberal marketplace. Rooted in, and referencing commercial impulses, it is thus undergirded by the earlier evolution of the successful Pentecostal churches of Ghana which crafted an integration of the material, commercial, and spiritual worlds. It is also grounded in the global circulation of popular, cinematic, and entertainment cultures, referencing the tropes, icons, and gestures of the global entertainment marketplace. It also serves to de-stabilize and undermine existing social and cultural structures and boundaries, specifically in relation to established religious and cultural authorities in Ghana. It is thus disruptive, potentially opening fissures in local and settled contexts that then can be filled by the circulations and practices of material circulations whose logics are more commercial and political-economic than they are moral or theological.

It might be said that what we have observed and described here is a case of a kind of liberation. Traditional and authentic resources, voices, and gestures, long suppressed by religious colonialism, are now becoming freed to find their own place and voice in the emergent public sphere of the Ghanaian roadside. And it seems self-evident that ATR does indeed find a more public place as a result of these affordances. But this emergence is not an unquestioned liberatory gesture. As we have seen, the representations of tradition present in these contexts are inflected with gestures, symbols, and affordances – most notably those involving remediations and framings through popular and cinematic cultural lenses – that frame and shape these representations in specific ways. Just as the leaders of the neo-Pentecostal "prosperity churches" of Ghana have adopted modern media of communication only to find that its logics and affordances increasingly condition what is possible and what is represented, these traditional practitioners find their way into publicity within the frames and expectations and logics of the emergent hypermediatic marketplace. The implications are many and are yet to be fully realized (in either case). This is also significant of the broader condition of religion in the media age: that the times bring with them significant challenges and nuances to the whole notion of religious authority. It is now shared, in important ways, with autonomous forces outside the boundaries of tradition or theology. In the present case, the evolving practical cultures, conventions, aesthetic preferences, and technical affordances of a collective of practitioners, connected only by the moral logic of a unique political economy, become important gatekeepers and voices in what is represented, and how. Neither ATR practitioners nor established bodies nor prosperity preachers, know exactly where this will all lead.

Works Cited

Ankutse, S. 2012 (Ghanaian Sign Artist) personal interview with Hoover, November 6.

Asamoah-Gyadu, J. K. 2005a. *African charismatics current developments within independent indigenous Pentecostalism in Ghana*. Leiden: Brill.

Asamoah-Gyadu, J. K. 2005b. "Of Faith and Visual Alertness: The Message of 'Mediatized' Religion in an African Pentecostal Context." *Material Religion: The Journal of Objects, Art and Belief*, 1(3), 336–356.

Asamoah-Gyadu, J. K. 2013. *Contemporary Pentecostal Christianity: Interpretations from an African context*. Eugene, Oregon: Wipf & Stock Publishers.

Clark, L.S. 2012. *Spiritual Marketplace*. New Brunswick: Rutgers University Press.

De Witte, M. 2001. *Long Live the Dead!: Changing Funeral Celebrations in Asante, Ghana*. Amsterdam: Aksant Academic Publishers.

De Witte, M. 2008. "Spirit Media: Charismatics, Traditionalists, and Mediation Practices in Ghana." Ph.D. Thesis. Universiteit van Amsterdam.

De Witte, M. 2011. "Business of the Spirit: Ghanaian Broadcast Media and The Commercial Exploitation Of Pentecostalism." *Journal of African Media Studies*, 3(2), 189–204.

De Witte, M. 2012. "Television and the Gospel of Entertainment in Ghana." *Exchange*, 41(2), 144–164.

De Witte, M. 2013. "Holy Spirit on Air in Ghana," *WACC Communication for All*. Toronto: World Association for Christian Communication.

Debrunner, H. W. 1967. *A history of Christianity in Ghana,*. Accra: Waterville Pub. House.

Gifford, P. 2004. *Ghana's new Christianity: Pentecostalism in a Globalizing African economy*. Bloomington, Ind.: Indiana University Press.

Goldstone, B. 2012. *The Miraculous Life: Scenes from the Charismatic Encounter in Northern Ghana*. Ph.D. Dissertation. Duke University.

Hoover, S. (ed.) 2016. *The Media and Religious Authority*. State College: Pennsylvania State University Press.

Lehmann, D. 2001. "Charisma and Possession in Africa and Brazil." *Theory, Culture & Society*, 18(5), 45–74.

Meyer, B. 1995a. "Beyond Syncretism: Translation and Diabolization in the Appropriation of Protestantism in Africa." In: *Syncretism/ Anti-Syncretism: the Politics of Religious Synthesis*, eds. C, Stewart and Rosalind S. London: Routledge, 45–68.

Meyer, B. 1995b. "Delivered from the Powers of Darkness': Confessions about Satanic Riches in Christian Ghana." *Africa* 65, 2: 263–55.

Meyer, B. 1998. "'Make a Complete Break with the past.' Memory and Post-Colonial Modernity in Ghanaian Pentecostalist Discourse," *Journal of Religion in Africa*, 28(3), 316.

Meyer, B. 1998. "The Power of Money: Politics, Occult Forces, and Pentecostalism in Ghana," *African Studies Review*, 41(3), 15.

Meyer, B. 2002. "Pentecostalism, Prosperity and Popular Cinema in Ghana," *Culture and Religion*, 3(1), 67–87.

Meyer, B. 2005. "Charismatic Christianity and Modernity In Ghana," *The Journal of African History*, 46(2), 372–374.

Meyer, B. 2008. "Powerful Pictures: Popular Christian Aesthetics in Southern Ghana," *Journal of the American Academy of Religion*. 76 (1) pp. 86–110.

Meyer, B. 2014. "Mediation and Immediacy: Sensational forms, semiotic ideologies, and the question of the medium," in J. Boddy and M. Lambeck (eds.) *A Companion to the Anthropology of Religion*. Wiley Online Library https://doi.org/10.1002/9781118605936.ch17 (accessed July 8, 2018).

Morgan, D. 2005. *The Sacred Gaze Religious Visual Culture In Theory And Practice*. Berkeley: University of California Press.

Opoku, K. A. 1978. *West African Traditional Religion*. Accra, Ghana: FEP International Private Limited.

Sanneh, L. 2003. *Whose Religion is Christianity? The Gospel Beyond the West*. Grand Rapids: Eerdmans.

Sanneh, L. 2005. "Introduction: The Changing Face of Christianity: The Cultural Face of a World Religion," in L. Sanneh and J, Carpenter (eds.) *The Changing Face of Christianity: Africa, the West, and the World*. New York: Oxford.

Ukah, A. 2008. *Roadside Pentecostalism – Religious Advertising in Nigeria and the Marketing of Charisma*, Critical Interventions: Journal of African Art History and Visual Culture, *Spring* (2), 125–141.

Woets, R. 2016. "The Art of Imitation: The (Re)Production and Reception of Jesus Pictures in Ghana," in M. Svašek and B, Meyer, (eds.) *Creativity in Transition: Politics and Aesthetics of Cultural Production Across the Globe*. Berghan Books, pp. 290–311.

Pradip Thomas
Religion, Media and Culture in India: Hindutva and Hinduism

This chapter focuses on the relationship between religion, media and culture in India, particularly on how this relates to the contested nature of Hinduism today, caught as it is between centripetal tendencies, largely advocated by the protagonists of Hindu nationalism, namely the family of Hindu organisations collectively committed to the project of *Hindutva* (the Hindu Nation) and centrifugal tendencies that are arguably germane to Hinduism. While there have been numerous expressions of Hindu extremism – from the '*Gau Rakshaks*' (cow protectors) who have lynched beef eaters such as Muslims and Dalits, to those involved in moral policing, the sharp edge of this contestation is reflected in the organized murder of rationalists throughout the country. After an introduction to some of the research trajectories and thematic expressions underlying academic work related to Hindu fundamentalism in India, it will highlight the war against rationalists in India waged by exploring the murder of the journalist Gauri Lankesh on September 5, 2017 in the South Indian city of Bengaluru. Her murder underlines the contested nature of secularism, and the fragile space for freedom of thought in religion, media and culture in India.

The advocacy of religious cultural nationalism in India has taken many forms. There has been a determined attempt to rewrite the cultural history of India from a Hindu nationalist perspective and celebrate Vedic civilization, a project that has fed into the writing of school textbooks (Banaji 2018; Mahajan 2018; Kamala 2009; Thapar 2000), Hindu revivalism exemplified by a resurgence in religious rituals and customs related to the reinforcement of caste-based divisions Naraynan 2014; Ray 2010) online archival projects aimed at offering alternative accounts of Indian history in which the contributions made by Mughal rulers have been noticeably edited out (Udupa 2018, 2016; Chopra 2006), the establishment of universities dedicated to Vedic studies and esoteric subjects such as astrology and Vedic science (Sundar 2018; Chopra 2016; Nelson 2015), the continuing efforts to build a temple to Ram on the ruins of the Babri Masjid that was destroyed by Hindu fundamentalists in 1989 (Subrahmaniam 2018; Chari 2018) the popular cultures of televised Hinduism (See Sengupta 2017), the imbrications between Bollywood, religion and the market in globalizing India. and the rise of 'Hate Speech' and the politics of intolerance (See George 2016).

Hindu extremists have been quick to decry academic writings that have celebrated the plurality, ecumenism and decentralised nature of Hinduism as for instance A. K. Ramanujan's essay *300 Ramayanas* that was removed from the undergraduate History syllabus in Delhi University because of pressure from Hindu right-wing groups (Biswas 2011). Another example of the pressure on academics is the case of Paula Richman and her publishers Oxford University Press who were taken to court for besmirching the unified, eternal story of the original epic by the sage Valmiki, *The Ramayana*. Paula Richman's (1991:11) edited volume *Many Ramayanas* includes fascinating accounts of the many inversions of the *Ramayana* made by non-dominant groups especially in South India. In her account the story of the *Ramayana* is a foundational South and South East Asian text that has become foundational precisely because it invites a plurality of meanings and retellings based on context and shaped by specific communities, local literary and artistic traditions and social relationships such as caste. For example, the book includes a chapter on folksong traditions by women in Andhra Pradesh "..several of the women's folksongs question Rama's integrity and foreground the theme of the suffering that husbandly neglect causes a wife"(Rama for example had doubted Sita's chastity and banished her after her rescue from the clutches of Ravana). In 2014, another book 'The Hindus', by Wendy Doniger was withdrawn from circulation by Penguin after protests from the Hindu right. It has been argued that the essentialised treatment of the two televised serials the *Ramayana* and *Mahabaratha* in the 1980s, resulting in a narrow re-telling of these stories and to the creation and validation of a pan-Hindu 'public sphere' that contributed to the ascent of the Hindu, political right in India (See Rajagopal 2001). There have been few critical readings of religion, media and culture given the real and perceived threats to those involved in hurting 'majoritarian sentiments' and this fear has led to academics and journalists taking a very cautious approach to dealing with this subject. There are some exceptions to this rule, notably Meera Nanda's writings that have explored the relationships between what she has termed the state-temple-corporate nexus in India. Over the last two decades, there has been massive growth in the Hindu God market, close correspondences between dominant Hindu politics and temple establishments throughout India, the monetization and globalisation of this market best illustrated by re-validations of ancient customs and practices in particular yoga, astrology and the Vedic 'sciences' on a variety of Hindu television channels and the availability of Hindu goods and services off and online.

The Ecumenicity of Popular Hinduism

These examples of the resurgence of muscular forms of Hinduism stand in marked contrast Hinduism's ecumenical traditions as for example its traditional culturescapes that include a variety of communication environments and performative traditions that reinforce continuities between the old and the new, that emphasize localized gods, goddesses and eclectic pantheons, and that connect worshipping communities to Hinduism's sacred geographies. The ability of Hinduism to absorb and make its own a bewildering variety of heterogenous practices has arguably been one of its strengths – a strength that is under threat from the forces of rational, national Hinduism. M. N. Srinivas (1995:227), one of India's best known social anthropologist best known for his concept of Sanskritisation describes Hinduism's catholicity in the following words "The presence, within Sanskritic Hinduism, of a vast and ever-growing mythology, the worship of trees, rivers and mountains, and the association of deities and epic heroes with local spots everywhere in India, makes easy the absorption of non-Sanskritic cults and deities . . . The Pantheistic bias in Hinduism also contributes to the Sanskritization of the deities and beliefs of low castes and outlying communities. The doctrine that everything in the universe is animated by God, and that all the various deities are only forms assumed by the same Brahma makes the process of absorption easier . . . The Gods of the lower castes are not denied, but affirmed, and affirmed in such a way that their subsequent Sanskritisation is rendered easier".

While one may or may not agree with Srinivas' interpretation of a seamless Hinduism that I believe is open to critique and the notion of Sanskritization that reinforces hierarchy and the immutability of tradition, it nevertheless points to a certain polycentrism within Hinduism that has come under question both from within the fold, as it were, and from secular rationalists, both of whom want to shape a Hinduism that is consonant with a globalising India with its pretensions to become a global leader in the 21st century.

The Study of the Cultures of Popular Hinduism

There are very few contemporary media and communication scholars in India who have produced work on the relationship between media, religion and culture and for the most part, the literature available is represented in the main by works from the Chicago School of anthropologists such as Robert Redfield and others who in the 1950s and 60s explored the continuities, the interfaces, the shared common consciousness between the symbolic universe shared by the Little traditions associated with popular Hinduism and Great traditions associated with Sanskritic Hinduism, shared mythological traditions, the role of ritual language, cultural performances and pilgrimages, cultural channels of communication, the social role of Hindu festivals, and the absorptive characteristics of the Great tradition. For the most part early studies concentrated on exploring the functional interdependence between the Great and Little traditions and the integrative aspects and consensual nature of culture in India. These studies suggested that cultural traditions evolved in two stages – through orthogenetic evolution and gradual heterogenetic encounters and that cultural performances related to a common body of myth sutured the continuities between the Great and Little traditions. It was taken for granted that all Indians shared in a common cultural heritage and therefore, consciousness, a conceit that continues to contribute to discussions related to the 'insider' and 'outsider' in contemporary India.

Shalini Kakar (2012) has written a short piece on cross-overs, the phenomenon of 'cinedevotion' the Madhuri Dixit Temple in Jamshedpur, a temple in which this Bollywood film star is represented as an incarnation of Goddess Durga. There are many examples of the worship of film stars, such as the Tamil actor politician MG Ramachandran whose illness resulted in numerous people taking their own lives in the hope that the Gods would spare his life. Santanu Chakrabarti (2012) has written a chapter in a book that I had co-edited on the politics of the maverick god-man and televangelist Baba Ramdev. Such studies are however few and far between. The resurgence of Hindu nationalism and the cultural politics of the Hindu nation has by far received the most academic attention in the recent past and while Hinduism online has begun to attract some scholarship, most of the latter is on the experiences of the Hindu diaspora connecting to Hinduism online (See Balaji 2018).

While the political economy of the God market is an area that needs to be explored further given that it involves all of the major religions in India, there is also a case for studies that explore the consumption of such products and for a lot more studies on visual cultures of contemporary Hinduism. What strikes me as a fascinating aspect of Hinduism is Hindu belief in the immanence of God in Hindu products, goods and services – a boon to the Hindu God market but that also suggests the key relevance of orthopraxy to any understanding of Hinduism. Nicole Karapanagiotis (2013:59) in an article on the Ontology of Cyber-Gods and Goddesses argues that ". . . many Hindu devotees do . . . understand cyber-forms of God on the Internet to be full and ontologically real forms of God. Virtual Visnu *is* Visnu and cyber-Siva *is* Siva, and their cyber-forms are believed to be no less real than their forms cast in gold, metal and granite". This mode of belief was illustrated by the phenomenon of worship in front of television sets prior to the telecast of Hindu mythologicals most notably, the Ramayana and the Mahabaratha in the 1980s among both local as well as diasporic Hindus. Hinduism is a religion in which 'seeing the Divine' is the very essence of worship. As Diana Eck (1980:3) describes it "Since in the Hindu understanding, the deity is present in the image, the visual apprehension of the image is charged with religious meaning. Beholding the image is an act of worship, and through the eyes one gains the blessing of the divine". So it is not altogether surprising that the mediation of images across many traditions of media has been enthusiastically embraced by Hindus – the latest being the on line world. The sacred gaze – the title of a book by David Morganic, reminds of the absolutely central role of visual cultures in Hinduism and therefore the need to study it. The latest manifestation of this is a variety of online worship services including saranam.com, e-prarthana, e-puja among many others that offer a monetized mediation of worship rituals mainly to diasporic audiences. The business model is based on franchises given to mediators resident in the vicinity of a given temple who physically visit these temple on behalf of their clients, perform the necessary rituals and who post the offerings back to their clients – not unlike Christian evangelists in India who allocate prayer requests to Christian priests who in turn pray for the individuals requesting such prayers. Madhavi Mallapragada (2010:114–115) describes online darshan as an example of remediation in which "new media involve the repurposing of older media and . . . how the latter is refashioned to adapt to the new media environment . . . Digital darshan foregrounds the remediation of 'digital' as analog media forms such as photographs, iconic calendar art and books reconfigured as digital bits . . . Correspondingly, 'old media' imagery is purposefully used to sacralize 'new' digital representation".

Arguably, there are traditions within popular Hinduism that are less sanguine about the prospect of or indeed the necessity for an all-India wide, centralized Hinduism with Ram as the first in the Vedic pantheon of Gods. An example of this turn towards defining a historical Hinduism include the attempts to elevate Lord Ram as a pan-Indian God. Rama is the hero of the epic Ramayana and he embodies moral and physical courage, duty, heroism and devotion, austerity and tenderness for his wife Sita. Krishna, on the other hand, the other great hero of the other epic the Mahabaratha, especially one of its parts the Bhagavadgita is a much more complex figure. Krishna is of course known for his dalliance with milkmaids, his eroticism, his flute playing that has been immortalised in popular dance dramas throughout India via many traditions of Krishnalila – the dance of divine love. As Jurgen Lutt (1995:143) explains, "Krishna is sensuous, soft, gentle, but his love cannot be counted upon, he is incalculable, polygamous and adulterous. His worshippers languish for him, they lose all control of themselves, and get lost in joy and delight". It is not surprising therefore that in the context of the project of muscular Hinduism and India's aspiration to become a first world country, a nuclear power with a permanent seat on the Security Council that Ram trounces Krishna as the preferred poster God of Hindu nationalism.

In the Afterword in Fuller's recently revised edition of a study of popular Hinduism, *The Camphor Flame*, the author offers some insights and reasons why it has been difficult for the forces of Hindutva to centralize and reproduce their version of all India-wide Hinduism while at the very same, making inroads into popular Hinduism.

> because the Sangh Parivar (family of right-wing Hindu organisations) cannot determine what all Hindus do and Hindutva ideology is not hegemonic; in particular, people's understandings and actions are always intimately connected to their own local position and interests, which may be opposed to those of Hindu nationalists, so that Hindutva ideology is changed into an array of diverse and contested meanings. (2018:288)

However Fuller also points out that "religious beliefs and practices have often been affected, to a greater or lesser extent, by nationalist discourse and agitation, even for people who certainly do not support the nationalist movement." Similarly, Raminder Kaur (2005) has observed in her ethnographic study of the Ganapati Utsava, a major festival in Western India – this kaleidoscopic spectacular (consisting of parades, floats, rituals, displays, competitions, performances) involving right wing Hindu parties, mainstream political parties, businesses, media conglomerates, regulatory bodies, has not been entirely taken over by Hindu nationalists. "The presence of a Hindu god in the public field need not be a prefix for communalism" (2005:xv). While ". . . emergent Hindutva forces avail themselves of the . . . 'emotional thread', entailed in such festivals to elicit sympathy for their cause . . . .. such measures are resisted by those of more liberal persuasion . . . the festival is amoeboid enough to accommodate fissiparous tendencies" (Kaur 2005:23).

Traditions of popular Hinduism include those who chant and recite the Ram story including the Ramnamis from North India who belong to the lower castes and who have traditionally contested the Brahmanic version of Hinduism and placed stress instead on an anti-orthodox piety are part of greater Hinduism although they have traditionally had the leeway to value Gods according to custom and need. There are as previously mentioned, many traditions of Ramanayas in India – some that even invert the story so that the evil persona of the demon king Ravana becomes the good guy. These types of role reversals are probably best illustrated by the worshippers of the Goddess Bhagavathy in Kerala. In the words of Gentes (1992:295), the festival in Kodungallur,

> The Cock Festival (or Minam Bharani Festival) at Sri Kurumba Kavu in central Kerala is known for the raucous, erotic, and insulting devotional practices of its participants. Thousands of devotees take part annually in the singing of highly explicit sexual songs and in the ceremonial pollution of the goddess Sri Kurumba's shrine. This festival is controversial but popular, and resembles in many ways descriptions of the ecstatic cults of the ancient Near East that spread throughout the Greco-Roman empire. Oracles of the goddess, called veliccappatus (illuminators), reveal her wishes through trance and in their possessed state cut their foreheads with swords as they dance.

Another example is that of the largest religious festival in the world, the Kumbh Mela that brings together all the sects of Hinduism to four fairs, held rotationally in the holy sites of Haridwar, Allahabad, Nashik and Ujjain on the River Ganges. Although this festival has become politicised it nevertheless represents the agglomeration that Hinduism is, and represents practices that cannot easily be reconciled with the project of a singular, all India wide Hinduism. Vineeta Sinha who is among the most perceptive sociologists of religion has this to say on the tradition of Hinduism in Singapore that also has also incorporated elements of Taoism.

> The evidence from Singapore reveals the presence of the following elements that typically define the 'folk' variety of Hinduism: the centrality of a non-Sanskritic pantheon of deities, the privileging of spirit mediums and trance sessions, the need for an intimate familiar, unmediated approaches to divinity (and the absence of religious intermediaries), the importance of devotion, intuition, emotion and religious experience, the offerings of non-vegetarian items, alcohol and cigars to the deity, the absence of formalised, standardized and textually ritual procedures for approaching the deity, valuing rituals of self-mortification and other 'extreme' bodily rituals. (2006:104)

She notes that the impetus for reform of this type of Hinduism in Singapore stems from bureaucrats and administrators and their disciplining processes and not from adherents who are comfortable worshipping both 'folk' and 'Sanskritic' deities.

The Attack against Free Speech

Siddhartha Deb (2018) writing in the *Colombia Journalism Review*, has highlighted the violence that affects the profession of journalism in India.

> According to the 2017 Press Freedom Index compiled by Reporters Without Borders, India ranked 136 out of 180, a position quite out of keeping with India's image as the world's most populous democracy. Zimbabwe, before the fall of Robert Mugabe, came in at 127, while Afghanistan, mired in a grinding war, ranked 120th. Since 1992, according to the Committee to Protect Journalists, 43 journalists have been killed in India. The number tallied by the International Federation of Journalists is far higher: 73 journalists killed since 2005. Nine journalists were killed in 2015, one of them allegedly set on fire by policemen working for a politician accused of rape. Five were murdered in 2016. In the cases of 30 journalists murdered since 2010 being tracked by the Indian media watchdog The Hoot, there has been exactly one conviction.

Gauri Lankesh was a journalist and editor of the Lankesh Patrike, a small circulation, weekly tabloid in the South Indian language, Kannada. She had been a forthright critique of muscular forms of Hinduism and her activism and commitment to a movement within her own community, the Lingayats, and recognition as a separate religious status from Hinduism, along with attempts to question the Fascist overtones of Hindu religious nationalism turned her into a target. She had begun a forum for communal harmony in 2005, the Komu Souharda Vedike (the Karnataka Communal Harmony Forum), and was a follower of the 12th century Hindu reformer Basavanna, and Dalit leader Dr BR Ambedkar. Basavanna was a reformer committed to a caste-less Hinduism and Gauri Lankesh occasionally spoke at and recited Basavanna's poems to Lingayat assemblies that owed allegiance to Brahmanism (See Rajghatta: 2018). She was the fourth writer to be murdered (along with Narendra Dabholkar, Govind Pansare and M. M. Kalburgi) for their 'rationalist' views in a short space of time (See Sharma 2019 and Roy 2017).

On November 27, 2018, a police investigation released its report in the killing after arresting 18 people who were involved in the killings of the four rationalists – including Parashuram Waghmare, Amol Kale, Sujith Kumar alias Praveen and Amit Degwekar. They belonged to fringe Hindutva groups and followed orders to murder issued by the Sanatan Sanstha, Hindu Janjagruti Samiti and the Hindu Yuva Sena (See Express Web Desk 2018).

Religion, Media and the Culture of Hindu Fundamentalism

In the context of both religious revivalism associated with the project of Hindu nationalism and the expansion of religious populism, the protection of turf at whatever cost has become a critical project. In the states of Maharashtra and Karnataka there are any number of right-wing Hindu organisations whose major project is the protection and extension of *Sanatana Dharma* – the eternal truth of Orthodox Hinduism as a world religion and the duties associated with it as opposed to the duties associated with *ssvadharma:* "one's own duties as a member of a specific caste or sect." The protection of a universal Hinduism has become sacrosanct. While attempts by rationalists to cleanse religion of its superstitions has been a counter narrative within India's turn towards modernity under colonial rule, in contemporary India it is arguable that the major attempts to legitimise the boundaries of what is 'popular' Hinduism is being carried out by the advocates of orthodox Hinduism. That the many fringe organisations are supported both tacitly and explicitly by the ruling party in power, the BJP, and the fact that the present prime minister of India, Narendra Modi, rarely if ever, speaks out against such violence against rationalists, minorities and those who advocate for free speech, are examples of the impunity and silence that have cut short democratic processes in India. While the government in the Western state of Maharashtra did pass the oddly worded Bill, the *Maharashtra Prevention and Eradication of Human Sacrifice and other Inhuman, Evil and Aghori Practices and Black Magic Bill* four days after Dabholkar's murder on August 20, 2013, there is little appetite to enforce legal actions against those involved in reviving superstitious practices (See Maharashtra Ordinance No. XIV OF 2013). In India the line between religion and superstition is thin and the law, despite such Bills, has been unable to make a dent in this rather catholic understanding of religion. At the same time, and arguably, despite the need for interventions by rationalists, their attempts to tar all superstitions with the same brush, all rituals that require a suspension of disbelief, their inability to distinguish between the multi-millionaire God man and the local fakir, along with their complete and utter reliance on science and scientific explanations – do confuse people whose everyday belief structures includes negotiations with the unseen, spirit world. "e-Hindu" sites know this perfectly well and most of them list a number of interventions to ward off the evil eye.

Johannes Quack (2012) in his book *Disenchanting India* has explored the world of organised rationalism in India and the 'culture wars' that this has ignited. This war pits mainly post-colonial scholars such as Ashis Nandy against scholars such as Meera Nanda who has openly castigated the tendency for post-colonial scholars to celebrate indigenity at all costs since the project of indigenity, as they see it, has suffered under the onslaught of Western modernity, science and the rational. In Meera's Nanda's way of thinking "Enchanting India" has now become a massive arena for a Hindutva, a reenchantment project in which commercialised television plays an important role. Post-colonial scholars see the limits of secularism and that of secular humanists in India as a form of cultural arrogance that was diametrically opposed to the lives that ordinary people led and that was rooted in religion. To these people, religion was their framework for life and as they saw it secularism and science questioned this security and certainty that left people with nothing to hold on to. Nanda however questions their inability to see the cultural and material basis for dominant Hinduism within neo-liberal India as the means to reinforce a politicised and commercialised Hinduism that is supportive of the status quo and its worst excesses including support for the extension of traditions of 'incredulity' in the name of religion. From a personal point of view I think that there are issues with both the uncritical embrace of Hindu traditions by post-colonialist scholars and the fundamentalism of rationalists. There is a need to distinguish between the everyday practice of ordinary popular Hinduism practiced by millions around the country that are extraordinarily diverse and inclusive and the mediatised versions of popular Hinduism that tend to veer towards Sanatana Dharma.

Online Contestations

The arena in which there is a potential for this contestation to become polarised is online – although with the exception of a few attempts by Dalit groups to claim this space, online Hinduism has for the most part followed the Hindu diaspora and become the arena for the propagation of traditional Hinduism and for the extension of virtual, online darshans and pujas, often from specific temples to diaspora communities. Although religious platforms in India cater to this diversity and the everyday needs of the faithful, it can also – as the distribution of posts on lynchings by 'gau rakshaks' on platforms and the many mobilisations by the Hindu right reveal– be used to mobilise around a very specific politics. These include apps from powerful Hindu right wing groups such as the Vishwa Hindu Parishad and the Bajrang Dal, although arguably, apart from the explicitly religious nationalist platforms, the bulk of such fare is in social media such as Facebook and in the messaging service owned by Facebook (250 million users in India), Whatsapp (the default communications mode in India) and Instagram. During the 2017 elections in Uttar Pradesh, India's most populous and political bell-weather state that the incumbent BJP won, 6000 Whatsapp groups were created by the BJP for targeted messaging. Vindu Goel (2018) in an article in the *New York Times*, describes the ease with which such groups can be formed and its potential to act as a conduit for fundamentalist content.

> WhatsApp has several features that make it a potential tinderbox for misinformation and misuse. Users can remain anonymous, identified only by a phone number. Groups, which are capped at 256 members, are easy to set up by adding the phone numbers of contacts. People tend to belong to multiple groups, so they often get exposed to the same messages repeatedly. When messages are forwarded, there is no hint of where they originated. And everything is encrypted, making it impossible for law enforcement officials or even WhatsApp to view what's being said without looking at the phone's screen. (Goel 2018)

What is fascinating about these virtual sites is the fact that these virtual arenas have become public spaces for the reinvention of tradition and cultural practices that arguably are based on irrational criteria. It would seem the case that these platforms and apps are catering primarily to the devotional needs of local and diasporic Hindus, extending efficiencies in the delivery of religious goods and services, in particular facilitating the virtual apprehending and experiencing of the local. Platforms such as AadiShakti offers over a 150 services to clients inclusive of "astrology, face reading, palm reading, reflexology, Vaastu, yoga, reiki, past life regression, acupuncture, naturopathy, feng shui consulting, aromatherapy, crystal healing, Chinese astrology, numerology etc. Consultation is available on a wide array of subjects such as legal problems, ancestral problems, financial problems, mental distress, relationship problems, career and marriage related issues"

(Sharma 2016). The internet has of course been used by forces from the Right for a number of years although also sporadically by those contesting the hegemony of Brahmanic Hinduism. The site Dalitistan.org was shut down by the Indian government in July 2006 allegedly for their strident critiques of Brahmins and for their online Dalit Holocaust museum although Kumar (2004) has observed that there are ". . . 51 sites, which provide information about dalits in India and abroad. A few important sites are www.ambedkar.org, www.dalitusa.org, www.dalitistan. org, www.dalitawaj.com, www.dalitindia.com, etc. Similarly Dalits also run e-magazines like such as Dalit-International@yahoogroups.com, dalits@ambedkar.org, Buddhistcircle@yahoogroups.com, and Sakyagroup@yahoogroup . . ." –sites that probably have multiplied a decade or more later in the context of generalised caste-based violence against the lower castes in India. Caste remains a major issue in contemporary Hinduism and the Indian government has tried its utmost to deflect and downplay international discussions related to casteism within a human rights framework. The issue however is real given that casteism remains a reality in India despite much legislation and the fact that diaspora Indians too carry their castes with them and perpetuate caste-based discriminations – an issue that has been recognised and taken up by the European Union and the UK governments.

I've hoped to provide here an introduction to contemporary struggles related to the imagining of Hinduism and Hindu futures. The efflorescence of many forms of religious nationalism, often aided and abetted by the powers that be, has opened up multiple fissures in Indian society that have major repercussions for the future of secularism and the fate of minority cultures, traditions and religions in India. There is strong evidence that various media forms have as well played important and complex roles in these trends. Understanding media and religion in relation to Hinduism and Hindutva remains a complex matter that will benefit from continuing research and reflection.

Works Cited

Balaji, M. (ed) 2018. *Digital Hinduism*. Lanham: Lexington Books.
Banaji, S. 2018. "Vigilante Publics: Orientalism, Modernity and Hindutva Fascism in India," *The Javnost* 25 (4) 333–350.
Biswas, S. 2011. "Ramayana, an 'epic' controversy," *BBC Online* Oct. 19. Available at: https://www.bbc.com/news/world-south-asia-15363181.
Chakrabarti, S. 2012. The Avatars of Ramdev: The politics, economics and contradictions of an Indian televangelist (149–170) from Thomas, P. N. & Lee, P. Eds. Global and Local Televangelism, Palgrave Macmillan, Basingstoke and NY.

Chari, M. 2018 "Hindutva rallies marking Babri's demolition have the police on edge across North India," *Scroll.in* Dec. 8. Available at: https://scroll.in/article/904909/hindutva-rallies-marking-babri-demolition-have-the-police-on-edge-across-north-india.

Chopra, S. 2006. "Global primordialities: Virtual identity politics in online Hidutva and online Dalit discourse," *New Media & Society* 8 (2) 187–206.

Chopra, S. 2016. "The Hindu right is quietly funding and lobbying American universities," *Quartz India* Jan. 14. Available at: https://qz.com/india/590909/the-hindu-right-is-quietly-funding-and-lobbying-american-universities/.

Deb, S. 2018. "The killing of Gauri Lankesh," *Columbia Journalism Review*, Winter 2018. Available at: https://www.cjr.org/special_report/gauri-lankesh-killing.php/.

Fuller, C. 2018. *The Camphor Flame: Popular Hinduism and Society in India.* Princeton: Princeton University Press.

Gauri Lankesh murder probe: Here's what has happened so far, The Indian Express, Express Web Desk, Nov. 27. Available at: https://indianexpress.com/article/india/gauri-lankesh-murder-case-probe-sit-arrests-hindu-outfits-5462349/

Gentes, M. 1992. Scandalizing the Goddess at Kodungallur (295–322), *Asian Folklore Studies*, 51.

George, C. 2016. "India: Narendraa Modi and the harnessing of hate," Chapter Four in *Hate Spin: The manufacture of religious offence and its threats to democracy*. Camridge: MIT Press.

Goel, V. 2018. In India, Facebook's Whatsapp plays a central role in elections, New York Times, May 14. Available at: https://www.nytimes.com/2018/05/14/technology/whatsapp-india-elections.html

Kakar, S (2012), "Starring" Madhuri as Durga: The Madhuri Dixit Temple and Performative Fan-Bhakti of Pappu Sardar, International Journal of Hindu Studies, 13 (3), 391–416.

Kamala, V., M. Witzel, N. Manjrenka, D. Bhog and U. Chakravarthi 2009. "The Hindutva view of history: Rewriting textbooks in India and the United States," *Georgetown Journal of International Affairs* 10 (1) 101–112.

Karapanagiotis, N. 2013. "Cyber Forms, *Worshipable Forms*: Hindu Devotional Viewpoints on the Ontology of Cyber-Gods and Goddesses," *International Journal of Hindu Studies*, 17 (1) 57–82.

Kaur, R. 2005. *Performative Politics and the Cultures of Hinduism: Public uses of Religion in Western India.* London: Anthem Press.

Kumar, V. 2004. Understanding Dalit diaspora (114–116), Economic & Political Weekly, 39 (1)

Lutt, J. 1995. "From Krishnalila to Ramrajya: A court case and its consequences for the Reformulation of Hinduism (142–153)," in V. Dalmia and H. von Stietencron (eds) *Representing Hinduism: The Construction of Religious Traditions and National Identity.* London: Sage.

Mahajan, S. 2018. "Hindutva agenda and history writing: Imaginings of nation," *Revista Canaria de Estudies Ingleses* 76, April 211–221.

Maharashtra Ordinance No. XIV OF 2013, the Maharashtra Prevention and Eradication of Human Sacrifice and other Inhuman, Evil and Aghori Practices and Black Magic Ordinance. Available at: http://bombayhighcourt.nic.in/libweb/ordins/2013/2013.14.PDF

Mallapragada, M. 2010. "Desktop deities: Hindu temples, online cultures and the politics of remediation," *South Asian Popular Culture*, (2) 109–121.

Naraynan, N. 2014. "Karnataka bans temple ritual that involves rolling over Brahmin's leftover food," *The Scroll* Sept. 26. Available at: https://scroll.in/article/680938/karnataka-bans-temple-ritual-that-involves-rolling-over-brahmins-leftover-food

Nelson, D. 2015. "India's next gift to the world could be Vedic mathematics," *The Telegraph* Jan. 7. Available at: https://www.telegraph.co.uk/news/worldnews/asia/india/11331533/Indias-next-gift-to-the-world-could-be-Vedic-mathematics.html

Rajagopal, A. (2001), Politics after Television: Hindu Nationalism and the Re-Shaping of the Public in India, Cambridge University Press, Cambridge.

Quack, J. 2012. *Disenchanting India: Organised rationalism and criticism of religion in India*. New York: Oxford University Press.

Rajghatta, C. 2018. When Gauri Lankesh decided to give "a piece of her my mind to the local Lingayats" in a small town in Karntaka. Excerpt from the book by Rajghatta, C. (2018), Illiberal India: Gauri Lankesh and the Age of Unreason (Context, New Delhi) in The Caravan, May 12. Available at: https://caravanmagazine.in/vantage/gauri-lankesh-piece-of-my-mind-local-lingayats-small-town-karnataka

Ray, S. 2010. Khap Panchayats: reinforcing caste hierarchies, Mainstream Weekly, 48 (30), July 23, Available at: https://www.mainstreamweekly.net/article2205.html

Richman, P. (ed) 1991. *Many Ramayanas: The Diversity of a Narrative Tradition in South Asia*. Oxford New Delhi: University Press.

Roy, N. 2017. "Gauri Lankesh, Journalist-Activist, 1962–2017," *The Financial Times*, Sept. 9. Available at: https://www.ft.com/content/961c5e1c-93b5-11e7-83ab-f4624cccbabe

Sengupta, R. 2017. "Iconography of violence in televised Hinduism: The politics of images in the Mahabaratha," *Continuum* 31 (1) 150–161.

Sharma, A. 2016. "This Bengaluru-based start-up has built an on-demand marketplace for spiritual gurus," *Geektime* July 10. Available at: https://www.geektime.com/2016/07/10/this-bengaluru-based-startup-has-built-an-on-demand-marketplace-for-spiritual-gurus/.

Sharma, K. 2019. Why we should remember Gauri Lankesh, *The Wire* Jan. 29. Available at: https://thewire.in/rights/why-we-should-remember-gauri-lankesh

Sinha, V. 2006. "Problematizing received categories: Revisiting 'Folk Hinduism' and 'Sanskritization'", *Current Sociology* 54 (1) 98–111.

Srinivas, M. 1965, *Religion and Society among the Coorgs*. Bombay: Asia Publishing House.

Subrahmaniam, V. 2018. "Babri Masjid's destruction laid the foundation of Modi's new India of today," *The Wire* Dec. 6. Available at: https://thewire.in/politics/babri-masjid-narendra-modi-bjp

Sundar, N. 2018. India's higher education troubles," *New York Times* Aug. 3. Available at: https://www.nytimes.com/2018/08/03/opinion/india-higher-education-modi-ambani-rss-trouble.html

Thapar, R 2000. "Hindutva and History: Why do Hindutva ideologues keep flogging a dead horse?" *Frontline* October 13, 15–16.

Udupa, S. 2016. "Archiving as history making: religious politics of social media in India," *Communication, Culture & Critique* 9 (2) 212–230.

Udupa, S. 2018. "Enterprise Hindutva and social media in urban India," *Contemporary South Asia* 26 (4) 435–467.

Contributors

Kwabena Asamoah-Gyadu is Baeta-Grau Professor of African Christianity and Pentecostal Theology and President of the Trinity Theological Seminary, Ghana. He teaches in the areas of Contemporary African Christianity; Religion and Media in Africa; and Pentecostal Theology. He is a Fellow of the Ghana Academy of Arts and Sciences.

Magali do Nascimento Cunha who holds the doctorate in Social Communication, is coordinator of the research group "Communication and Religion" of the Brazilian Society on Interdisciplinary Studies on Communication (INTERCOM) and researcher of the Institute of Religion Studies (ISER) in Brazil on issues related to media, religion, culture and politics.

Nabil Echchaibi is Associate Professor of Media Studies and Associate Director of the Center for Media, Religion and Culture in the College of Media, Communication, and Information at the University of Colorado Boulder, USA. His work focuses on Muslim media, Arab cultural production and aesthetics, and decoloniality.

Florence Pasche Guignard is Assistant Professor in religious studies at the Université Laval (Quebec City, Canada). Her research explores issues at the intersection of religion and ritual, digital and material cultures, embodiment, and gender. She brings her interdisciplinary scholarship in conversation with anthropology, ritual studies, media studies, as well as with gender and women's studies.

Stewart M. Hoover is Professor of Media Studies and Director of the Center for Media, Religion, and Culture in the College of Media, Communication, and Information at the University of Colorado Boulder, USA. A theorist of media audiences and audience research, his research is located at the intersection of religion and modern media of communication.

Steven Hu is a Ph.D. candidate in the Department of Religious Studies at the University of California Santa Barbara, USA. His research examines Christian urbanism, digital religion, and global evangelicalism.

Deborah Justice holds a doctorate in ethnomusicology from Indiana University. She currently teaches at the Sentor School of Music and Department of Art and Music Histories at Syracuse University, and directs the Cornell Concert Series at Cornell University in Ithaca, New York, USA.

Solmaz Mohammadzadeh Kive is an Assistant Professor at the University of Oregon, USA. She holds a masters degree in architecture and a Ph.D. in design and planning. Her research explores identity politics in art/architecture historiography and museum studies.

Seung Soo Kim is full-time lecturer in media and cultural studies on the Faculty of Arts at Chulalongkorn University, Bangkok, Thailad. His research interest centers on the mediation and materiality of Korean religions in the context of the postcolonial modernity of South Korea.

Kathleen M. Ryan is a documentary filmmaker and Associate Professor in the School of Media, Communication and Information at the University of Colorado Boulder, USA. Her research and creative work focuses on transformations in storytelling in shifting media technologies. Specifically, she explores the intersection of theory and praxis within evolving media forms such as the interactive documentary. Her hybrid projects deal with issues of gender, self-identity, visuality and user/participant agency.

Pradip Ninan Thomas is at the School of Communication and Arts, University of Queensland, Australia. He has published extensively on the media in India, communication and social change and religion and media.

Devin Wilson is an educator and artist. He holds an MFA from the University at Buffalo's Department of Media Study (USA), and his work can be found at devinwilson.net.

Index

300 Ramayanas 206

AadiShakti platform 214
Adams, R 90
African Traditional Religion 17, 181–182, 185, 193–195, 197–202
Africans 147
age of exploration 4, 11, 31, 36, 181
agnosticism 52, 56
altar call 144
Althusser, L 163
anatta 99–101, 103
Anderson, B 12, 76, 162
animé 147
Adams, A 83–84, 87–92, 94–95
Appadurai, A 11, 31, 162
apps 15, 41–43, 44, 53, 58, 60, 141–143, 146–148, 150–156, 214
Asamoah-Gyadu, K 187
Asante 196
Assmann, H 130
atheism 52, 56, 168
Auslander, P 65, 68–70, 79
avatar 103

Bagherzadeh, F 115
Bakhtin, M 68
Banaji, S 205
banalization 200
Barnes, Marian
Bharani 210
BigPharma 44
Bird, W 65
birth control methods 43
birth control pill 55
BJP 212, 214
Blau, E 144
Bobel, C 45–48
Bollywood 205, 208
Borelli, V 133
Boyd, R 143
Braga, J 126, 132
Brahmanism 210, 215
Brasher. B 142

Brazil 1, 9, 14, 17, 26, 125, 127–129, 132–133, 139, 219
breastfeeding 51
Brexit 1, 26, 34
Bright, B 144–147
Britain 26
Buddhism 51, 99–100, 103, 185

Campos, L 134, 137–138
Campus Crusade for Christ 141, 143
Castoriadis, C 162
Catholic 50–51, 55, 127, 130–132, 134, 146, 181, 184–186
Catholicism 13, 15, 52, 127, 129, 131, 182, 192
Center for Media, Religion, and Culture V, 161, 219
Chakrabarty, D 4, 6, 8, 31, 34, 164, 169, 173, 177
Chaves, M 64
Chen 161
Christian evangelism 142
Christian music 134
Christianity 16–17, 26, 28, 37, 65–67, 74–75, 89, 127–129, 132–133, 139, 146–147, 155, 160, 164–165, 167–168, 173, 181, 183–186, 193, 199–200, 219
citizenship 27, 87, 154
civility 143, 153–156
Clark, Lynn Schofield 68, 192
climate change 46
colonialism 3, 5, 7, 11–12, 13, 18, 26, 36–37, 170, 181, 193, 200, 212–213
commodification 3, 9–10, 13, 15–16, 32, 37
Communication 23, 25, 30–32, 36–38
community 27–28, 49, 61, 66, 70, 76, 78, 112, 116, 135, 138–139, 154, 156, 162, 190, 192, 211
control over religious symbols 138
Couldry, N 8, 161, 163, 176
cultural flows 33
curation 14, 193, 199–200

Dalitss 212, 214–215
Dart 144

David Loy 100
de Witte, M 185
Debrunner, H 182
deconstructionism 100
denominations 67, 144, 186, 192
Derrida, J 100
Diagne, S 38
diasaporic 209
digital age 32, 36
digital media 3, 10, 32, 68, 137–138, 160–161, 176–177, 190
digital preaching 66
digital religion 60, 132, 137
digital revolution 30
diversity 3–4, 18, 24, 32, 42, 49, 106, 109, 210, 213
Dunaway, 83, 86
Durkheim, 170

earthrise 21–22, 24, 31
East Asia 16
Echchaibi, V, 1, 8, 21, 24, 32, 60, 161, 219
ecumenism 136
Eck 208
Eden 86
electronic churches 135
Eisenstein, E 198
emergent religions 34
Emerich, E 45
enchantment 195
enlightenment 23, 33–34
Environmental Edens 83, 92, 95
Eshleman, P 144–145
ethics 32, 42, 59
ethnoscapes 31
Europe 4, 6, 8, 26, 28, 34, 36, 47, 84, 105, 146, 164, 169, 173, 177
Evangelicals 127, 131, 159–164, 166, 168, 170, 173, 175–176
evangelism 16, 132, 141–142, 144, 153, 155–156, 159, 167
Evernden 86

Facebook 48, 53, 58, 69, 159, 170, 214
Fajardo, A 136

Farinelli, F 22
fertility 10, 13, 41–47, 49–60
Foresta, Mary 92
formal civility 143
forums 48–50, 52, 152
Four Spiritual Laws 147
francophone Canada 47–61
free speech 211–212
Fukuyama, F 26
fundamentalism 205, 212–213
funerals 188, 190

Garfield 101
games 69, 99, 101–103
Gaonkar, D 163
Gauri Lankesh 205, 211
Genesis Project 144
Gentes 210
Ghana 17, 151, 181–186, 198–201, 219
Giddens, A 23
global village 31
globalism 185
globalization V, 1–4, 11–17, 21–25, 31–39, 130, 141, 144, 146–147, 156, 164, 167, 169, 181–183, 185, 187, 201, 207
Good News Bible 141
Gorsky, P 26, 30
Graham, Billy 28, 144
Costikyan, HG 101
Bateson, HG 101

Hall, S 112, 161, 169
Hartford Institute of Religious Research 65
Hays, S 49
health 41–45, 47, 49–50, 53, 55–60, 194–195
Hepp, A 8
Heyman 144
Hindi 145
Hindu nationalism 209
Hinduism 17, 26, 185, 205–215
Hindutva 9, 17, 205, 210, 212–213, 215
Hirschkind, C 153
historical universalism 176

Hjarvard, S 8
Hoover, S V, 1, 9–10, 16, 21, 28, 60, 138, 161, 181, 184, 192, 198, 219
Huizinga, J 101
hypermediation 8, 19, 24, 32–33, 36, 201

imaginaries 28, 32, 37
imperialism 21
individualism 85, 132
Indo-European 108
Inglehart, R 26
interactive media 31
International Artists Agency 144
International Curch of the Kingdom of God 129–130
Iran 14, 105–120
Iran Bastan Museum 107–108, 115, 120
Iranian Cultural Heritage Organization 114
Islam 26, 50–51, 106, 116, 120–121, 182, 185–186
Islamic art 105
Ito, M 152

Juul, J 103
Jenkins 3
Jesus People 75

Karapanagiotis, N 208
Kardecist Spiritualism 128
Kaur 210
Kazerooni 116
Kellner, D 133
Klassen P 49
Kolo Group 152
Korea 159
Korean Media Rating Board 166
Kramnick, I 165
Kumar, S 215

La Torre, C 119
Lady Gaga 159
laïcité, 51
Larson, C 74
LCBC Church 66, 69–77
Lehman 182
Limerick P 93
Little traditions 207

live music 64, 66, 77
LOHAS 45
Lövheim, M 8
Lupton, D 42
Lutt 209

Mallapragada, M 209
magic circle in gaming 101
Mahabaratha 206, 208–209
Mainline Protestantism 166
Maisel, D 83, 93
Mami Wata 194, 197
Manifest Destiny 84
maps 22, 31, 90
markets 1, 11, 14–16, 27, 29–30, 32, 37, 44, 47, 53, 130–131, 134–135, 166, 183–186, 192, 194, 201, 205–206, 208
Martin-Barbero, J 8–10, 17, 125–127, 135
Marx, Leo 93, 95
materialities religion 10
media change 30
media marketplace 17, 37, 132, 134, 184, 192
mediatic religion 15, 183, 193
mediation 1–2, 3, 5–10, 32, 34–36, 39, 42, 45–46, 48–49, 51, 75, 78, 135–136, 139, 156, 177, 181, 197, 219
mediatization 8–14, 47–48, 64–70, 126–135, 137
megachurches 66, 185
Meyer B. 9, 49, 153, 186–187, 192–193, 197
Mignolo, W 11
MitchellW 24
modern 24
modernity 5, 12, 14, 16, 23, 25, 32–33, 37, 87, 162, 164, 168–170, 173, 191, 195–196, 212–213, 219
modernization 107, 162, 164, 166–167, 169, 173, 175–177
Modi 212
Moors, A 153
moral values 42
Muir, J 85
multi-site churches 64, 66, 70–76
muscular Christianity 18
museums 105
music 13, 63–64, 66–80, 120, 134, 136–138

mystical religion 132
myth 83–86, 208

National Park Service 86
nationalism 205
natural childbirth 50
natural parenting 44–60
neo-liberalism 32
neo-pentecostalism 133, 136
networked religion 152
New Media Bible 144
new religious movements 34
Newhall, N 87
Noll, M 147
"notself" 99, 103

O'Leary, S 142
online forums 50
other, the 48, 137, 147, 164, 166–169, 173–176

Papacharissi, Z 143
Pentecostalism 17, 26, 182–186, 195 200–201, 219
Peperkemp, E 145
Perigoe, R 167
Persian Empire 106–107, 114
Peters, J 165
photography 9–10, 13, 84, 88, 90, 93
planetarism 31
play 21, 34, 56, 66, 70, 101–103, 119, 134, 186
Poland 1, 146
politics 21, 26–28, 30–35, 37–38
Pope Francis 132
Pope, A 108
popular culture 12, 42–43, 59–60, 131–138, 199–201, 209–213
populism 1–9, 26–28
post-colonial 200
pre-modern 162–177
print media 2, 134
property 21–22, 135
Protestantism 9, 15–16, 27–28, 65–66, 127, 146–170–176, 181–186
provincialization 4, 8
public discourse 34

public sphere 17, 182–187, 191, 199, 201, 206
publics 23, 35, 152
Puritanism 84

Qibla 117
Quack 213

radio 30, 69, 129–130, 133–138, 184–185, 191
Ramachandran 208
Ramanayas 210
Ray, S 205
Rede Record Network 130
reflexivity 12–13, 23, 156
Reformation 37, 198
religion journalism 35
religiosity 83–87, 128, 131, 181, 183
religious authority through media 138
religious identity 112
religious nationalism 212, 215
religious privatization 2, 4
religious radio 129, 134, 136
Reporters Without Borders 211
resistance 16, 32, 119–120, 160–162, 176
River Ganges 211
roadside signs 186
Roman Catholic Church 56, 130, 146
Roohfar, Z 115

sacred geographies 207
Said E 6, 31, 163, 167, 169
Sanneh L 183
Sanskritic Hinduism 207
Sassanid Empire 109
Sbardelotto, M 138
secular media 134
secularization 26, 33, 35
Sen, A 21–22
sermons 63–64, 66, 69–71, 73–77, 80
Shaheen, J 169
Kakar, S 208
Shreve, A 145
Siddhartha, De 211
Sierra Club 86
Sikkhism 185
singing 78

social imaginaries 1, 162–163, 170, 176–177
Soviet Union 146
spectacle 9, 91, 132, 136–137, 184, 191, 210
spirit 83, 86–87, 103, 108, 112, 114, 120–121, 154, 181, 195, 211, 213
Srinivas, M 207
Stoler 163–164, 173, 175, 177
Subrahmaniam 205
Sufism 185
Sumiala, J 163
Sundar, N 205
surveillance 46
sustainability 45, 48–50, 57, 60
syncretism 15, 131
Szarkowski, 88

tacitness 200
Taylor, S 144, 161–163, 175, 177
technology 3, 8, 11–12, 41–49, 53–60, 64, 67, 73–74, 78, 115, 121, 127, 137, 141–142, 146, 152–153, 161, 177, 195–197, 200, 220
telenovelas 131, 134
Televangelism 184
The Ramayana 206
"the religious" 6, 8, 12, 16, 21–22, 25, 28, 34–36, 38, 51, 114, 119, 127–131, 133–136, 161, 177, 181–182, 186–187, 191, 199, 201

theology 10, 22, 76, 138, 147, 201
Thich Nhat Hanh 103
Thoreau, H 85–88, 95
Tomlinson, J 24, 29, 79
Tradition 195
traditional media 1
Trump 1, 26–27, 34
Turino, T 78–79
Turner 75

Ukah, F 187
Umbanda 128

Valaskivi, K 163
video 2, 53, 63–64, 66–67, 69–71, 73–78, 133, 141, 145–148, 151–152
Virtual Visnu 208
visuality 17, 30, 54, 90, 109–111, 118–119, 121, 184, 186–188, 191–194, 197, 199–200, 208–209

Walsh, K 11, 145
Warner, M 142, 145, 152, 155
western medicine 56
Whatsapp 214
Wuthnow, R 67, 79

Yellowstone National Park 86

www.ingramcontent.com/pod-product-compliance
Lightning Source LLC
Chambersburg PA
CBHW031426150426
43191CB00006B/410